Info-line Guide to Training Evaluation

An Info-line Collection

Info-line is a series of "how-to" reference tools; each issue is a concisely written, practical guidebook that provides in-depth coverage of a single topic vital to training and HRD job performance. *Info-line* is available by subscription and single copy purchase.

ISBN 1-56286-117-4

Library of Congress Catalog Card No. 99-072464

Printed in the United States of America.

ASTD
1640 King Street
Box 1443
Alexandria, VA 22313-2043
PH 703.683.8100, FX 703.683.8103
www.astd.org

Info-line Guide to Training Evaluation

An Info-line Collection

Editor
Cat Sharpe

Graphic Production
Anne Morgan

Essentials for Evaluation

Issue 9705

Essentials for Evaluation

Issue 9705

Essentials for Evaluation

Issue 9705

Essentials for Evaluation

Issue 9705

Essentials for Evaluation

AUTHOR:

Alice K. Waagen, Ph.D.
Waagen and Associates
1557 Hiddenbrook Drive
Herndon, VA 20170-2817
Tel: 703.834.7580
E-mail: aaw5@aol.com

Alice Waagen has over 16 years experience in designing and implementing corporate training. She has developed full systems of training measurement and evaluation, including cost of training, training volume and activity, training customer satisfaction, and ROI. Dr. Waagen holds M.S. and Ph.D. degrees in education.

Editor
Cat Sharpe

Associate Editor
Patrick McHugh

Designer
Steven M. Blackwood

Copy Editor
Kay Larson

ASTD Internal Consultant
Dr. Walter Gray

Essentials for Evaluation

We all know the lingo: reengineering, downsizing, rightsizing, competition, globalization—the list seems endless. What all the "ations" and "isms" represent is the accelerated climate of change in corporate organizations today. Faced with maturing markets and global competition, corporate leadership has become extremely critical in its analysis of existing business processes and procedures.

One aspect of this introspection is the desire to eliminate waste and redundancy. Corporate overhead—or those support functions not directly responsible for generating revenue—has come under great scrutiny. The support functions that have survived this scrutiny best are those that, early on, learned how to operate like independent businesses themselves—providing optimal customer service while emphasizing value for the dollars spent.

Leading-edge training and development organizations, whether internal staff or contractors providing services to many corporations, know that the success of their businesses depends on demonstrating the value of training investment. The simplest way to prove training's value to a client is to document that the training has achieved its desired outcome.

Herein lies the fundamental secret to evaluating training: The evaluation process and procedure must be incorporated at the start; it must be an integral part of any program development process. If program development follows the classic steps of assessing needs and generating objectives, the evaluation criteria that follow are then based on measuring how well the program components—students, instructors, and materials—have met these objectives and answered the needs.

For more information on needs analysis and objectives refer to the following *Info-line*s: No. 8502, "Be a Better Needs Analyst"; No. 9808, "Task Analysis"; No. 8505, "Write Better Behavioral Objectives"; No. 9611, "Conducting a Mini Needs Assessment"; No. 9401, "Needs Assessment by Focus Group"; No. 9712, "Instructional Objectives"; and No. 9713, "The Role of the Performance Needs Analyst."

A broad range of methods and tools is available for every evaluation approach. Options include direct observation, comparisons of tests taken before and after training, interviews, reports, follow-up testing, questionnaires, and surveys. The most effective approach includes combinations of the aforementioned methods. Depending on your objectives, the nature of the training, and focus of the evaluation, some methods are more appropriate than others. For example, the best choice for measuring machine repair skills is direct observation, the worst evaluation tool is a survey.

This issue of *Info-line* outlines the basics of training program evaluation. Different methods of evaluation will be discussed and matched to assorted training program designs. You will learn the advantages and disadvantages of the various types of evaluation. And finally, the emphasis on reporting results to management will be discussed, as well as keeping the evaluation process *client focused* and closely tied to business results.

Benefits of Evaluation

Evaluation methods help determine whether training achieves its objectives. Programs that are structured and designed properly have objectives or elements that specify what the training must accomplish and in what time period these accomplishments must be realized.

A sound system of evaluating training provides valuable information for the client, training management, and senior corporate management. The information elicited from training evaluations should be the final instrument upon which training decisions such as program additions, changes, or deletions should be made. Good evaluations document results of training programs, which subsequently can be used to prioritize training needs at the corporate level. Then, financial and other resources can be shifted from training that has less impact on corporate goals to those objectives that have the most favorable cost/benefit ratio.

Evaluation of Training

Some specific benefits of evaluation are:

- a tool to assess the value of courses, seminars, and workshops

- built-in quality control of training programs that documents whether or not course objectives have been met

- a method for identifying programs that need improvement

- a basis upon which decisions to continue or eliminate a program can be made

- a way to identify the proper audience for future programs

- a method for managing training programs

- a mechanism to review and reinforce essential program points

- a way to get top management and participants to "buy-in" to the program

When structured to elicit open-ended comments, training evaluations can serve two purposes: first, as a demonstrator of present-day benefits and second, as an indicator of future training program needs.

Finally, summary or "macro" evaluation information can be proffered to senior management or key clients on a regular basis. This educates them as to the value of the training enterprise. Good evaluation reports should also document, in both statistical and qualitative terms, how training has helped the organization meet its goals.

There are a number of ways to evaluate training and each method is designed to elicit different information. These various methodologies are often described as "levels" of information, from the simplest that obtain and quantify (reaction surveys), to the more complex and detailed (corporate results).

There are several levels of program evaluation criteria based on participants' reactions: what they've learned, their skills performance, their on-the-job behavior, and the effects and results the training has had on the entire organization.

Each of the main evaluation methods will be discussed in terms of their strengths and weaknesses. Rather than thinking of these methods as a hierarchy from least valuable to most valuable, think of them all as useful tools in your training tool kit. If your client is most interested in seeing reaction data, this is a perfectly acceptable and useful form of evaluation; it should not be passed over for something more complex.

Following is a breakdown of how each level can be applied to help you develop a systematic approach to evaluating what your programs have accomplished.

Participant Reaction Surveys

Participant reaction surveys or "smilesheets" are questionnaires that are typically distributed at the end of each training program. They ask students to rate their perceptions about the quality and impact of the specific program. These questionnaires can range from a simple handful of questions regarding program design, instruction methods, and facilities to elaborate multipage forms for students to rate all facets of the program and provide input on future programs. This evaluation tool can serve as a valuable measure of attendee satisfaction and is relatively easy to administer, tabulate, and summarize in a results report.

Guidelines for Designing Reaction Surveys

Reaction surveys can provide quantifiable customer service data, giving you direct information from your program consumers. When designed with uniform overall questions, these surveys produce data that can be used to make comparisons between courses and participants. This allows program design decisions to be based on a broad range of perceptions, not just the responses of a few disappointed or disgruntled participants.

Reaction surveys provide the following results:

● Protection against making decisions based on a limited number of either satisfied or disappointed participants.

● Clues for improving programs, but no indication of how the training will affect job performance or organizational results.

Steps for Evaluating Reactions

The best instruments for reaction evaluations focus on points that are most important to the evaluator. They are straightforward and simple to fill out.

Evaluate reactions by using the following steps:

1. Determine what you want to know. Concentrate on specific areas such as methods, facilities, materials, and so on.

2. Design a comment sheet for tabulating and quantifying reactions. Experts suggest using a form designed for the particular program rather than a standardized or generic form.

3. Include sufficient space for questions and comments that cannot be quantified or tabulated.

4. Do not require participants to sign their evaluation forms. If participants are forced to identify themselves, they may feel obligated to be overly positive.

5. Keep the form simple and make sure it takes only a short time to complete. If you are interested in reactions, design sheets focusing on program content, not administration, for example.

6. Use a final comment sheet to gather additional or follow-up information. If you have already collected two or more previous evaluations, use a final one to clarify and complete information.

7. Establish standards of performance by converting reactions to numerical ratings. An example of this is a scale with numbers representing grades of quality: 1 poor, 2 adequate, 3 good, 4 very good, 5 excellent.

What Have Participants Learned?

A number of different tools can be designed to measure what participants have learned in the training program. Paper and pencil tests, administered before and after training, can be used to measure acquisition of knowledge and information. Skills can be evaluated concurrently with the training through simulations or in-class activities, which allow students to demonstrate instructed skills. Regardless of the assessment method used, all of these tests must be designed to relate directly to the course objectives.

Participant learning evaluations are difficult and more time consuming to develop and administer, but they are essential if the nature of the training requires that the learning be demonstrated and documented. Learning assessments are most commonly used in training programs that lead to licensing, certification, or involve skills that contain elements of risk. Computerized simulators, used for airplane pilot and locomotive engineer training, are examples of learning assessment tools. One reason learning evaluations are difficult to design is that they must be customized for every instructional program and *must* reflect the conditions of the specific job.

It is important to remember that learning evaluations accurately measure the amount of knowledge and skills acquired *at the time the test is administered*. In no way do these tests indicate long-term knowledge or skill retention, nor are they an indicator of how knowledge and skills are applied to the job. They simply serve as a snapshot in time denoting that students have mastered the course objectives at the time the instruction was offered.

Components of Learning Evaluations

Effective tests must be thoroughly and thoughtfully designed. Most course developers will design questions as they author the course rather than wait until they are done. All evaluation instruments must be "dry run" on subject experts as well as sample student audiences. Be especially watchful for unclear or ambiguous wording in questions and instructions.

Paper and pencil tests and performance tests are the standard methods for measuring knowledge and skills. The first type measures knowledge, the second measures skills. The material in these tests relates directly to program objectives and the specific knowledge and skills learners work to acquire during training.

Evaluation tests may be based on standardized tests, but the ones that yield the best results are custom written for each specific program.

Designing Paper and Pencil Evaluations

You may want to use the following suggestions for designing and administering effective tests:

Increase your research resources by drafting sample questions before and during program development. Use these questions to make sure you have touched on all program areas; delete the ones pertaining to areas you could not cover during the session.

Plan thoroughly. Tests must be planned out in complete detail. Pay close attention to every part of the test including the schedule, timing breaks, review of instructions, administration, and scoring.

Give participants the opportunity to show what they have learned. Tests should be representative of the training, allowing learners to demonstrate their new knowledge. Relevant tests are more meaningful to learners and yield more valid results to instructors.

Use objective questions such as multiple choice and true or false instead of open-ended essays.

Present only one correct answer. More than one right answer confuses test-takers, makes scoring more difficult, and reduces the validity of the test.

Never present misleading information. Trick questions invariably result in wrong answers, and are a waste of time for you and your learners. If trainees will be faced with difficult on-the-job decisions, represent these situations with challenging but fair questions.

Write questions for easy comprehension. Remember, your object is to test participants' knowledge of the training material, not their reading skills.

Write questions to reveal how well the participants understand the material, not how well they can memorize it.

Use a random arrangement of answers to keep test-takers from guessing the pattern of correct responses (two false, three true).

Use multiple choice items that do not allude to answers of subsequent questions. A block of answers that are tied together seriously affects a participant's score if he or she incorrectly answers the first question. Again, this kind of situation can affect the results and validity of your test.

Vary the level of difficulty throughout the test. Use a mixture of challenging, relatively difficult, and comparatively easy questions.

Try not to cue or signal the correct answer by varying the size of fill-in spaces or by letting one multiple choice item stand out from the rest of the list as the only reasonable possibility.

Make the mechanics of test-taking simple. Remember, your objective is to measure participants' knowledge, not their ability to follow complex test instructions.

Review the test before you administer it. Is it valid? Does it meet the objectives of both the program and the evaluation process? Ask training colleagues to review the test and make suggestions for improving it.

Provide thorough and consistent directions. All learners must receive identical, clear, and concise instructions. Poor instructions can influence the outcome of the evaluation. When administering tests, be sure to provide whatever information is necessary such as blueprints, tables, charts, diagrams, reference books, and so on. If possible, the instructor should use a beta test to present samples of how trainees are expected to answer evaluation questions.

Use procedures for objective evaluations. Determine standards in advance and prepare learners so they will understand the requirements for satisfactory test performance.

Evaluating Skills Performance

Follow these suggestions to evaluate how well new skills have been learned:

- Design performance tests to objectively measure skills in quantifiable terms.

- Ensure that tests cover key requirements of the skills performance specified during training.

- Present the test to participants by clearly and simply explaining instructions, tabulation methods, and performance standards. Tell trainees precisely what they are expected to accomplish.

- Concentrate on improving participants' job performance rather than giving them more training material or information.

- Be sure evaluations reflect how the training has changed skill levels. To do so, carefully prepare and design evaluations. Research your procedures during program pilots and use "control" as well as "experimental" groups to gather data.

- Consult with design experts and other resource people to check the validity and value of your design methodology.

If the test is to be used to qualify a person for a specific job, use outside expertise to evaluate the test for validity and fairness. If test scores can be used to deny employment or promotion opportunities, they must be demonstrably sound or you will open your employer to discrimination charges. If you do not have the expertise yourself or in your staff to validate tests, seek validation from an industrial psychologist or other professional possessing this expertise.

A final note on testing: Be cautious of managers who ask for test results on individual students. Some managers may want to use learning evaluation scores as grounds for discipline, termination, or even promotion. Remember, these tests document a snapshot view of knowledge and skill acquisition. By no means do they accurately reflect on a person's job performance. Using test results as performance indicators can be misleading and even illegal. When in doubt, consult with your Human Resources or Legal departments.

On-the-Job Behavior Evaluation

The ultimate goal of any training program is to improve job performance. Often, training clients want to know more than "has the student acquired new knowledge and skills by the end of the program?" They also want to know if the student can apply the knowledge and skills on the job. Behavior evaluations are designed to measure changes in on-the-job behavior and document improved performance directly related to training.

Job performance evaluations measure whether or not the trainee can accomplish program objectives. These evaluations must be based on the actual task or job performance. This can be documented by observing on-the-job behavior; managers, peers, or subordinates can serve as observers, plus offer oral and written reports regarding performance changes.

If available, performance data can also be gathered and analyzed. For instance, most manufacturing facilities have detailed records of work units produced by employees. In the "soft skills" training programs, action plans can be developed based on observable results. Again, co-workers can be used to record the presence of these observable behaviors.

Evaluation Checklist

Training evaluations can make the difference between a company's losses and gains. Accurate methods and tools for measuring training outcomes can mean significant improvement in organizational performance—increased productivity and savings, decreased costs and personnel problems. To get valuable data from an evaluation, plan your approach by thinking through the following checklist:

☐ What questions do you want to answer? How did participants feel about the training? What did they learn? How did the training affect their attitudes and behavior? What were the organizational results?

☐ How will you measure the items addressed in your questions? Will you administer paper and pencil tests, questionnaires, or surveys? Will you require participants to demonstrate their new knowledge and skills in a role play or simulation?

☐ What are the objectives of your training program? Are your evaluation criteria based on these objectives?

☐ Do the criteria indicate improvement between expected and actual performance when measured against the results of your needs analysis?

☐ What data sources are already available to help you measure results (productivity reports, sales and revenue analyses, and so on)?

☐ Are there alternative methods for gathering this data such as interviews and on-site observations?

☐ What are the best and most cost-effective methods for measuring the results of training? Can you think of less costly, more efficient ways of administering the evaluation?

Components of Behavior Evaluations

The key to developing effective behavior change evaluations is to have clear, observable objectives. These objectives must be based on a systematic appraisal of on-the-job performance as well as interviews with employees and management about requisite levels of the task's performance. Essentially, the difference between current performance and desired performance should correlate to the content of the training.

Methods for gathering this kind of information include:

● on-site observations of performance by trained observers (supervisors, co-workers or professional observers)

● analyses of individual performance records

● observable results of action plans developed during training to improve specific performance areas

● comments from managers, employees, or subordinates, describing behavior changes of their supervisors, co-workers, or support staff

Steps for Data Collection

To determine the effectiveness of a program in behavioral terms, follow these steps and be sure measurements are objective and quantifiable:

1. Make a systematic appraisal of on-the-job performance both before and after the training.

2. Collect comments and performance appraisals from trainees, superiors, subordinates, and co-workers.

3. Compare pre- and posttraining performances and how they relate to the program's instruction.

4. Conduct posttraining evaluations at least three months after program completion to allow trainees sufficient time to practice and test their new skills and knowledge. Additional appraisals will add to the validity of your evaluation.

5. Use control groups that do not receive training to compare against those that do receive training. This helps you measure the effectiveness of your program and its impact on job performance.

One note of caution: In addition to skills or knowledge, behavior change is based on many factors. Training programs can be successful in knowledge and skill transfer yet not result in changed behavior on the job. Participants may choose not to change their behavior due to various reasons: lack of management support for the new behavior, lack of sufficient rewards to motivate change, or perhaps the workplace itself may not be conducive to change.

Since the cause-and-effect relationship between training and behavior change is complex, one should elicit more than just performance observations to have an accurate evaluation system. Posttraining interviews with employees can be used to discover why there has been a behavior change or resistance to change. If there has been no change, ask employees why they have not used the new skill or knowledge on the job. Keep this information confidential. The answers may reveal significant environmental barriers to the change. Until these barriers are identified and eliminated, performance measures will fail to produce positive results. Once the barriers are removed, training can more effectively produce the desired performance objectives.

Evaluation of Organizational Results

Evaluating organizational results measures and documents the effects of training interventions as they relate to the achievement of corporate goals and objectives. Essentially, this documents the overall "macro" result of training programs and is frequently sought when senior managers ask the question: "What real difference does training make? If we stopped training tomorrow, what effect would I see on my bottom line?"

Trainers who need to document their program's impact on the corporation should first look at the corporation's annual goals and strategic direction. They also need to examine any measures that are currently used at divisional or departmental levels to support these goals. Some of these metrics might include: new or existing reports and records covering profits and production, quality, sales, customer service, costs, waste, defects and efforts, efficiency, employee absenteeism, turnover, and so on.

After determining corporate objectives, trainers can relate the evaluation of results to organizational gains and improvements. The benefits of training can include:

- increased productivity
- increased savings
- better quality
- decreased absenteeism
- fewer errors, grievances, and safety problems

To analyze the effects of the training program on the organization, practitioners compare pre- and posttraining data. Results evaluation measures the fiscal or financial impact of a program and is much more difficult than the simple reaction measurement, but possesses the highest value for an organization.

There is an inherent difficulty when measuring training in terms of results. This is because training is only one of many variables that affect organizational performance. Additionally, since many corporate performance metrics are developed irrespective of the training, they can measure factors that may not directly relate to employee performance. These include things such as stock prices or equipment efficiency. Trainers must be cautious when stating that training impacts a measure not directly linked to the objectives of the program. For this reason, many organizations opt only for reaction, learning, and behavior evaluations.

Choosing the Right Format for Questions

Selecting the right kind of questions for your particular program evaluation is essential for obtaining good results. Tests may consist of one or all of the following types of questions:

Multiple choice. This format provides a selection of possible responses; the trainee is told to choose the most accurate one.

Open-ended. These tests offer unlimited responses. Learners write lengthy answers in blank spaces following each question. For example: An angry customer arrives at your office complaining about your delivery service. How would you calm the customer down and resolve the situation?"

Checklist. This type of test presents the learner with a situation and a list of items which may or may not apply. The trainee must choose those items most applicable to the given situation. For example:

"Match the proofreader's symbols to their proper use."
   a. paragraph
   b. insert comma
   c. let it stand
   d. capital letter
   e. lower case letter

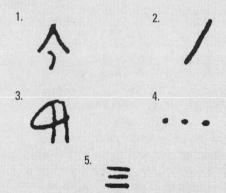

Two-way. This format poses alternate answers. Learners choose *yes* or *no* or else *true* or *false* responses. For example:

"Adult learners are mainly interested in highly job-relevant training."
   a. True
   b. False

Rating scale. This type of test asks learners to rank lists of items according to particular scale.

Guidelines for Measuring Results

Evaluations measuring the impact of training on the organization require hard data—new or existing reports and records covering profits and production, quality, sales, customer service, costs, waste, defects and efforts, efficiency, employee absenteeism and turnover, and so on.

Use the following guidelines to assist you when gathering evaluation material:

1. Gather accurate data from results evaluations; isolate the effects of the program in order to evaluate them objectively.

2. Be aware of external factors that are not related to training. Some of these include:

    • changes in procedures, processes, and new technology

    • the job experience and maturity of trainees

    • the trainee recruitment method; volunteer participation usually results in more positive performance than mandatory attendance

3. Ensure validity by using the following methods:

    Control groups. These are employees who have not received training. Check organizational gains, such as increased productivity and decreased errors, against a performance comparison of trained and untrained employees. Note differences in on-the-job behavior and whether they are related to training or other factors.

    Sampling. This is a representative selection of the entire trainee population. Choose a sample that represents different backgrounds and levels of experience.

4. Analyze evaluation data carefully before making connections between training and organizational achievements. Review the data to make sure it is consistent and accurate. Scan reports and studies for excessive and unrealistic values and eliminate incorrect or incomplete items.

5. Never exclude relevant data. Valid, though often negative, information that does not support the desired outcome must be included with the positive data.

6. Keep your statistical and data analyses as simple as possible. Limit your methods and interpretations to a particular focus for drawing accurate conclusions.

7. Focus on bottom-line results directly related to organizational goals. Increased production or sales, for example, are frequently essential objectives for many companies. Calculate changes by comparing totals before and after the training program.

8. Determine the benefits of reducing time in production, processing, and construction. The valuable and visible result is improved service, or a decrease in the amount of time it takes to deliver products and services to customers.

9. Calculate the value of improved quality by comparing pre- and posttraining reports on the numbers of mistakes and necessary corrections, client dissatisfaction, and product liability.

Be sure to evaluate results in quantifiable and accountable terms. For example, assign a dollar value to cost savings, remembering to adjust costs experienced over time since they are likely to increase beyond the value of actual savings. Assign dollar values to the time saved by employees trained to perform their jobs faster and more efficiently. To calculate time savings, multiply the labor costs per hour by the amount of hours saved.

A final note on results evaluation: Many training managers have concluded in recent years that there is "no Return-on-Investment (ROI) when measuring the ROI of training." Results measurement is by far the most difficult, complex, and costly evaluation methodology. Be cautious of building elaborate systems of measurement and reporting unless your clients and management have specifically requested them.

If management requests that you demonstrate training's impact on corporate goals, research thoroughly the resources you will need, both in staffing, computer power, statistical and analytical support, and so on. Prepare a cost analysis of the results evaluation project and present it to management before you begin.

Testing Methods

Comparisons of pre- and posttest scores are very good indicators of program effectiveness. Higher test scores show that the program has improved and strengthened trainees' skills, knowledge, and abilities. Following are types of tests used in Human Resource departments:

■ *Norm-referenced*
Rather than rate learners according to program objectives, these tests compare individuals or groups to the norm, the average trainee performance. This kind of test identifies the best and weakest performers, the class rank of each person, the median score for the group, and the percentile standing of each participant. Norm-referenced tests are most useful in a program with a large learner population where score average and individual ranking are significant.

■ *Criterion-referenced*
These are objective tests that require specific and precise responses based on program objectives. Criterion-referenced tests (CRTs) have predetermined cut-off scores and measure according to precisely defined program objectives. Rather than analyze how learners rank among each other, the CRT focuses on assessing, analyzing, and reporting what learners have achieved based on the combination of performance standards and program objectives. For example, the criteria for a typing test would follow from a program objective such as: "At the end of training, learner will be able to type 60 words per minute with no more than two errors." If the learner successfully meets this standard and accomplishes the objectives, he or she will have mastered the typing skills as specified in the training program.

■ *Performance or Simulations*

These tests permit the learner to physically demonstrate skills or the uses of knowledge in a program. Some types of skills exhibited may include: analytical, manual, interpersonal, verbal, or any combination of the aforementioned. Most often, practitioners use performance tests to demonstrate activities in specific job-related training. For example, "Demonstrate the correct procedures for coding an HTML document for a Web page."

Supervisory and management training involves performance testing as role plays and skill practice exercises. Learners may be asked to demonstrate problem-solving or communications skills by acting out scenarios with each other.

Evaluation Tips

1. The basic steps for evaluation can be used in any kind of organization. The techniques and procedures have broad application, but never try to overlay evaluation results from one department or organization onto another department or organization.

2. Always give your participants enough time to complete evaluation forms in class. Experts agree that "take-home" forms usually stay at home. If you save only the last few minutes of the session for evaluations, the forms will show tell-tale signs of the time crunch—hurried and incomplete responses. Before the wrap-up segment of the program, put aside some time to review the program and answer questions about the evaluation forms.

3. To get a comprehensive picture of your program, try to ask the same number of questions about strengths and weaknesses. A "mixed review" can be more accurate and helpful than overly positive or negative responses.

4. Share responses with the group. Express your interest in their opinions and ideas by preparing a summary of the written evaluations and discussing the issues that seem most important. This gives individuals a sense of how others responded as well as how their own reactions compare with the group's response.

5. Conduct evaluations more than once during the training no matter how long or short the program. An eight-hour workshop can be evaluated at midpoint and improved for the remaining half. If you evaluate only at the end, you will not be able to share comments, use suggestions, or follow up for additional information.

6. When it is not feasible to stop and evaluate the program at different points, use a method of ongoing evaluation. Instead of evaluating only at the end of the program (during long programs it can be difficult to remember important details), hand out evaluation forms at the beginning and instruct learners when and how to fill them out. Give them a few minutes after each topic to evaluate the material, presentation, and presenter.

7. Review your evaluation methodology with your human resources and legal professionals to ensure that your tests are valid and nondiscriminatory. This is especially important if the test results are used to qualify a person for hiring, promotion, or to serve in a specific job. An invalid or discriminatory test can create a legal risk for the corporation. Also, determine with your legal partners how long test results must be stored for future reference.

8. Legal departments also use training attendance and completion records to demonstrate "due diligence" effort of corporations in sexual harassment or Equal Employment Opportunity (EEO) types of litigation. If a corporation can demonstrate that it takes an active role training its employees on appropriate behavior in the workplace, the organization can shift responsibility for subsequent misbehavior from the corporation to the individual. Partner with your legal staff to determine how training results need to be documented.

9. Keep all employee test results confidential and secured. Misuse of this information, especially low or failing scores, can be devastating to the employee and to the credibility of your entire training effort. Again, seek legal counsel as to the length of retention for this type of information and destroy it once obsolete. Keep all paper records locked and secured; password protect all electronic files.

Follow-Up Evaluations

After the last program evaluation, conduct a related follow-up evaluation that involves feedback questionnaires, interviews, and observations.

Use follow-up evaluations to:

- Measure lasting results of training.

- Identify areas where learners show the greatest and the least improvement.

- Compare follow-up and end-of-program evaluation responses.

Guidelines for Follow-up Evaluations

To find out the degree of improvement since the program, measure the success of the training according to participants' on-the-job accomplishments and how they are using the training to improve performance.

- Make sure learners are prepared for the follow-up. At the end of the program announce your intention to conduct a follow-up evaluation and explain what kind of information you need. Providing this type of explanation will increase your response rates.

- Explain that the follow-up is mandatory, not optional; the evaluation is crucial in determining the effect and value of the program.

- Pose questions that are the same or similar to those that appeared on the end-of-program evaluation forms.

- Find out if the training worked.

- Share follow-up data with all managers and supervisors.

- The kinds of questions you ask will give you a reliable basis for accurate data comparison and analysis. For example, if learners were asked to estimate their increase in productivity resulting from the training, follow up by asking about their actual rate of increase.

- Encourage participants to identify reasons why they have or have not improved and what factors obstructed their progress. Isolating the negative effects can be as useful as identifying the positive ones.

- It is vitally important to share follow-up evaluations with participants' managers or supervisors. These individuals need to know the program results and follow-up information and should also be involved with the participants' practice and application of the training.

- As a final effort, assign follow-up activities when and if appropriate. For example, if a learner needs clarification in some aspect of the training, practitioners can instruct them to complete a task or achieve a goal related to the program's content. This helps learners to better evaluate the program.

Reporting Results to Management

At a minimum, training evaluation data should be reported to the training manager and on up to the senior level. At each level, the data should be increasingly summarized and extracted. No manager wants to wade through tomes of data, so reports should be condensed to provide the most relevant information for each level.

The fundamental question to ask in reporting any data is: "What business decision will the reader make after reading this information?" To answer this question, you need to determine the decision-making authority and span of control belonging to the reader. If the manager cannot use the report to assist in his or her decisions, it is "nice to know" information and will probably end up discarded and unread.

Evaluation Methods

Paper and Pencil Test. This method measures how well trainees learn program content. An instructor administers paper and pencil tests in class to measure participants' progress.

Attitude Surveys. These question-and-answer surveys determine what changes in attitude have occurred as a result of training. Practitioners use these surveys to gather information about employees' perceptions, work habits, motivation, value beliefs, working relations, and so on. Attitude surveys also reveal respondees' opinions about their jobs, the workplace, co-workers, supervisors, policies, procedures, and the organization. If you conduct a program to change attitudes, before and after surveys can assess improvement.

Simulation and On-Site Observation. Instructors, or managers' observations of on-the-job performance in a work simulation, indicate whether a learner's skills have improved as a result of the training.

Productivity Reports. Hard production data such as sales reports and manufacturing totals can help managers and instructors determine *actual* performance improvement on the job.

Post-training Surveys. Progress and proficiency assessments by both managers and participants indicate perceived performance improvement on the job.

Needs/Objectives/Content Comparison. Training managers, participants, and supervisors compare needs analysis results with course objectives and content to determine whether the program was relevant to participants' needs. Relevancy ratings at the end of the program also contribute to the comparison.

Evaluation Forms. Participants' responses on end-of-program evaluation forms indicate what they liked and disliked about the training.

Professional Opinion. Instructional designers critique and assess the quality of the program design.

Instructor Evaluation. Professional trainers administer assessment sheets and evaluation forms to measure the instructor's competence, effectiveness, and instructional skills.

Cost Analysis. The training manager compares costs of instructor's fees, materials, facilities, travel, training time, and the number of trainees to determine the hourly cost of training for each participant.

Consider using these suggestions for including management in the evaluation process:

- Involve line managers in developing evaluation objectives and determining criteria.

- Explain the process to managers and use their input to develop data collection methods and techniques that focus on the criteria and indicate the effects of training.

- Include managers in identifying significant results. They also can help determine the best ways to report results.

- Reach agreement on a reporting method—written, formal presentation, or informal discussion.

- Decide who should receive the reports: participants, administrators, department managers, supervisors, as well as the best times for distributing or presenting the reports.

Essential Corporate Partners

To the new trainer, developing good training evaluations can be a daunting task. But there are many skilled professionals within a corporation who can help you with this task. In return, you can make them special clients of training, offering them your training counsel and expertise. Actively seek out partners in the following departments:

■ *Information Systems Specialists*
These are the computer hardware and software gurus who can help you automate all your record-keeping and reporting. And no, there is no one miracle computer program out there that will do it all. Once you get into the intricacy of data collection and retrieval, you will need expert help in setting up programs to manage it.

■ *Human Resources*
Talk regularly with your corporation's recruiters. Ask them what positions are difficult or costly to fill. Then talk to the organizational development (OD) staffing experts about the possibility of retraining existing staff for these positions. OD, leadership, and executive development professionals can also provide you with keen insight about organizational difficulties that might be addressed through training.

Inquire from the compensation staff whether there are any requirements for training in the performance review process. If so, this will impact your training volume shortly before review time. The words trainers hate to hear are: "My performance review is next week and I have to take Course XYZ before then. Why aren't you offering it?"

Likewise, talk frequently with the Employee Relations and EEO people. They hear a lot of the negative stories about management and employee behavior; sometimes training can raise awareness and alleviate some of these problems.

■ *Legal*
Partner with the legal department to obtain help regarding the legal side of testing, surveying, record retention, and reporting.

■ *Finance/Accounting*
Somewhere in every finance department are people with expertise on statistics and modeling. They also are well versed on reporting complex statistical information in ways that are easy for management to comprehend. Get their advice to fine-tune your data reporting.

Financial experts can also provide you with models that determine the cost of training. Many corporations use standard algorithms to compute average employee salary costs. You need to use the same calculation for your reports.

■ *Employee and Corporate Communications*
These people not only have vehicles (e-mail lists and newsletters) to reach all employees, they are often the consummate word smiths. They can help you with the appearance and readability of your reports.

This is but a small sampling of the corporate staff that can help you with training evaluation and reporting. Network frequently with these people and they will help ease your reporting burden.

References & Resources

Articles

Barron, Tom. "Is There an ROI in ROI?" *Technical & Skills Training,* January 1997, pp. 21-26.

Benabou, Charles. "Assessing the Impact of Training Programs on the Bottom Line." *National Productivity Review,* Summer 1996, pp. 91-99.

Bernthal, Paul R. "Evaluation That Goes the Distance." *Training & Development,* September 1995, pp. 41-45.

Birnbrauer, Herman. "Improving Evaluation Forms to Produce Better Course Design." *Performance & Instruction,* January 1996, pp. 14-17.

Blickstein, Steve. "Does Training Pay Off?" *Across the Board,* June 1996, pp. 16-20.

Bushnell, David S. "Input, Process, Output: A Model for Evaluating Training." *Training & Development Journal,* March 1990, pp. 41-43.

Dixon, Nancy M. "New Routes to Evaluation." *Training & Development,* May 1996, pp. 82-85.

Dust, Bob. "Understanding Financial Terminology." *Training & Development,* May 1996, pp. 99-100.

Geber, Beverly. "Prove It! (Does Your Training Make a Difference?)" *Training,* March 1995, pp. 27-34.

Jedrziewski, David R. "Putting Methods to the Madness of Evaluating Training Effectiveness." *Performance & Instruction,* January 1995, pp. 23-31.

Lapp, H.J. "Rate Your Testing Program." *Performance & Instruction,* September 1995, pp. 36-38.

Lewis, Theodore. "A Model for Thinking About the Evaluation of Training." *Performance Improvement Quarterly,* vol. 9, no. 1, 1996, pp. 3-22.

McLinden, Daniel J. "Proof, Evidence, and Complexity: Understanding the Impact of Training and Development." *Performance Improvement Quarterly,* vol. 8, no. 3, 1995, pp. 13-18.

Phillips, Jack J. "How Much Is the Training Worth?" *Training & Development,* April 1996, pp. 20-24.

————. "ROI: The Search for Best Practices." *Training & Development,* February 1996, pp. 42-47.

————. "Was It the Training?" *Training & Development,* March 1996, pp. 28-32.

Pulley, Mary Lynn. "Navigating the Evaluation Rapids." *Training & Development,* September 1994, pp. 19-23.

Shelton, Sandra, and George Alliger. "Who's Afraid of Level 4 Evaluation?" *Training & Development,* June 1993, pp. 43-46.

Smith, Jack E. and Sharon Merchant. "Using Competency Exams for Evaluating Training." *Training & Development,* August 1990, pp. 65-71.

Williams, Leigh Ann. "Measurement Made Simple." *Training & Development,* July 1996, pp. 43-45.

Willyerd, Karie A. "Balancing Your Evaluation Act." *Training,* March 1997, pp. 52-58.

Books

ASTD. *The Best of the Evaluation of Training.* Alexandria, Virginia: American Society for Training & Development, 1991.

————. *The Best of the Return on Training Investment.* Alexandria, Virginia: American Society for Training & Development, 1991.

Basarab, David J., and Darrel K. Root. *The Training Evaluation Process: A Practical Approach to Evaluating Corporate Training Programs.* Norwell, Massachusetts: Kluwer Academic, 1992.

Bassi, Laurie J., et al. *The ASTD Training Data Book.* Alexandria, Virginia: American Society for Training & Development, 1997.

Dixon, Nancy M. *Evaluation: A Tool for Improving HRD Quality.* Alexandria, Virginia: American Society for Training & Development, 1991.

Fisk, Catherine N. (ed.). *ASTD Trainer's Toolkit: Evaluation Instruments.* Alexandria, Virginia: American Society for Training & Development, 1991.

Head, Glenn E. *Training Cost Analysis: The How-To Guide for Trainers and Managers.* Alexandria, Virginia: American Society for Training & Development, 1993.

Kirkpatrick, Donald L. *Evaluating Training Programs: The Four Levels.* San Francisco: Berrett-Kohler, 1994.

References & Resources

Medsker, Karen L., and Donald G.
  Roberts (eds.) *ASTD Trainer's Toolkit:
  Evaluating the Results of Training.*
  Alexandria, Virginia: American Society
  for Training & Development, 1992.

Phillips, Jack J. *Handbook of Training
  Evaluation and Measurement Methods.* Houston, Texas: Gulf Publishing,
  1991.

Rae, Leslie. *How to Measure Training
  Effectiveness.* Brookfield, Vermont:
  Gower Publishing, 1991.

Robinson, Dana G., and James C. Robinson. *Training for Impact.* San Francisco: Jossey-Bass, 1989.

Info-lines

Callahan, Madelyn R. (ed). "Be A Better
  Needs Analyst." No. 8502 (revised
  1998).

———. "Write Better Behavioral Objectives." No. 8505 (revised 1998).

Gilley, Jerry W. "How To Collect Data."
  No. 9008 (revised 1998).

Hacker, Deborah Grafinger. "Testing for
  Learning Outcomes." No. 8907
  (revised 1998).

Martelli, Joseph T. and Dennis Mathern.
  "Statistics for HRD Practice."
  No. 9101.

Long, Lori. "Surveys From Start to
  Finish." No. 8612 (revised 1998).

O'Neill, Mary. "How to Focus a Training
  Evaluation." No. 9605.

Robinson, Dana Gaines and James C.
  Robinson. "Measuring Affective and
  Behavioral Change." No. 9110 (revised
  1997).

———. "Tracking Operational Results."
  No. 9112.

Younger, Sandra M. "Benchmarking the
  Training Process." No. 9405 (out of
  print).

Internet Sites

American Society for Training and
Development
http://www.astd.org

Evaluation and Training Institute (ETI)
http://www.otan.dni.us/webfarm/eti/

Evaluation of Web Based Training
http://www.ucalgary.ca/%7Egwnichol/for
meval/formeval.html

A System Approach to Training
http://www.nwlink.com/%7Edonclark/hrd/
glossary.html

Catalogue of Evaluations and Evaluation
Summaries (Evsums) Overseas Development Administration
http://www.oneworld.org/oda/publica-
tions/catalogue1.html

Industrial and Commercial Training.
Journal Contents and Abstracts.
http://www.mcb.co.uk/services/contents/li
blink/webpages/

Education, Training and Development
Resource Center for Business and Industry
http://www.tasl.com/tasl/home.html

Network for the Evaluation of Education
and Training Technologies
http://socserv2.mcmaster.ca/srnet/evnet.
htm

Job Aid

Evaluation Guide

I. Client Needs

A. State the objectives of the program.

B. Describe evaluation criteria based on these objectives.

II. Participant Reaction

A. How will participants' reactions during and after the program be measured? State what methods will be used: questionnaires, surveys, interviews, observations.

B. Describe what measurement standards will be used. Examples of these are relevance ("Was the program relevant to your specific job needs?) and ease of learning ("Were you able to complete the activities and exercises with relative ease, or were they too difficult?).

C. List specific issues to be addressed. Some examples include: program design, class size and arrangement, and the value of program's content.

D. How will the information be collected and tabulated?

E. State and describe back-up sources for information. These may include participants' remarks to the trainer, and their questions concerning program exercises and content.

III. Performance Skills and On-the-Job Behavior

A. List the methods for evaluating learning during and at the end of the training. Examples include tests, questionnaires, and company documents.

B. Describe the measurement standards. Use these questions to help establish standards. How much of the material do the participants understand? How well do they understand it and apply it?

C. List specific program areas that will be questioned. Focus on program structure, presentation, activities, and examples.

D. How will the information be collected and tabulated?

E. List and describe back-up sources. Look at the amount of time the training program required and note whether all or some of the content was covered. Check trainee performance on exercises, during demonstrations, and on the job. (Are trainees using the new skills and information successfully?)

IV. Organizational Results

A. How did the training affect the organization. Did it have a positive impact on organizational performance?

B. Using annual reports, corporate, strategic, and annual plans, list the organization's goals or objectives against which you will measure the training's impact.

C. Describe the measurement standards that will be used to evaluate organizational results.

D. How will the information be collected and tabulated?

E. List back-up data sources. Some of these may be interviews and discussions with management, personnel, and clients.

F. Include observations of procedures and processes.

Level 1 Evaluation: Reaction and Planned Action

Issue 9813

Level 1 Evaluation: Reaction and Planned Action

AUTHORS:

Jack Phillips, Ph.D.
Performance Resources
    Organization
P.O. Box 380637
Birmingham, AL 35238-0637
Tel.: 205.678.9700
Fax: 205.678.8070
Email: roipro@wwisp.com

Joan O. Wright
First Union National Bank
301 South College Street,
    Suite 1500
Charlotte, NC 28288-0957
Tel.: 704.374.6569
Email: Joan.Wright@
    FirstUnion.com

Sandra I. Pettit-Sleet
First Union National Bank
301 South College Street,
    Suite 1500
Charlotte, NC 28288-0957
Tel: 704.383.0391
Email: Sandra.Pettit@
    FirstUnion.com

Editor
Cat Sharpe

Contributing Editor
Ann Bruen

Production Design
Anne Morgan

Why Measure Reaction?

There are many ways to evaluate training, but the starting point of any evaluation program is a measure of participants' reaction to the training itself. Measuring how trainees feel about the program is the basis for planning additional programs, expanding current programs, or even changing existing programs. It also is a sound and value-added way for organizations to stay on the cutting edge of training. In this ever-changing world of "just-in-time" and "just-enough" training and technologically alternative training—that is, training via the Internet, video, satellite broadcast, or computer—the evaluation tool must be as flexible as the types of training offered.

Measuring participant reaction is, according to the Donald Kirkpatrick four-level approach to evaluation, a Level 1 evaluation. This is defined as what participants thought of the program, or in Kirkpatrick's words, "Evaluating reaction is the same thing as measuring customer satisfaction." In this case, trainees are the customers, and the evaluation measures how well they liked or disliked the program in regard to materials, instructors, facilities, methodology, content, and so on. Participant reaction can be a critical factor when redesigning or continuing HRD programs.

Level 1 evaluation is important because it determines customer satisfaction and reaction. The participant must see some value in the program and usefulness of the skills and knowledge acquired from the program. Managers want the investment in training and development to produce a measurable impact on business performance standards. Reaction evaluation provides a fundamental first step for measuring these essentials through objective data that in turn can be used in making future training decisions.

You can use Level 1 evaluation data for any of the following purposes:

- determine trainee satisfaction level with the program

- identify the strengths and weaknesses of the training program

- evaluate instructor ability to present programs

- determine participant needs

- obtain quantitative data that can be communicated to management

- analyze quantitative data that can be used to establish performance standards for future programs

- help decide who should participate in future programs

- collect data that will assist future marketing programs

In addition, Level 1 evaluation is an opportunity to see how participants plan to apply what they have learned. Other approaches expand Level 1 evaluation to include enabling factors that address the availability of various resource inputs necessary for a successful intervention as well as other subjective input of participants. Regardless of the approach, Level 1 evaluation can drive important changes in any part of the training delivery process.

The concept of different levels of evaluation is instructive in understanding the measurement and evaluation process. Donald Kirkpatrick created a four-level model of training evaluation that has been used for several decades:

1. Reaction and planned action.

2. Learning.

3. Application.

4. Business impact.

These levels have been expanded to add a fifth level: measuring return-on-investment (ROI).

Although business results and ROI are desired, evaluation at the other levels is important. A chain of impact should occur through all levels as skills and knowledge learned are applied on the job to produce business results. If measurements are not taken at each level, it is difficult to conclude that a program actually caused the results. This issue of *Info-line* is the first of five that take an expanded view of the levels discussed above. This framework expands Level 1 evaluation to include participant reaction to the program as well as how participants plan to apply what they have learned.

Case Study: First Union National Bank

First Union National Bank, headquartered in Charlotte, North Carolina, is one of the largest banks in the United States with approximately 50,000 employees. As a growing bank, First Union continues to increase its investment in and dependence on training and has its own training and development division—First University. Recently, First University has increased its emphasis on evaluation of training and magnified the focus on Level 1 evaluation. To create an effective Level 1 tool, processes were challenged, forcing individuals to think and act creatively.

Since First University had used Level 1 evaluation for several years, it already had defined the "purpose"—identifying the impact of training on participants. With the continued growth and increased focus on Level 1, stakeholders were surveyed to pinpoint unaddressed needs. Three trends having a direct impact on evaluation were also identified:

- increase in banking industry mergers

- shift from traditional classroom training to alternative delivery methods

- projections that training would rely heavily on technology by the year 2000

By incorporating the *purpose* with the *needs* and the impact of trends, First University established criteria to link the final evaluation product to the purpose and needs.

Data Collection

With a large merger approaching, First University had to prepare for a continued growth in training, which would affect how much Level 1 data had to be collected. A system was needed to handle the increased volume, yet adhere to budget limitations. In addition, there had to be an accommodation for the growing use of technology-based training and how it affected data collection.

With no single computer system in place, First Union decided to use hard copy, scannable OMR (Optical Mark Reader) Level 1 evaluation forms for each training program participant. This also ensured participant anonymity. As a means of transitioning to technology-based data collection, First University is currently striving to develop alternative formats—CBT or CD-ROM—but these will be expanded to include other forms of delivery, such as videotapes and satellite broadcasts.

A customized database was already in existence for reporting Level 1 data; so the decision was made to invest in upgrading and enhancing the existing database to improve its analysis and reporting capabilities. This also allowed for linkage of selected data from the database to other software programs and for further analysis of data without weighing down the database with extra tables, queries, and reports.

To ensure accurate data collection, First University decided to provide trainers with methods for capturing accurate and necessary Level 1 feedback. First University modified the Level 1 form to provide incentive for completing the evaluation and ensure a means for accurate completion of the form. The revised form was color-coded to draw attention to the information that would normally be provided by a facilitator. The incentive is *Course Credit*, which is documented for each First Union employee. In addition, the form provides a toll-free number for addressing questions relating to the program, materials, or evaluation form.

Data Analysis and Reporting

First University chose a database program over a spreadsheet because its ability to sort and retrieve information from Level 1 data was more valuable than performing mathematical calculations. By using a customized database, First University had the flexibility of reporting data in a variety of ways, depending on client requests and needs.

After completing the database and before implementation, the consistency and accuracy of the reporting was verified. Test data were imported into the database and used to print a variety of reports. The results were compared for consistency among reports and against the results of a spreadsheet that was created to check the accuracy of the mathematical calculations.

Application of Data

To ensure success of the tool, and even before the new Level 1 form was designed, First University had to look at potential uses for the Level 1 data and set objectives for utilizing the results. The objectives were a guide for providing data results to clients and assisting them in the follow-up use of those data.

Instrument and Process Development

Standards

Standards had to be set for realistic data benchmarking. First University faced the challenge of establishing an unbiased company- and industry-focused means of data comparison. Currently, the internal standard is set as the highest-ranking college in each overall section of Level 1 data and each college's prior years' scores. To get an external comparison, First University also needed to benchmark against the industry. This is difficult with the diversity in Level 1 criteria among businesses.

Prior to converting to the new Level 1 evaluation form and process, First University created a process booklet and distributed it to all First University employees. The contents were as follows:

- an explanation of Level 1 and its importance to First University

- First University's vision, goals, and objectives relating to Level 1

- a copy of the new form and an explanation of the changes

- details of the entire process flow

- report samples

- a phone number and e-mail address for questions and concerns

As a follow-on to the booklet, a videotape and satellite broadcast were used to promote the new form and process and to address frequently asked questions. To provide a consistent, efficient, and user-friendly means for using the Level 1 evaluation instrument and process, forms were set up on the e-mail system for ordering evaluations, requesting reports, obtaining the status on completed evaluations, and getting answers to questions.

Too often, a Level 1 evaluation is implemented and the data disappear into a black hole, resulting in a waste of time and expense. The purpose for implementation and the uses of the data must be established before development of a successful Level 1 instrument and process can be justified. So, before you can actually develop the instrument for a successful Level 1 evaluation, you must determine why you are conducting the evaluation. This is easily accomplished by stating or defining the purpose of the evaluation and then determining stakeholder needs that can be satisfied by the data obtained from the evaluation.

For example, your organization is planning on converting to a new software system. This system is completely different from the existing one and will integrate many parts of the business, including order processing, which is handled by customer service representatives who receive calls and process orders for fulfillment. To effect the change, all call center employees will participate in a staggered, three-day training program to introduce and teach the new software. Since the purpose of the conversion is to upgrade the system and provide better service to customers (both internal and external), service representatives must be able to convert to and use the new system seamlessly. Immediately following a pilot training class, participants are asked to fill out a reaction questionnaire that will measure their response to the training, as well as determine how participants plan to use their newly acquired skills.

So why is the reaction and planned action evaluation being done? *Answer:* To ensure that the training program designed for customer service representatives will be well received, easily learned, and more important, able to be applied immediately, on the job. Given this data, an instrument can be designed and developed to measure participant reaction. For a specific example of the development of an evaluation instrument and process, see the case study at left.

Step 1: Establishing Evaluation Criteria

After recognizing the value and diverse needs of the Level 1 evaluation instrument and the information it can provide, you will begin by setting criteria that match the final product to the identified purpose and needs. Here are some considerations for these criteria.

- Design the evaluation so that its content can produce the desired results. Always ask, "How does this input affect the outcome?"

- Create an "apples to apples" comparison of all training throughout the company, while accommodating the need for external benchmarking.

- Develop evaluation questions so they can be converted easily into quantitative data. In other words, develop as many questions as possible to choice-driven response statements.

- Determine the appropriate number of possible responses on the question response scale and the scale's corresponding labels.

- Incorporate feedback on planned action of the way in which the participant plans to use the training.

- Include at least one open-ended comment and determine how it will be consolidated with the numerical ratings for reporting purposes.

- Decide on the number of facilitators to be evaluated. (Generally, either the hardware or software will limit the number of evaluated trainers per class.)

- Obtain honest reactions by guaranteeing participant anonymity.

For help in designing evaluations, see *Evaluation Reactions: A Guide to Success* opposite.

Step 2: Creating Data Collection Tools

Once the criteria have been established, the next step is to ensure that the collected data will have integrity and will be processed in a timely manner. The end-of-course questionnaire, more commonly referred to as the *smile sheet*, is the most typical format of a Level 1 evaluation. This method, has several advantages. It is:

- cost effective

- time efficient

- consistent through its distribution and reporting capabilities

Questionnaire design is a simple and logical process. The following steps will help ensure that a valid, reliable, and effective instrument is developed.

■ Determine the Information Needed
The first step of any instrument design is itemizing the subjects, skills, or abilities presented in the program, along with other factors related to the success of the program. Questions are developed later. It might be helpful to develop this information in outline form so that related questions can be grouped together.

■ Select the Type(s) of Questions
Determine whether open-ended questions, checklists, two-way questions, multiple-choice questions, or a ranking scale is most appropriate for the intended purpose. Consider the planned data analysis and variety of data to be collected.

■ Develop the Questions
Develop the questions based on the type of question(s) planned and the information needed. The questions should be simple and straightforward enough to prevent confusion or leading the participant to a desired response. Avoid terms or expressions that are unfamiliar to the participant.

■ *Test the Questions*

After the questions are developed, test them for understanding. Ideally, the questions should be tested on a group of participants in a pilot program. If this is not feasible, the questions should be tested on employees at approximately the same job level as the potential participants. Collect as much input and criticism as possible, and revise the questions as necessary.

■ *Prepare a Data Summary*

Develop a data summary sheet so that data can be tabulated quickly for summary and interpretation. This step will help ensure that the data can be analyzed quickly and presented in a meaningful way.

■ *Develop the Completed Questionnaire*

Finalize the questions in a professional questionnaire with proper instructions. Select the appropriate questionnaire type based on the number of respondents. With large groups, use a checklist or alternate response questionnaire for simple processing and data comparison. Checklists are suitable for presenting data in quantified form.

The key to success with any evaluation method is making sure the input is sufficiently accurate to produce measurable output. Some concerns in collecting appropriate and accurate data include:

● Getting participants to follow marking and question scale instructions.

● Dealing with responses that contradict open-ended comments.

● Motivating participants to provide open-ended feedback.

● Capturing open-ended comments without having them manually input.

● Receiving more program-specific feedback without using two separate evaluation forms.

For ways to enliven Level 1 assessment tools, see *Measuring Level 1 and Making It Fun* on the next page.

Evaluation Reactions: A Guide to Success

The best instruments for reaction evaluations focus on points that are most important to the evaluator. They are straightforward and simple to fill out. Here is a seven-step method for measuring reactions.

1. Determine what you want to know. Concentrate on specific areas such as methods, facilities, materials, and so on.

2. Design a comment sheet for tabulating and quantifying reactions. Use a form designed for the particular program rather than a standardized or generic form.

3. Include sufficient space for questions and comments that cannot be quantified or tabulated.

4. Do not require participants to sign their evaluation forms. If participants are forced to identify themselves, they may feel obligated to be overly positive.

5. Keep the form simple and make sure it takes only a short time to complete. If you are interested in reactions, design sheets focusing on program content, not administration, for example.

6. Use a final comment sheet to gather additional or follow-up information. If you have already collected two or more previous evaluations, use a final one to clarify and complete information.

7. Establish standards of performance by converting reactions to numerical ratings. An example of this is a scale with numbers representing grades of quality: 1 for poor; 2 for adequate; 3 for good; 4 for very good; and 5 for excellent.

Adapted from "Essentials for Evaluation,"
Info-line No. 9706. Copyright ASTD.

Measuring Level 1 and Making It Fun

Without a doubt, Level 1 evaluation instruments of one form or another are the most commonly used assessment tools for measuring training outcomes. Unfortunately, Level 1 instruments are frequently undervalued resulting in valuable data not being collected or properly processed. If a conscientious effort is made to develop, deliver, and analyze Level 1 instruments, they can be of substantial value. They can provide a "first line of defense" against huge expenditures of time and resources that ultimately produce unsatisfactory results.

Interactive Measurement Technologies Corporation, operating as InterACT, is a company that specializes in assessment and evaluation of training programs at Levels 1, 2, and 3. They provide assessment services on a global scale, working for some of the largest and most successful corporations and universities. Their view of how to succeed with Level 1 instruments is straightforward.

Keep It Simple

Most of us need to fill out forms on a regular basis, whether for business or just as a part of our daily lives. Many find the depersonalization of completing lengthy, monochromatic questionnaires tedious at best. Throw in the requirement of darkening bubbles on a machine-readable response sheet (read: "Darken the bubble completely. Carefully erase all stray marks. Always use a No. 2 pencil."), and you will find your class participants nervously shifting in their seats, looking for the nearest exit.

InterACT tries to eliminate as much of the tedium as possible. First, their forms are colorful, often reflecting the colors of the logo of the organization being serviced. No black-and-white questionnaires or faded pink forms with bubbles are allowed. The forms are bold, with larger than normal font sizes used to capture attention and improve the ease with which they are read. Gone, too, are the requirements to use No. 2 pencils, or to darken tiny circles. Instead, raters will find large boxes with colorfully shaded grids that invite their creative, childlike side to

express themselves. Indeed, the raters are instructed to draw a mark across a shaded grid with complete abandon at a point that indicates their level of agreement with the item statement just preceding it. A mark at the center of the grid indicates agreement. A high mark suggests the statement was not worded strongly enough to capture the sentiment, and a low mark suggests disagreement.

Keep It Short

A Level 1 form is rarely more than 10 items in length. If you ask, they will tell you that if you ask an adult 10 things in the right way, you will get more information by a country mile than you will if you ask 50 things, no matter how carefully you word them.

According to business manager and psychometrician Susan Calcagno, respondents will carefully consider their opinions about a class if asked 10 things. If probed for more, they get tired of being questioned and pay less attention. "When we ask for a reaction, we are asking the participant to do us a favor by providing us with guidance about how we can do better. Asking for too many favors all at once, like filling out 30-50 reaction items soon becomes an imposition. Ask only about what you need to know and can correct, and leave the rest alone. People like to help, but they don't want to be called upon to analyze every aspect of the training experience. That's the training manager's job."

Make It Fun to Complete

Fun is perhaps an ambitious term for an assessment instrument, but does hold the conviction that if the instrument is colorful, bold, and elicits an emotional reaction through proper wording of item statements, it need not be boring. The previously described grid helps to break some of the tedium and allows respondents to express their opinion graphically rather than digitally. Using a 1-to-5 or a 1-to-10 scale not only forces a respondent to react to an item statement at an emotional level, it requires a shift in thinking to classify numerically the intensity of the reaction.

Assume Respondents Have Sound Judgment

This principle translates into eliciting comments aggressively. Many of the company's Level 1 forms are actually two-part forms. The top sheet allows the respondent to mark the grid, while causing the mark to create an impression on the sheet below. The impression created on the second sheet may indicate that an extreme reaction has been captured.

If a reaction is a bit intense, whether positive or negative, the instructions request that the respondent write a brief comment as to why he or she felt so strongly. This gentle prodding often yields data that would otherwise be lost. It seems that people love to justify themselves, especially if they think they will be heard. The forms allow plenty of space for open-ended comments, suggesting that somebody is interested. This approach yields three to four times more commentary than conventional forms.

Get the Information Back Fast

Perhaps the single greatest success is the speed with which InterACT processes and reports information. Using the latest technology to convert slash marks into numeric scores, they are able to scan as many as 4,000 response sheets per hour. The data are moved electronically into a large database for processing and subsequent reporting, which emerges as bold and colorful graphs and charts.

Step 3: Collecting the Data

Once you have created the instrument, the following administrative guidelines can improve the effectiveness of the data collection method.

■ *Keep Responses Anonymous*
Anonymous feedback is highly recommended. It allows the participants to be open with comments that can be helpful and constructive. Otherwise, the input can be extremely biased and perhaps stifled because of concern about the direct reaction from the facilitator.

■ *Have a Neutral Person Collect Forms*
In addition to anonymous responses, it is helpful to have a neutral person collect the feedback questionnaires. In some organizations, the program coordinator or sponsor will conduct the evaluation at the end, independent of the facilitator. This action increases the objectivity of the input and decreases the likelihood of the instructor or facilitator reacting unfavorably to criticism contained in the feedback.

■ *Provide a Copy in Advance*
For lengthy evaluation forms covering programs that span several days, it is helpful to distribute the feedback questionnaire early in the program so that participants can familiarize themselves with the questions and statements. Participants can also address specific topics as they are covered and can take more time to think through particular issues. They should be cautioned, however, not to reach a conclusion on general issues until the end of the program.

■ *Explain the Purpose of the Evaluation*
Tell participants why you are asking for feedback and how it will be used. Although this is sometimes understood, it is best to repeat where the information goes and how it is used in the organization. There is still some mystery surrounding the use of feedback data. Restating the process in terms of the flow and use of data can help clarify this issue.

■ *Explore an Ongoing Evaluation*

For lengthy programs, an end-of-program evaluation may leave participants unable to remember what was covered at what time. An ongoing evaluation can be used to improve this situation. One approach is to distribute evaluation forms at the beginning of the program and instruct participants when and how to supply the information. After each topic is presented, participants evaluate the topic and facilitator. Participants can easily recall the information, and the feedback is more useful to program evaluators. Another approach is to use a daily feedback form to collect input on program pacing, degree of involvement, unclear items, and so forth. (See the Job Aid at the back of this issue for a sample daily feedback form.)

■ *Consider Quantifying Course Ratings*

Some organizations attempt to solicit feedback in terms of numerical ratings. Although still subjective, overall ratings can be useful in monitoring performance and making comparisons. For example, the American Management Association (AMA) collects an overall rating in their public seminars. AMA monitors these overall ratings to compare them with similar programs and to track changes over time. With a large number of programs repeated several times, these ratings can be useful in making comparisons. In some cases, targets or norms are established to compare ratings. When using a norm scale, a rating that is usually considered good may prove to be quite low when compared with the norm of the factor being rated. Another caution is needed since these ratings are subjective: Comparing numerical values may create an impression that the data are objective. This point should be considered in evaluation communications.

■ *Allow Ample Time to Complete Form*

A time crunch can cause problems if participants are asked to complete a feedback form at the end of a program, particularly if they are in a hurry to leave. Consequently, participants may provide incomplete information in an effort to finish and be on their way. A possible alternative is to allow ample time for evaluation as a scheduled session before the end of the program. This evaluation session could be followed by a wrap-up of the program and the last speaker. A 30-minute session will provide an opportunity to enhance the quality and quantity of information.

Step 4: Data Analysis and Reporting

If the data collection process has been carefully and thoroughly developed, the requirements for data analysis and reporting will be minimal. Below are some recommendations that should be addressed at this stage in the evaluation process flow.

- Decide what means of analysis to employ to make certain that the correct software is being used. (For example, spreadsheets are excellent tools for performing mathematical calculations, while databases quickly sort and retrieve information. If possible, use software that can be linked.)

- Ensure that the mathematical analysis is consistent for all Level 1 output and appropriate for user interpretation.

- Verify the accuracy of all mathematical calculations. Begin this process by documenting all data entered into each calculation.

You will also want to determine the types of reports needed. Consider the following questions when making this decision:

- What data need to be reported—the date of training, location, facilitator's name, number of participants, number of responses for each question response scale, reprinting of the evaluation question, totals for each question, totals for each section, summary totals, and so on?

- How should the data be displayed—counts, averages, percentages, bar graph, pie chart?

Technology Trends Affecting Level 1 Evaluation

Implementation of technology for Level 1 evaluation is perhaps one of the most crucial needs among members of the training community. As the need for evaluation continues to grow, it stands to reason that technology will be utilized to enhance the efficiency of such processes. To ensure this efficiency is reached, it will be imperative for organizations to purchase, vendor out, or design a system that is flexible, adaptable, and provides the appropriate data integration and reporting that fits the organization's needs.

When planning a Level 1 evaluation, you will want to consider trends affecting your organization and industry. Issues of how technology has and is affecting training are described briefly below.

■ *Rapid Change of Technology*
With technology changing at an exponential rate, technology training programs are also undergoing rapid change. Today, test designers need immediate feedback in order to make necessary changes and improvements to programs. As a result, it is more important than ever for Level 1 data to be turned around quickly via a smooth, efficient, and reliable Level 1 evaluation process. To report data quickly, many companies are employing basic or customized spreadsheet and database software to simplify the capture and analysis of the data. There are a number of off-the-shelf software packages available that can organize, filter, and calculate evaluation data into comprehensive reports. Some companies are even using scannable forms or outside vendors to automate the actual data processing and reporting. As companies move toward paperless transactions, a greater emphasis on electronic data gathering will be necessary.

■ *Decreased Cost of Learning Technologies*
Lower technology costs make it more viable to offer training programs via learning technologies. For example, a Web-based program can be developed many times more quickly and more inexpensively than possible just a few years ago. In addition, the trend of increasing the capacity and capability of hardware and software has made the process much more adaptable to the training environment.

■ *Web-Based Training and Applications*
The trend toward Web-based training and applications creates an even greater challenge for posttesting evaluations. The use of technology to gather Level 1 data will shift from standard processing to full, real-time data inte-

gration. As new methods of program delivery become available, new methods of collecting post-program data will have to be developed. Today, many companies offer training programs and applications via an intranet or the Internet. Very few of these companies are gathering the necessary evaluation data electronically, however, and are losing some of the efficiency of automation. With some slight enhancements, many of these types of programs can be easily amended to handle electronic data collection and reporting.

Disadvantages of Technology

Using technology to enhance training programs and evaluation methodology creates situations that need to be addressed.

Increased expenses for the short term. It may be difficult for many organizations, large or small, to justify the large up-front expenditures required to invest in the technology that will reap long-term benefits.

Hardware and software selection. Given the explosion of technology variations in software and hardware, it is difficult, if not daunting, to make the right selections. Basically, it becomes almost impossible to decide what is appropriate for a given organization, unless you have the on-staff expertise. Otherwise, you will need to hire a specialist in this area. If you make the wrong decision, or worse yet, no decision, chaos results and puts your organization and its programs behind its competitors. This builds a case for the need for appropriate evaluation processes that accurately assess implementation. The important challenge in this data automation is that someone will have to design the process and support it in a way that allows for flexibility and ease of use.

Staff resistance to new technology. While many staff members are champions of technology, others may resist, preferring to stick with what they know best and their own level of comfort. This will have to be challenged, and the methods by which data were previously captured, calculated, and reported will disappear. Staff skills will need to be enhanced to include interpreting evaluation data and reporting results to stakeholders and line managers so they can assist in the application of learning on the job. Acquiring these new skills can also add to resistance.

- Do the data need to be sorted—by course, facilitator, location, date?

- Is there a need for reports with varying degrees of detail?

The analysis and reporting of data should meet the needs and requests of the clients. The database or spreadsheet used should be flexible enough to report the data in a variety of ways. Reporting and analysis should allow for sorting around demographic variables as well as evaluation response variables. Such variables include:

- course group
- course code
- facilitator
- location
- division
- date
- position
- number of employees
- education (level of)
- training delivery method
- data utilization

Accumulating sound, accurate reaction data and providing useful reports are important steps in the evaluation process, but these steps go hand in hand with documenting how the results must be used to enact program improvements. Too often instructors or program evaluators use the data to feed their egos and let it quietly disappear in their files, forgetting the original purposes for its collection. Several specific uses of Level 1 data are reiterated below.

■ *Monitor Customer Satisfaction*
Because this input is the principal measure taken from the participants, it provides a good indication of their overall reaction to, and satisfaction with, the program. Thus, program developers and owners will know how well the customers are actually satisfied with the product.

■ *Identify Strengths and Weaknesses*
Feedback is extremely helpful in identifying weaknesses as well as strengths in the HRD process. Participant feedback on weaknesses can often lead to adjustments and changes. Identifying strengths can be helpful in future design so that they can be replicated.

■ *Develop Norms and Standards*
Because Level 1 evaluation data can be automated and the information is usually collected with 100 percent of programs, it becomes relatively easy to develop norms and standards throughout the organization. Target ratings can be set for expectations; particular course results are then compared to those norms and standards.

■ *Evaluate Instructors*
Perhaps one of the most common uses of Level 1 data is instructor evaluation. If properly constructed and collected, helpful feedback data can be provided to instructors so that adjustments can be made to increase effectiveness. Some caution needs to be taken since instructor evaluations can sometimes be biased, and other evidence may be necessary to provide an overall assessment of instructor performance.

■ *Evaluate Planned Improvements*
Feedback data from the Level 1 questionnaire can provide a profile of planned actions and improvements. This can be compared with on-the-job actions as a result of the program and can provide a rich source of data in terms of what participants may be changing or implementing because of what they have learned.

■ *Link With Follow-Up Data*
If a follow-up evaluation is planned, it may be helpful to link Level 1 data with follow-up data to see if planned improvements became reality. In most cases, planned actions are inhibited in some way through on-the-job barriers.

■ *Help Marketing Programs*
For some organizations, participant feedback data provide helpful marketing information. Participants' quotes and reactions provide information that may be persuasive to potential participants. Program brochures often contain quotes and summaries of data from Level 1 feedback in the marketing material.

Step 5: Communication

The final step in developing a successful Level 1 evaluation tool and process involves clear, company-wide communication of the process flow to ensure understanding and compliance by all involved. This communication should include, but is not limited to, an explanation of the following:

- The meaning and purpose of the evaluation, as well as what it measures. (It is recommended that a copy of the instrument be provided to clarify this explanation.)

- The importance of the evaluation within the company and its value to stakeholders.

- The entire process flow for receiving, using, and returning evaluations, along with the process for obtaining and distributing reports.

- The means for measuring the effectiveness and efficiency of the process.

- The way in which this information is delivered depends on the company's culture and the Level 1 budget, as well as the number of people involved and their accessibility.

Planned Action

When a Level 1 evaluation includes planned applications of training, the important data can ultimately be used in ROI calculations. With questions concerning how participants plan to use what they have learned and the results that they expect to achieve, higher-level evaluation information can be developed. The questions presented at right illustrate how these types of data are collected with an end-of-program questionnaire for a supervisory training program. Participants are asked to state specifically how they plan to use the program material and the results they expect to achieve. They are asked to convert their accomplishments to an annual monetary value and to show the basis

---

Planned Improvements

As a result of this program, what specific actions will you attempt as you apply what you have learned?

1._____

2._____

3._____

Please indicate what specific measure, outcomes, or projects will change as a result of your actions?

1._____

2._____

3._____

As a result of the anticipated changes in the above, please estimate (in monetary values) the benefits to your organization over a period of one year. _____

What is the basis of this estimate?

_____

_____

What confidence, expressed as a percentage, can you put in your estimate (0% = No Confidence; 100% = Absolute Certainty)?   _____ %

for developing the values. Participants can moderate their responses with a level of confidence to make the data more credible while allowing them to reflect their uneasiness with the process.

When tabulating data, managers multiply the confidence level by the annual monetary value, which results in a more conservative estimate for use in the data analysis. For example, if a participant estimated that the monetary impact of the program would be $10,000, but was only 50 percent confident, a $5,000 value is used in the calculations.

ROI at Level 1

The use of ROI with Level 1 data is increasing, and some organizations have based all of their ROI calculations on Level 1 data. Although it may be very subjective, it does add value, particularly when it is included as part of a comprehensive evaluation system.

Continuing with the planned action form from above, you can develop a summary of the expected benefits by first discarding any data that are incomplete, unusable, extreme, or unrealistic. Next, make the adjustment for the confidence level as discussed earlier. Then adjust the total value again by a factor that reflects the subjectivity of the process and the possibility that participants will not achieve their anticipated results. This figure can be derived with input from management or can be established by the training staff. For one organization, the benefits were divided by two to come up with a number to use in the equation. Then finally, you can calculate ROI by using the net program benefits divided by the program costs. This value, in essence, becomes the expected return-on-investment after the two adjustments for accuracy and subjectivity. For more complete information on ROI, refer to *Infoline* No. 9805, "Level 5 Evaluation: ROI."

References & Resources

Articles

Bassi, Laurie J., and Daniel P. McMurrer. "Training Investment Can Mean Financial Performance." *Training & Development,* May 1998, pp. 40-42.

Benabou, Charles. "Assessing the Impact of Training Programs on the Bottom Line." *National Productivity Review,* Summer 1996, pp. 91-99.

Bramley, P., and B. Kitson. "Evaluating Training Against Business Criteria." *Journal of European Industrial Training,* volume 18, number 1 (1994), pp. 10-14.

Dixon, Nancy, M. "The Relationship Between Trainee Responses on Participant Reaction Forms and Posttest Scores." *HRD Quarterly,* volume 1, number 2 (1997), pp. 129-137.

Garavaglia, P.L. "Applying a Transfer Model to Training." *Performance and Instruction,* volume 35, number 4 (1997), pp. 4-8.

Heideman, James, and Bruce Sanderson. "Zooming In On Training Goals." *Technical & Skills Training,* July 1997, pp. 26-28.

Kaufman, R., J. Keller, and R. Watkins. "What Works and What Doesn't: Evaluation Beyond Kirkpatrick." *Performance and Instruction,* volume 35, number 2 (1995), pp. 8-12.

Kidder, Pamela J., and Janice Z. Rouiller. "Evaluating the Success of a Large-Scale Training Effort." *National Productivity Review,* Spring 1997, pp. 79-89.

Kirkpatrick, D.L. "Revisiting Kirkpatrick's Four-Level Model." *Training & Development,* January 1996, pp. 54-59.

Thornburg, Linda. "Investment in Training Technology Yields Good Returns." *HRMagazine,* January 1998, pp. 37-41.

Watson, Scott C. "Five Easy Pieces to Performance Measurement." *Training & Development,* May 1998, pp. 45-48.

"Why Go to Level 3 & 4 Evaluation? Gap Inc. Finds the Training Payoff." *Training Directors' Forum Newsletter,* July 1997, pp. 1-3.

Willyerd, Karie A. "Balancing Your Evaluation Act." *Training,* March 1997, pp. 52-58.

Books

Basarab, David J. Sr., and Darrell K. Root. *The Training Evaluation Process.* Norwell, MA: Academic Publishers, 1992.

Bassi, Laurie J., and Darlene Russ-Eft (eds.). *What Works: Assessment, Development, and Measurement.* Alexandria, VA: ASTD, 1997.

Bramley, Peter. *Evaluating Training Effectiveness.* London: McGraw-Hill, 1996.

Brown, Stephen M., and Constance J. Seidner (eds.). *Evaluating Corporate Training: Models and Issues.* Boston: Kluwer Academic Publishers, 1997.

Burnham, Byron R. *Evaluating Human Resources, Programs, and Organizations.* Malabar, FL: Krieger Publishing, 1995.

Dixon, Nancy M. *Evaluation: A Tool for Improving HRD Quality.* San Diego: University Associates, 1990.

Fink, Arlene. *The Survey Handbook.* Thousand Oaks, CA: Sage Publications, 1995.

Fisk, C.F. *Evaluation Instruments: ASTD Trainer's Toolkit.* Alexandria, VA: ASTD, 1991.

Kirkpatrick, D.L. "Techniques for Evaluating Training Programs." In *Evaluating Training Programs.* Alexandria, VA: ASTD, 1975.

———. *Evaluating Training Programs: The Four Levels.* San Francisco: Berrett-Koehler, 1994.

Newby, A.C. *Training Evaluation Handbook.* San Diego: Pfeiffer, 1992.

Parry, Scott B. *Evaluating the Impact of Training.* Alexandria, VA: ASTD, 1997.

Phillips, Jack J. *Handbook of Training Evaluation and Measurement Methods.* (3d edition). Houston: Gulf Publishing, 1997.

Rea, Louis M., and Richard A. Parker. *Designing and Conducting Survey Research: A Comprehensive Guide.* (2d edition.) San Francisco: Jossey-Bass, 1997.

Schwarz, Norbert, and Seymour Sudman (eds.). *Answering Questions.* San Francisco: Jossey-Bass, 1996.

References & Resources

Info-lines

Austin, Mary. "Needs Assessment by Focus Group." No. 9401 (revised 1998).

Fisher, Sharon, et al. "Write Better Behavioral Objectives." No. 8505 (revised 1998).

Phillips, Jack J., et al. "Level 2 Evaluation: Learning." No. 9814.

————. "Level 3 Evaluation: Application." No. 9815.

————. "Level 4 Evaluation: Business Results." No. 9816.

————. "Level 5 Evaluation: ROI." No. 9805.

Plattner, Francis. "Instructional Objectives." No. 9712.

Shaver, Warren, Jr. "How to Build and Use a 360-Degree Feedback System." No. 9508 (revised 1998).

Waagen, Alice. "Essentials for Evaluation." No. 9706.

Other

Pettit-Sleet, Sandra. "1998 Level One Evaluation Process." Learning Services, First University, First Union National Bank, 1997.

Wallace, Debi. "Learning Evaluation Reference Guide." Commercial College, First University, First Union National Bank, 1997.

Daily Feedback Form

Here is a sample daily feedback questionnaire you can customize for your specific training class.

1. What issues presented today still remain confused or unclear?

_____

_____

_____

_____

2. The most useful topics presented today were:

_____

_____

_____

_____

3. It would help me if you would:

_____

_____

_____

_____

Job Aid

4. The pacing of the program is:

   ☐ Just right.

   ☐ Too slow.

   ☐ Too fast.

   Comment: _____

5. The degree of participant involvement is:

   ☐ Just right.

   ☐ Too slow.

   ☐ Too fast.

6. Three very important items you should cover tomorrow are:

   A. _____

   B. _____

   C. _____

7. Comments

   _____

   _____

   _____

   _____

Level 2 Evaluation: Learning

Issue 9814

Level 2 Evaluation: Learning

AUTHORS:

Jack Phillips, Ph.D.
Performance Resources
 Organization
P.O. Box 380637
Birmingham, AL 35238-0637
Tel.: 205.678.9700
Fax: 205.678.8070

Robert Shriver
Lockheed Martin Energy
 Systems, Inc.
701 Scarboro Rd.
Oak Ridge, TN 37831-8240
Tel.: 423.574.0684
Fax: 423.576.4179

H. Steve Giles
Tenera Energy LLC
3619 Knoxville Hwy.
Wartburg, TN 37887
Tel.: 423.324.5555

Editor
Cat Sharpe

Contributing Editor
Ann Bruen

Production Design
Anne Morgan

Tests to Measure Learning

Evaluations of training programs are usually undertaken to provide reasonable assurance that the programs are producing competent employees who are capable of performing their jobs safely and efficiently. Evaluations are conducted to serve the following purposes:

- to improve the design or delivery of learning events

- to increase the use of the learning on the job

- to make decisions about learning in the organization

Before a participant completes a training module, he or she should be evaluated in the instructional setting. This on-the-spot, before-they-leave-the-setting evaluation is the centerpiece for all instruction and a key checkpoint in the training evaluation process.

Evaluation at all levels, 1 through 5, is an iterative cycle with numerous opportunities to gather data and important feedback as it relates to the participants, facilitator(s), and instructional content. Evaluation has components that touch the formative (pretraining/development-stage work), as well as the summative (posttraining assessment) side of training programs.

Evaluating systematically, rather than as an afterthought, creates prospects to make improvements to the training process. Evaluation steps build on one another. For example, once the individual effects of a program are assessed, it is possible to use that data to determine if a program is on target in its overall design and application. While there may be other program development tools, none is more effective in determining whether learning objectives are relevant and productive in the work environment than this systematic, phase-by-phase, analysis.

Measuring learning also provides the following:

- a valid, reliable indicator of an employee's knowledge, skills, and abilities related to job requirements

- a self-assessment tool used to determine an employee's progress

- the ability to determine if employees possess knowledge of work policies and procedures that will enable them to safely perform their duties (a critical issue in manufacturing and process industries)

This issue of *Info-line* will provide the guidelines for performing Level 2 evaluations, including a discussion of various test types, test formatting and design, and administration issues. It is one of five *Info-line* issues covering the different levels of evaluation as defined by the model where:

Level 1 is reaction and planned action.

Level 2 is learning.

Level 3 is application.

Level 4 is business impact.

Level 5 is return-on-investment.

Most employees have been tested by objective tests at some point during their careers. These tests include true-false, matching, and multiple-choice questions. It is possible to check for a "higher level of knowledge" using the multiple-choice question format. This refers to Benjamin Bloom's taxonomy of learning objectives, which includes the following six progressive levels for measuring cognitive learning objectives:

1. Knowledge.

2. Comprehension.

3. Application.

4. Analysis.

5. Synthesis.

6. Evaluation.

Test Design

Test design and development is not a mechanical process that blindly applies testing principles. It is important to test areas that are meaningful to job performance. For this purpose, a job analysis may provide direction for your entire program. Effective testing requires that learning objectives for current and future instruction be thoughtfully selected prior to test development.

■ *Length and Scope*
Keep the overall number of test items reasonable. You need to limit each section or subject area and keep questions from a minimum of two to a maximum of 10 per instructional objective. If you develop tests that take longer than one hour, you should plan to include a break period. For multiple-choice questions, a good rule of thumb is to allow about one minute per question.

■ *Language and Cultural Factors*
Test language should be targeted to your audience. For example, individuals being tested on how to place part X on widget Y on an assembly line do not need a test written at the level of graduate school exams. You also may need to take steps to ensure that multilanguage and cultural factors are addressed for non-English-speaking employees.

■ *Subject Matter Experts (SMEs)*
Subject matter experts, or SMEs, are invaluable for their expertise. Use SMEs to determine the significance and accuracy of test material.

For more information on test design and construction, refer to *Info-line*s No. 8905, "Lesson Design and Development"; No. 9706, "Basics of Instructional Development Systems"; and No. 8907, "Testing for Learning Outcomes."

Training programs and training materials are usually designed to encourage and enable participants to comprehend, apply, and even synthesize information—not just recall facts. As a result, there is value in checking learning at several levels or dimensions within a test. It is also crucial for course objectives and tests to be aligned.

Test experts agree that all tests are, at best, estimates of an employee's knowledge of a particular subject. Even so, a test is still the more objective and reliable measure of an employee's knowledge. For more information on design and construction, see *Test Design* at left.

Testing Formats

There are advantages and disadvantages to the various testing formats. For example, essay tests are usually easier to prepare and evaluate. They simply ask a short list of open-ended questions. But essay tests, along with problem-solving tests, cannot cover as much material because of how long it takes to answer questions. Essay tests are often treated more subjectively when graded, while it is easy to unintentionally build in biases in objective tests. Test developers need to prepare for the most objective, effective test conditions possible.

When considering the testing environment, there is also a balance to achieve. It is the balance between setting up a controlled environment that elicits precise measures of achievement and one that students perceive as a natural work setting—or as "real"—at the same time.

Knowledge Tests

While knowledge tests reveal differences in student achievement, in most cases, this is not the only method for assessing progress. Other tools include performance checks, interaction assessments, and information collected from observations. Follow these guidelines when preparing knowledge tests:

● Ask important questions.
● Word questions clearly.
● Provide examples when possible.
● Familiarize yourself with the test material.
● Consider the knowledge level of the students.

● Select the best format for the material.

● Provide clearly written instructions.

Oral Tests

Oral tests are usually conducted face-to-face. There may be some variations to this approach, such as using two evaluators per student to minimize partiality in the test administration. Normally, the oral format provides an opportunity for evaluators to ask follow-up questions—to probe for more details. The following list characterizes many consistent features of oral tests:

● a pass-fail structure

● more interpersonal since the evaluator sees facial expressions and gets a feel for the personality and stress level of the participant

● flexible, allowing for a change of pace depending on the evaluator's level of experience

● may be more time consuming and expensive to administer

Other influences in the evaluation of student performance may make this approach less valid than others. It is easier to conceal—intentional or unintentional—evaluator bias. Personality conflicts could play a role as well. The pressure of this intense face-to-face examination style may place less socially adept students at a disadvantage. If language and presentation skills have no relevance to the overall learning objectives, it is probably best to reconsider the use of this type of test.

Essay Tests

Essay tests are often used because they are so easy to prepare. Unfortunately, they often lack the careful review given to objective tests because of their open-ended style. Usually there is neither rating scale nor standard answers, and the evaluator is in a position to adjust the assessment regardless of the quality of the answers. Essay tests are sometimes favored as an assessment tool because participants must draw upon a wide range of knowledge and write an organized summary of

facts and principles. Equally important is how the participant argues his or her point. Recognize that essay tests do not produce consistent results. Here are some guidelines for when to best employ essay tests in your evaluation process.

● The group is small.

● Tests will be used only once.

● Testing ability to provide written answers is important.

● Time to prepare is less than time to assess progress.

True-False Tests

True-false tests provide a simple, yet reliable means of checking information recall. This requires that participants have, for the true-false test to be of value, language comprehension as well as the ability to determine accuracy of test statements. Guessing on true-false tests can be a problem, but generally the success rate of guessing is limited.

One misconception about true-false questions is that they are used to test insignificant facts. This test format does allow you to ask complex questions that examine knowledge and comprehension of principles and processes. The advantages of true-false tests are:

Efficient—they cover many questions in little time.

Effective—as much so as a multiple-choice test of the same length.

Easy—to develop.

Test developers should be able to defend answers easily; that is, the answers should be quite obvious to a participant who has taken the instruction and studied the material. Throughout the test, keep items short, simple, and consistent. Here are additional hints to keep in mind when developing true-false tests: Write more false than true items, and write items in such a way that having only a superficial knowledge leads to an incorrect answer.

Multiple-Choice Tests

There are many good reasons for using multiple-choice tests. Foremost is that they are more direct and less ambiguous than true-false tests, and answers are easier to defend. Selecting an answer from several alternatives is often just as difficult as writing out an answer to a question. Both essay tests and multiple-choice tests can measure the same levels of achievement and have the same level of effectiveness.

When writing the opening statement—or stem—of a multiple-choice question, use the direct approach. You will want to develop multiple-choice tests that provide participants with a learning opportunity while serving as a vehicle for assessing skills. When developing a multiple-choice test that enhances both, remember to do the following:

- Strive for parallel responses.

- Stay away from negative statements.

- Keep answers short and clear.

- Use "all of the above" responses occasionally.

- Write two to three believable distracters per question.

- Order numerical responses from low to high.

Distracters, correct-sounding statements that challenge a student's accurate comprehension of subject matter, provide an excellent testing methodology for multiple-choice items. One good method for developing a "bank" of plausible distracters is to first give the test as a fill-in-the-blank test. Then, use plausible wrong answers given by participants as the multiple-choice test distracters. You also want to avoid unintentionally giving away the answer. This can happen with improper use of grammatical cues. For example, making the correct answer singular and the incorrect answers plural is a common mistake. Also avoid making right answers longer than wrong answers.

There are other types of tests you can use, such as short-answer, completion, matching, and problem tests. Short-answer questions may call for word, phrase, or sentence completion; these kinds of items are typically used to check factual information. There is little or no concern with guessing to short-answer questions. When developing short-answer, completion, and problem tests, remember to:

- Word questions to elicit a single answer.

- First determine the correct response, then write the question.

- Place the fill-in-the-blank space at the end of the question item.

- Ask direct questions; do not use language to confuse the test taker.

- Do not accidentally incorporate the answer in the question.

When developing matching tests, remember to:

- Group like items to create a more challenging test segment.

- Use fewer and shorter premises to be matched with more possibilities.

- Give clear directions.

- Organize lists alphabetically.

Measuring Simulation Learning

Another technique to measure learning is job simulation. This involves the construction and application of a procedure or task that simulates or models the activity being conducted. The simulation is designed to represent, as closely as possible, an actual job situation.

Simulation offers an opportunity for participants to practice what is being taught in a training program and have their performance observed in a simulated job condition. It also can provide accurate evaluations if the performance is objective and can be clearly measured. Simulations can be employed during the training program, at the end of the program, or as part of the follow-up evaluation. There are several advantages to using simulations.

■ Reproducibility
Simulations permit jobs or parts of jobs to be reproduced in a nearly identical manner to the real thing. This enables you to shorten the time required to perform an actual task in the "real" environment.

■ Cost Effectiveness
Sometimes expensive to construct, simulations can be cost effective in the long run. For example, it is cost prohibitive to train or recertify pilots using million-dollar aircraft. As a result, simulators are used to replicate flying conditions, which enables pilots to demonstrate or learn skills and techniques—such as landing on aircraft carriers—before actually piloting the aircraft.

■ Safety Considerations
Safety is a major factor for using simulated environments. Using the aircraft example, it would be too dangerous for a pilot to learn how to land a jet on an aircraft carrier without the use of a simulator. The nature of many jobs requires participants to be trained in simulated conditions instead of on the job. For example, firemen are trained in simulated conditions prior to actual fire exposure, and law-enforcement officers are trained in simulated conditions prior to being put into field operations.

There are a variety of simulation techniques used to evaluate program results. These are the most commonly used techniques:

■ Electrical or Mechanical Simulation
This technique uses a combination of electronics and mechanical devices to simulate real-life situations and is used in conjunction with programs to develop operational and diagnostic skills. Two very expensive examples are simulated "patients" or a nuclear power plant operations simulation.

■ Task Simulation
This approach involves performing a simulated task as part of an evaluation. For example, in an aircraft company, technicians are trained on the safe removal, handling, and installation of a radioactive source used in a nucleonic oil-quantity indicator gauge. Technicians attend a detailed training program and, to become certified, must be observed and evaluated during a simulation. Only after demonstrating their proficiency and passing safety performance standards are technicians certified. The task simulation serves as the program's evaluation.

■ Business Games
Games can be used to simulate all or part of a business enterprise where participants are asked to change the business variables and then observe the effects of the changes. These games often reflect real-world situations and can effectively predict patterns and outcomes of future business scenarios. Typical objectives in this type of simulation are methods to maximize profits, market share, or return-on-investment.

■ In-Basket
This technique is particularly useful in supervisory and management training programs. Portions of a supervisor's job are simulated through a series of items that normally appear in the in-basket—everyday memos, letters, personnel issues, and reports. Participants must determine action plans for each item while considering HRD principles. Performance and outcomes of the in-basket items also represent an evaluation of the program.

■ Case Study
Possibly less effective, but still popular, the case study provides a detailed description of a problem and typically contains a list of questions pertinent to the case. The participant is asked to analyze the case and determine the best course of action. The problem should reflect the content in an HRD program and the conditions in the real-world setting. The most common categories of case studies include:

● Exercise case studies—participants practice the application of specific procedures.

● Situation case studies—participants analyze provided data and make decisions based on their particular situation.

- Complex case studies (an extension of the situation case study)—participants are required to sort through a mountain of information, some or much of which may be irrelevant.

- Decision case studies—participants are required to go a step further by presenting plans to solve an assigned problem.

- Critical incident case studies—information is withheld from participants until participants request it.

- Action maze case studies—here a large case is presented in a series of small units, and participants are required to predict outcomes at each stage.

Objectivity on the part of the evaluator is an inherent difficulty with case studies. Frequently there can be many possible courses of action, some as plausible as others, which makes it difficult to consistently attain an objective, measurable performance rating.

■ Role Play

This is sometimes referred to as skill practice, where participants practice newly learned skills while being observed. Participants have assigned roles with specific instructions, often including an ultimate outcome. Participants then practice their skills, interacting with others to accomplish the objective. The role play is intended to duplicate a workplace setting. A facilitator is frequently used to keep the role play on track and help guide participants to a favorable outcome. Essential to the success of this technique as an evaluation tool is the judging ability of the observers.

■ Assessment Center Method

Using this method, feedback is provided by a group of specially trained observers called assessors. Assessors are not HRD staff members. This tool has been effective when used for employee selection and shows great promise as an evaluation tool of HRD program effectiveness. While not actual "centers," the term refers to a procedure for evaluating performance.

In a typical situation, an employee is assessed on his or her mastery of a variety of exercises that demonstrate particular knowledge, skills, and abilities, usually called KSAs or job dimensions. The assessment may take from a few hours to a few days to complete. Participants are evaluated on each dimension, then individual ratings are combined to lessen subjectivity and determine a final rating for each participant.

These dimensions are vital to on-the-job success. For example, one manufacturing organization identified the following job dimensions for first-line supervisors:

- analysis
- delegation
- initiative
- judgment
- leadership
- management identification
- oral communications
- planning and organization
- reading skills
- sensitivity
- technical knowledge
- written communication

Measuring Learning Through Activities

An informal assessment of learning may be sufficient if resources are scarce. In some situations, it is important to have an informal check of learning that provides some assurance participants have acquired skills, knowledge, or perhaps even some changes in attitudes or behavior. Using an informal approach is appropriate when other levels of evaluation are pursued. For example, if a Level 3 on-the-job application evaluation is planned, it may not be critical to have a comprehensive Level 2 evaluation.

Following are some alternative approaches to measuring learning that you can use if inexpensive, low-key, informal assessments are needed:

Exercises and Activities

Many programs contain specific activities, exercises, or problems that must be explored and developed. Some are constructed in terms of involvement exercises, while others require individual problem-solving skills. When integrated into the program, there are several specific ways to measure learning.

- The results can be reviewed and scored by the instructor. This becomes a measure of learning and part of the overall score for the course.

- The results can be discussed within a group comparing various approaches and solutions. A joint-group assessment of each individual can be reached. While not always practical, this can work with narrowly focused applications.

- Solutions can be shared with the group, and participants provide self-assessments that indicate the degree of skills or knowledge obtained. This also offers reinforcement value since participants have access to correct solutions.

- The instructor reviews individual progress to determine success. This works in small group settings but can be difficult and time consuming with large groups.

Self-Assessment

For many applications, participants can self-assess the extent of skills and knowledge they have acquired. This is particularly applicable when Level 3, 4, and 5 evaluations are planned, and it is important to know if actual learning is taking place. A few techniques can ensure the process is effective.

- The self-assessment should be anonymous so individuals feel free to express a realistic and accurate assessment of what they have learned.

- The purpose of the data and what the data will be used for should be explained. This is especially true if the data are used to alter course or test design.

- If the self-assessment indicates little or unsatisfactory improvement, an explanation should be offered to participants. This helps ensure that accurate and credible information was provided.

Instructor Assessment

This is another assessment technique for instructors and facilitators. Although subjective, this approach may be appropriate when a Level 3, 4, or 5 evaluation is planned. One of the most effective ways to accomplish this is to provide a checklist of the specific skills that need to be acquired. Instructors can then check off their assessment of individual skills. Also, if there is a specific knowledge that needs to be acquired, the categories could be presented with a checklist to ensure that individuals have a good understanding of those items.

Team Assessments

Team assessments are conducted to determine and address performance problems that might otherwise go unnoticed in a self-directed work group. Assessing team performance is important when discussing Level 2 evaluation since a significant amount of group learning can be acquired from this kind of continuous process improvement. A number of positive results come out of team assessments; for example, they:

- may take the form of an independent audit by an outside group in addition to the internal review (self-assessment)

- can provide feedback on team performance problems—whether conducted as an internal self-assessment or as an external audit

- enable teams to focus their improvement efforts and make more informed decisions as a result of findings uncovered in a study

The team assessment process can be burdensome, but it can also provide a vehicle for research or data gathering—helpful when used to determine future activities and directions.

Observing Behavior Change

When observing posttraining task performance, a unique kind of evaluation is taking place. Special skills are needed to observe and measure behavioral changes. Evaluators require particular training for this type of assessment. It is also important to ensure that students receive the correct information, including the site location, when an observation has been set up. Before implementing an observation process, decide whether the student should be stopped if a step is performed incorrectly. At this point, the observer should determine if the student is competent to perform the task or needs more practice or additional instruction.

The evaluator needs to restrain himself or herself from coaching, asking questions, or talking with the individual performing the task. It is disruptive and possibly prejudicial to the process. Record observation results using either a form of field test instrument or an activity/performance checklist. In general, the student receives feedback on incorrect performance immediately after the task has been completed.

Interviews and Discussions

Occasionally, supervisors or training staff members will conduct field discussions or interviews to determine the level of knowledge before a student performs a job at the work site. This may happen before or after an observation is conducted, or it may be an independent one-on-one assessment relative to a specific set of questions. An interview generally proceeds along a script of questions.

Since the observable measures center on a specific procedure or piece of equipment, it may not be possible to conduct an interview in the classroom setting. This would apply in situations where an employee needs to demonstrate recognition of things such as product defects, equipment malfunctions, safety hazards, or other real-time concerns or problems. Other applications could include situations where an employee needs to explain, using a discussion format, how a control panel at an operator station works.

Asking appropriate questions at the appropriate time is a key evaluation item. Questioning students like this allows the interviewer to probe for answers more easily than with a structured, objective test. Though talking is necessary, interviewers should avoid coaching students.

Measuring Learning on the Web

With the recent explosion in the use of the World Wide Web for training and education, the issue of testing on the Web has received much attention. On one hand, there are advantages to training and testing on the Web, such as around-the-clock availability and accessibility anywhere there is a phone line or network connection. This translates into dollar savings, especially when using the Web as a means to demonstrate pretraining proficiency.

On the other hand, there are problems with protecting exam banks, ensuring that the persons taking the test are who they say they are, and that they are working on their own. These issues cause acute concern about the wisdom of offering testing on the Web. Here are some possible solutions to this problem.

- Use a random generator to pull a designated number of questions (perhaps for each objective) from an exam bank. This ensures that no two participants receive the same test.

- Assign passwords to participants and corresponding password protection to tests to provide some degree of security. In organizations with intranets or networked systems where computer security requirements for the issuance, use, and protection of user identification and passwords are strictly enforced, this can be very effective.

- Allow training on the Web, but require participants to come to a traditional testing center for written exams.

Developing Web-based tests should follow all the rules for developing traditional tests (refer to *Infoline* No. 9701, "Delivering Quick Response IBT/CBT Training.") If valid and reliable test banks already exist, there is no need to change the questions. Generally, Web test items tend to be more objective because the most commonly used question style is multiple-choice. True-false and matching items are certainly possible, but essay and short-answer tests are not as easily graded by current technology. In some cases, drag-and-drop style questions can be used when simulating a work situation or environment where the participant must make selection or routing decisions.

To reduce time and costs, templates can be developed for writing and programming Web tests. The developer can use a template in a word processing software program to make organization and style consistent. The programmer also can use a template when merging the text file to the test shell. For more information on Web-based testing, see *Online Testing Software Tools* on the next page.

Evaluation Validity and Reliability

For any type of objective test, it is useful if the instrument is a valid measurement tool. In a nutshell, do tests and their scores truly represent the knowledge, skills, and abilities (KSAs) being measured? For example, if a test is intended to measure high school chemistry knowledge, it should measure high school chemistry knowledge—not college-level chemistry or high school-level mathematics. Use the following validity review measures for your tests:

■ *Content Validity*
This review can be the simplest method to assess whether a test is valid. It is established by aligning test items and learning objectives. You do not need statistical calculations to determine content validity. Subject matter experts (SMEs) play a key role with this process, as they judge whether test items truly correspond to the learning objectives. The primary basis for this determination is the quality of the job analysis and learning objectives that follow, plus a careful SME review. Content validity is a minimum requirement for a good test and is founded on solid test development practices.

■ *Construct Validity*
This is achieved when one test compares favorably with another test—one already conducted by your organization or an equivalent national test of the same material (convergent validity). By the same token, the test does *not* correlate with tests of different material (divergent validity). For example, a new test of mathematical skills would be expected to strongly correlate with other tests of similar math skills (convergent construct validity). It would also be expected to *not* correlate with a test of running speed (divergent construct validity).

This validity measure is determined by administering a new test and the established test to a group, and finding the correlation between the test scores. To the extent that the results are related, there is an established level of construct validity. Statistical analysis is required to determine the level of convergent and divergent construct validity. Relatedness will yield a numerical value—a correlation coefficient. Refer to *Info-line* No. 9101, "Statistics for HRD Practice," or look to a number of statistical software packages to help calculate these data.

■ *Predictive Validity*
This measure is an important step when considering how well a test predicts future job success. Predictive validity is determined by administering a job performance test to a group of employees after training and then again after 90 days to six months on the job. How the two sets of data correlate is an indication of the measure of predictive validity coefficient. Predictive validity is established using similar statistics to construct validity. When measures of current job performance are correlated with test scores, the result is termed *concurrent validity*. Both predictive and concurrent validity are measures of how a test relates to job performance.

■ *Documentation*
Job, learning objectives, and test item documentation are important during any test validation project. Some companies have developed task-to-test matrices using a database to ensure that validity elements are aligned in a clearly defined manner.

Online Testing Software Tools

Adapted from Brandon Hall's book, *Web-Based Training Cookbook,* the following is a features requirement list to help you plan your own testing software.

Create Function

- interactive study guides
- templates
- quizzes
- tests
- surveys
- certifications
- screening instruments

Assessment Capacity

- knowledge
- skills
- aptitude
- strengths
- weaknesses

Design Features

- pictures
- video clips
- animation
- sound/music files
- editing buttons
- graphics
- audio
- video
- drag-and-drop
- hot spots

Navigation Features

- move between questions
- determine number of questions
- mark questions and return later
- review buttons for skipped or marked questions

Test Results

- displayed in tables or graphs
- groups scores or averages
- categorizes scores or averages
- 360-degree feedback system

Question Types

- choose one
- multiple-choice
- choose all that apply
- true-false
- short-answer
- rate on a scale
- fill-in-the-blank

Security Features

- passwords
- confidential questions and results
- makes answer-sharing difficult
- prevents mistakes
- prevents cheating
- controls who takes test
- controls how often test is taken

Time Features

- sets time limits
- time remaining indicator
- immediate results
- immediate assessments

Other Features

- design, cut, or paste from other Windows-based programs
- create instruments using existing instructor-led or Web-based courses
- unlimited number of questions
- unlimited number of answers per question
- unlimited number of users
- customizable assessment and data collection
- answers can change course of a program
- accommodates prescribed or random question order
- introductory or explanatory information displayed throughout test
- no programming required
- point-and-click interface for instruction creation
- integrates with e-mail systems
- developer or participant can attach documents, images, and audio clips

Relationship of Reliability to Validity

To arrive at test validity you need to evaluate the degree to which guess work (which is sometimes necessary) supports conclusions and actions. Whether an evaluation is accurate is determined by weighing the overall test scores or other modes of assessment with the more speculative components of the evaluation.

Reliability refers to the consistency of measurement and can be interpreted as an index of test results error. While there is no established standard for assessing test reliability, the validity rationale above can be applied here as well. Generally, tests with a reliability at or above 75 percent are considered adequate. For a real-world example of reliability analysis, see the case study at right.

Test validity determines that a test accurately measures what it is intended to measure, and test reliability determines how often it succeeds. Both indexes are used to determine whether inferences and actions based on test scores are on target.

Test validity incorporates several aspects of the testing process into a single judgment—the test is valid or it is not. This judgment should be based on several test result aspects including the following two considerations:

1. Is the test reasonably reliable (for example, free from significant measurement errors)?

2. Does the test content sufficiently cover the material presented in the training program, which is needed to perform the job safely and competently? Information regarding test content often is based on expert judgment and involves SME assessment of individual items. Item analysis can help guide this process, but it cannot take the place of true expert evaluation of item content.

Criterion-related information refers to a test's relationship to other measures of job performance, such as performance appraisals or other subjective performance standards. The key to the usability of this type of information is the accuracy of the assumptions used to bring the data together.

Case Study: Test Item Analysis

Test item analysis is often considered part of a Level 2 evaluation since it is one the methodologies used to assess learning by objectively analyzing the quality of test items. In 1996, a test item analysis was conducted by the evaluation group of the central training department of a large government contractor.

In response to a plant evaluation action plan, the evaluation group conducted a test item analysis for a safety compliance course as part of an overall evaluation plan to improve retention of the plant's radiological workers' knowledge. The specific purpose was to evaluate the psychometric properties of the safety compliance course in order to determine if multiple-choice test items effectively measured the constructs of interest. An arbitrary population sample was selected from plant personnel who had taken the examination during a three-month period in 1996. The selection yielded 85 usable examinations.

The compliance exam was categorized as a type designed to ascertain if respondents achieved an acceptable level of mastery on a given construct. These types of examinations are somewhat different in psychometric properties than examinations designed to measure depth of knowledge. The analysis found that both the A and B versions of the course exam appeared to have acceptable reliability and equivalency in terms of respondents' overall test performance. Nevertheless, the analysis suggested that the content of some test items be reviewed by subject matter experts (SMEs) to ensure that certain items were clearly worded, measured the appropriate constructs, and were not too easy. The analysis found numerous test items with easy item difficulty ratios (.90-1.00 range); this could suggest several things:

● The information was well taught.
● Distracters were not believable.
● Answers were cued in some way.
● The participants already knew the material.

Some test items indicated a degree of difficulty. Those with ratios of .60 or below suggested the information was taught poorly or not at all, the questions were badly worded, or the material was too difficult.

The item analysis correlated both test versions with performance on the separate practical test and found neither was significantly related. It was also noted that the reading level of the exam may have been too difficult for those individuals with limited vocabulary and comprehension skills.

Construct-related information refers to a test's ability to capture the overall composition of a topic, task, or skill. This means that it "captures the mood" of the item being measured without introducing extraneous information. Without proper construct, a test can easily muddy the waters and cause confusion, or it can lead to wrong assumptions.

Test Difficulty

Test reliability and validity are maximized if the level of difficulty for answering most test items is more than just a chance possibility, and at the same time, the degree of difficulty is not too high. If a test is too easy, it will show up in overall high grade averages, which in turn translate into poor job performance, on-the-job accidents, or damage to expensive equipment. If a test is too difficult, it will become apparent if the overall grade averages are low. A too-difficult test can produce the same potentially disastrous on-the-job performance results as a too-easy test.

A test or test item that appears to be on the easy side could mean:

- The information was well taught.
- Answers were cued in some way.
- The participants already knew the information.

When it becomes apparent that a test or test item is too difficult, consider these possibilities: It was not adequately presented in the training session or in the reading materials; or the item is so difficult that only the most knowledgeable participants are able to answer correctly.

Skillful test assembly achieved by taking into account all the test construct considerations discussed here will have a distinct impact on the day-to-day workings of an organization.

Split-Half Check of Reliability

This is a type of test reliability where one test is converted into two shorter ones. It is achieved by randomly assigning test items to one test half or the other. Each half is scored, and the correlation between the halves is calculated to provide a measure of response and consistency. Because only one test is administered at a time, this approach is often used to determine test reliability. You retest with the unused half, which overcomes the memory bias in a test-retest approach.

Test-Retest Check of Reliability

This approach does just what the name implies. The same test is administered twice to the same group of people, and the scores are compared. Memory can play a factor. With too short a period between tests, participants could simply remember the questions. With too long a period, other variables—such as exposure to new information—enter the equation. Timing is the critical issue in a test-retest check of reliability.

You can refer to some of the sources in the references and resources section at the back of this issue to find other helpful reliability checks.

Pilot Testing

Just as a course or a questionnaire is piloted, so too is a test piloted. This is especially true when the test and its parts evaluate an entire job function. The size and diversity of the test population or the information covered may also necessitate several pilots. Several drafts and technical reviews may be necessary before administering the first test. After you administer the test to a pilot group, there should be a period of review and open discussion with the participants to get their feedback for improving the test or the testing process.

Selecting a Pilot Group

This is an important step. The pilot group must represent a solid sample of the workforce population—not just people who are available at the time. A pilot is a part of the test development phase and is considered to be formative evaluation. It is the final phase before proceeding with project implementation.

Pilot group participants need be told how important their roles are to the process. Their comments and input will help ensure the project's success. It is also a nice idea to send thank-you letters to participants in recognition of their efforts.

Following are some pointers for pilot testing your evaluation instruments:

- Handle the pilot as if it is the real thing; this way any problems can be corrected realistically—up front.

- Update the test material based on feedback from the pilot.

- If customized scan forms are created, update these as well.

- Incorporate feedback from the pilot session into the overall program.

- Document the pilot process for use with future programs.

Test updates must be made as more current production, research, or quality assurance information becomes available. Updated tests will also need to be checked for reliability and validity.

Administrative Issues

Tests should have clearly written instructions explaining what to do, how to do it, and how to document the information. The format should include:

- general instructions
- specific section instructions
- specific item format instructions

Instructions should be presented orally to participants. Written instructions should be clear enough so the participant can complete the test without further assistance. Provide time for examinees to read the instructions and ask questions. A few things to consider are:

- Tell participants whether it is acceptable to ask questions during the test.

- Address answers to individual questions to the entire group.

- Tell participants the value of test items and how the tests will be scored.

- Clearly state and post all time limits.

Administrative Guidelines

A sample of the kinds of clear and concise test administration guidelines that must be developed are:

- Make test instructions clear and concise by using a different type size and style to make important points stand out.

- Hold an independent review of test instructions to check for inconsistencies or ambiguities.

- Include examples with the instructions when introducing difficult formats.

In general, effective administration and monitoring will help to ensure that all participants have an equal opportunity to understand and properly answer test questions. This can be accomplished by having independent administrators (not evaluators or instructors) facilitate the testing. Developing testing administration guidelines can also provide definitive procedures for the process.

Testing Conditions

Optimize, to the extent possible, testing conditions. This might include something as simple as scheduling tests during the morning hours if the classroom becomes hot in the afternoon. To enhance test performance, consider correcting the following problems if they exist in the test setting:

- high noise levels
- inadequate lighting
- lack of ventilation
- excessive heat or cold
- interruptions

While paying attention to the physical testing conditions, many may not give enough consideration to the emotional conditions related to testing. Make the purpose of the test clear and emphasize the need for accurate results. Create a positive climate to help motivate the test takers, reduce stress and anxiety, and enhance communication. Here are some other items to take into consideration.

■ *Confidentiality*

All exam results should be kept strictly confidential. Scores should be sent only to the employee and his or her immediate supervisor. An employee's scores should not be revealed in written program reports.

■ *Record Keeping*

If a detailed database of test scores is developed, it makes it possible to sort the data in a number of useful ways for application throughout the organization. It can be used to calculate such valuable information as:

- mean
- standard deviation
- range
- standard error
- count
- minimum
- maximum

■ *Scanning*

Using scannable test answer forms is recommended when large numbers of tests are to be administered. Scanners are now available that read ink as well as pencil markings and can be used to process data rapidly and directly into a database. The front and back of forms can be scanned, which makes it possible to include more items when needed. In recent years, hardware and software advances have significantly improved the scanning process.

■ *Standard Forms*

Software packages are available to help create customized scannable answer sheets that correlate to a test question booklet. This not only makes it easier for participants to complete the forms, it speeds data processing, too.

Putting It All Together

Measuring learning in the business setting is more than a simple question-and-answer session. It is foundational to the successful implementation of the subsequent levels of the five-level evaluation process. Such vital issues as safety, morale, optimal use and maintenance of expensive equipment, and, ultimately, the fiscal health of an organization hinge on expertly designed and executed testing processes. It must be a precise process because so much is at stake.

This issue presents a comprehensive overview of the various types of tests and their format, design, evaluation, and administration. These are tools to put you well on the way to achieving an efficient learning evaluation process for your organization.

References & Resources

References & Resources

Articles

Ackerman, P.L. "Individual Differences in Skill Learning: An Integration of Psychometric and Information Processing Perspectives." *Psychological Bulletin,* volume 102 (1987), pp. 3-27.

Anderson, J.R. "Acquisition of a Cognitive Skill." *Psychological Review,* volume 89 (1982), pp. 369-406.

Campbell, C.P., and T.G. Hatcher. "Testing that is Performance-Based and Criterion-Referenced." *Performance & Instruction,* May/June 1989, pp. 1-9.

Books

Aiken, L.R. Jr. *Psychological and Educational Testing.* Boston: Allyn and Bacon, 1973.

Basarab, D.J., and D.K. Root. *The Training Evaluation Process.* Norwell, MA: Academic Publishers, 1992.

Bassi, L.J., and D. Russ-Eft (eds.). *What Works: Assessment, Development, and Measurement.* Alexandria, VA: ASTD, 1997.

Bloom, B. *Taxonomy of Education Objectives: The Cognitive Domain.* New York: Donald McKay, 1956.

Brown, S.M., and C.J. Seidner. (eds.). *Evaluating Corporate Training: Models and Issues.* Boston: Kluwer Academic Publishers, 1997.

Chang, R.Y., et al. *Measuring Team Performance.* London: Kogan Page, 1994.

Cryer, J.D., and G.W. Cogg. *An Electronic Companion to Business Statistics.* New York: Cogito Learning Media, 1998.

Deming, B.S. *Evaluating Job-Related Training.* Alexandria, VA: ASTD, 1982.

Denova, C.C. *Test Construction for Training Evaluation.* New York: Van Norstrand Reinhold, 1979.

Ebel, R.L. *Essentials of Educational Measurement.* Englewood Cliffs, NJ: Prentice-Hall, 1989.

Gagne, R.M. *The Conditions of Learning.* New York: Holt, Rinehart & Winston, 1977.

Hall, B. *Web-Based Training Cookbook.* New York: John Wiley & Sons, 1997.

Jacobs, L.D., and C.I. Chase. *Developing and Using Tests Effectively.* San Francisco: Jossey-Bass, 1992.

Kirkpatrick, D.L. *Evaluating Training Programs.* (2d edition). San Francisco: Berrett-Koehler, 1998.

————. "Evaluation of Training." In *Training and Development Handbook: A Guide to Human Resource Development.* Edited by R.L. Craig. (2d edition). New York: McGraw-Hill, 1976.

Kubiszyn, T., and G. Borich. *Educational Testing and Measurement Classroom Application and Practice.* Glenview, IL: Scott, Foresman, 1990.

Lord, R.G., and K.J. Maher. "Cognitive Theory in Industrial/Organizational Psychology." In *Handbook of Industrial and Organizational Psychology.* Vol. 2. Edited by M. Dunnette and L.M. Hough. (2d edition). Palo Alto, CA: Consulting Psychologists Press, 1991.

Mager, R.F. *Measuring Instructional Results.* Carefree, AZ: David S. Lake, 1984.

Medsker, K.L., and D.G. Roberts. *Evaluating the Results of Training: ASTD Trainer's Toolkit.* Alexandria, VA: ASTD, 1992.

Newby, A.C. *Training Evaluation Handbook.* San Diego: Pfeiffer, 1992.

Parry, S.B. *Evaluating the Impact of Training.* Alexandria, VA: ASTD, 1997.

Phillips, J.J. *Accountability in Human Resource Development.* Houston: Gulf Publishing, 1996.

————. *Handbook of Training Evaluation and Measurement Methods.* (3d edition). Houston: Gulf Publishing, 1997.

————. *Implementing Evaluation Systems and Processes.* Alexandria, VA: ASTD, 1998.

Preskill, H., and R.T. Torres. *Evaluative Inquiry for Learning in Organizations.* Thousand Oaks, CA: Sage Publications, 1998.

U.S. Department of Education. *DOE Guideline: Guide to Good Practices for the Design, Development and Implementation of Examinations, STD-1011.* (No. FSC-6910-0007) Washington, DC: Government Printing Office, 1992.

Info-lines

Hacker, Deborah G. "Testing for Learning Outcomes." No. 8907 (revised 1998).

Phillips, Jack J., et al. "Level 1 Evaluation: Reaction and Planned Action." No. 9813.

————. "Level 3 Evaluation: Application." No. 9815.

————. "Level 4 Evaluation: Business Impact." No. 9816.

————. "Level 5 Evaluation: ROI." No. 9805.

Waagen, Alice. "Essentials for Evaluation." No. 9705.

Job Aid

Evaluation Standard Worksheet

Use this evaluation standard worksheet when preparing a Level 2 evaluation to measure learning. The worksheet will simplify your organization's task of creating and producing standards that are fair and objective.

Test # _____   Tools/Equipment: _____

Revision #_____   _____

Page # _____   _____

Task # _____   Performance Terminal Objective: _____

Task Title: _____   _____

Average Time to Perform Task: _____   _____

Instructions to Student: _____   Conditions: _____

_____   _____

_____   _____

Personnel/Equipment Safety: _____   Initiating Cue: _____

_____   _____

_____   _____

Action Step:	Standard:	Satisfactory/Unsatisfactory:
_____	_____	_____
_____	_____	_____
_____	_____	_____
_____	_____	_____

Oral Questions:	Comments:	Pass/Fail:
_____	_____	_____
_____	_____	_____
_____	_____	_____
_____	_____	_____

Terminating Cue:

_____

_____

The material appearing on this page is not covered by copyright and may be reproduced at will.

Level 3: Application

Level 3: Application

AUTHORS:

Jack Phillips, Ph.D.
Performance Resources
    Organization
P.O. Box 380637
Birmingham, AL 35238-0637
Tel: 205.678.9700
Fax: 205.678.8070
E-mail: roipro@wwisp.com

Connie Schmidt
Illinova University
370 South Main Street
E-07
Decatur, IL 62523
Tel: 217.425.4133

Editor
Cat Sharpe

Associate Editor
Sabrina E. Hicks

Production Design
Anne Morgan

Why Measure on-the-Job Application?

Organizations are rethinking the way traditional training programs are developed, implemented, and delivered. All over the world, organizations are concerned about the accountability of training—and they are exploring ways and techniques to measure the results of training. Training programs and interventions must link directly to the organization's important goals and strategic initiatives. More specifically, all training programs must link directly to job performance of participants in some way.

Measuring on-the-job performance after a training and development program, also known as Level 3 evaluation, is becoming a standard evaluation technique. Several key influences are driving the increased use of this level of evaluation. First, measuring on-the-job performance in a follow-up evaluation is a higher level evaluation than measuring reaction and learning (Levels 1 and 2). While it is important to measure participants' reaction and assess the extent of learning during the program, it is more important to determine specifically what has changed on the job as a result of the training and development program. From a client's perspective, this level of evaluation is more valuable and provides evidence of program success.

Second, one of the critical problems in the training and development profession is the lack of actual "transfer of learning" to the job. In some cases, employees do not use as much as 90 percent of what they learn in a training and development program. A Level 3 evaluation provides proof of whether or not transfer of training has occurred. In addition, this evaluation tool identifies specific obstacles and barriers to transfer. When obstacles and barriers are identified, you can minimize or remove them to enhance transfer and, consequently, job performance.

Third, workplace performance is the key indicator of if employees apply newly learned skills and knowledge on the job. This change in focus, from learning to actual on-the-job application and the change in job performance, is integral to the emerging shift toward performance improvement. Most organizations concentrate on performance improvement with learning as a way to drive the improvement process. This shift to performance has resulted in more follow-up evaluations that monitor actual changes in job performance.

Fourth, depending on the type of work done, it is important for employees to apply certain skills and behaviors on the job consistently. This is particularly true in areas such as customer service and team leadership. Follow-up evaluations ensure participants of training programs use their acquired skills appropriately.

Fifth, with the increased use of competencies, many organizations use training and development to build critical core competencies. To ensure that you develop competencies to desired levels, follow-up evaluations measure how much employees are changing or improving skills, motives, knowledge, tasks, and behaviors that constitute the previously established competencies. You should align competencies with other business measures and strategies.

Finally, many top-level executives are demanding increased accountability from the training function. One element of this accountability is actual participant job performance. Transfer of training is more important as organizations focus their attention on the payoff of training and development programs, corporate universities, Web-based training, and other learning strategies. Along with senior managers, many middle managers expect and often monitor actual changes in behavior resulting from training programs to determine if the training is improving job performance.

This issue of *Info-line* takes an in-depth examination of how to measure on-the-job application of training or Level 3 evaluation. It is one of five issues covering specific levels of evaluation. You may refer to *Info-line*s No. 9813, "Level 1 Evaluation: Reaction and Planned Action"; No. 9814, "Level 2 Evaluation: Learning"; No. 9816, Level 4 Evaluation: Measuring Business Impact"; and No. 9805, Level 5 Evaluation: ROI" for more information on these other levels.

Criteria for Level 3 Evaluation

Because of the time and cost involved in conducting Level 3 evaluations, not all training programs will have a follow-up unless the process is automated. You should select a program for Level 3 evaluation based on criteria that may include, but are not limited to, the following:

- a higher level of evaluation is planned (Level 4 or 5)

- the training program has high visibility

Improving Response Rate

You can explore a wide range of issues in a follow-up questionnaire or survey. The challenge is to tackle questionnaire design and administration for maximum response rate. Questionnaire design is a critical issue when the questionnaire is the primary data collection activity and most of the evaluation hinges on its results. Take the following actions to increase response rate:

- Provide advance communication.
- Communicate the purpose.
- Explain who will see the data.
- Describe the data integration process.
- Keep the questionnaire as simple as possible.
- Simplify the response process.
- Obtain local manager support.
- Let the participants know they are part of the sample.
- Consider incentives.
- Have an executive sign the introductory letter.
- Use follow-up reminders.
- Send a copy of the results to the participants.

Collectively, these items help boost response rates of follow-up questionnaires. Using all of these strategies can result in a 50 to 60 percent response rate, even with lengthy questionnaires that take as long as 30 minutes to complete.

- the training program is important in meeting business objectives

- a needs assessment has been conducted

- the extent to which behavior change is a critical issue, such as in customer service

- the ease of conducting the evaluation

- the training program is expensive

- on-the-job application is important information for marketing the training program to others

Level 3 Data Collection Methods

Perhaps the single most disruptive phase of evaluation to an organization is data collection. Though time consuming, no other phase of evaluation will produce such rich data while providing an opportunity to obtain application (Level 3) data. Fortunately, you can employ a variety of methods to capture data at an appropriate time after the training. These methods include the following:

- surveys
- questionnaires
- interviews
- focus groups
- observation
- action plans
- follow-up sessions

Follow-Up Questionnaires and Surveys

Probably the most common data collection method is the follow-up questionnaire or survey. Ranging from brief assessment forms to detailed follow-up tools, you can use questionnaires to obtain subjective information about items ranging from skill application to document measurable business results.

You can also use questionnaires to obtain subjective information about participants, as well as to objectively document transfer of learning or behavior change. The questionnaire's versatility and popularity make it the preferred method for capturing Level 3 data in some organizations.

You should also involve management in the survey process, either as a client, sponsor, supporter, or interested party. If possible, managers most familiar with the program or process should provide information on specific issues and concerns that often frame the actual questions planned for the questionnaire. Some managers may want to provide input on specific issues or items. Not only is manager input helpful and useful in the questionnaire design, but it also builds ownership in the measurement and evaluation process.

You should address specific design issues when formulating the questionnaire. The design process should be simple and logical. Nothing is more confusing, frustrating, and potentially embarrassing than a poorly designed or an improperly worded questionnaire. To ensure that you develop a valid, reliable, and effective instrument, use the following steps:

■ *Step 1: Select Type*
The first step in questionnaire design is to select the types of questions that will best result in the specific data needed. You should consider the

planned data analysis and variety of data to be collected when deciding which questions to use.

Next, you should develop these selected questions based on the type of questions planned and the information needed. Questions should be simple and straightforward to avoid confusion or lead the participant to a given response. A single question should only address one issue. If multiple issues need to be addressed, separate the question into multiple parts or develop a separate question for each issue. Avoid terms or expressions unfamiliar to the participant.

■ *Step 2: Assess Reading Level*
To ensure that the target audience understands the questionnaire, assess the reading level of the questionnaire. A word processing program can perform this function for you. Many programs have features that will evaluate the reading difficulty according to grade level. Assessing the reading level of the questionnaire in this manner ensures that it is appropriate for your audience.

■ *Step 3: Field Testing*
Field testing the proposed questions is an ideal test for understanding. Test questions on a sample group of participants or a sample group of employees at approximately the same job level as participants. You should also guarantee the confidentiality of responses to encourage participants to answer the questions honestly. One way to do this is to let the participants answer the questionnaire anonymously—unless there are specific reasons why you need to identify the individuals.

This sample group can provide feedback, critiques, and suggestions that improve the questionnaire design. Testers should view each question in terms of data tabulation, data summary, and analysis. If possible, outline and review the data analysis process with the testers. This step avoids the problems of inadequate, cumbersome, or lengthy data analysis caused by improper wording or design.

■ *Step 4: Develop Appearance*
The final step includes integrating the questions to develop an attractive questionnaire. Insert proper instructions so that you can administer it effectively. In addition, develop a summary sheet to tabulate the data quickly for analysis.

Questionnaire Content

Perhaps the most difficult task in developing a questionnaire is determining the specific content issues (such as assessing the progress of program objectives or determining the relevance of the program). One of the most important questions should focus on job application (Level 3 data). This question should present specific skills and knowledge areas and inquire after the amount of change the participant perceives since attending the program.

The rest of this section on content reviews selected parts of a sample questionnaire to illustrate content concerns. Designers of the sample questionnaire decided it was the appropriate evaluation tool for a one-day program on self-development. They designed the evaluation to capture behavior change skill transfer to the workplace.

Progress with objectives. Sometimes it is helpful to assess progress with the objectives in the follow-up evaluation, as illustrated in question 1 of the sidebar on the following page. While such Level 1 data is usually assessed during the program, you may find it helpful to revisit the objectives after the participants have had an opportunity to apply what they learned. For more information on objectives, refer to *Info-line*s No. 8505, "Write Better Behavioral Objectives" and No. 9712, "Instructional Objectives."

Action plan implementation. If the program requires an action plan, the questionnaire should reference the plan and determine the extent to which the organization has implemented it. If the action plan requirement is very low, perhaps you should devote only one question to the follow-up on the action plan, as illustrated by the last objective of the *Progress with Objectives* sidebar. The action plan itself may be very comprehensive and contain an abundance of Levels 3 and 4 data. If so, the questionnaire takes a secondary role and most of the data collection will focus directly on the status of the completed action plan.

Relevance of the program. Although the relevance of the program is often assessed during the program as Level 1 data, you may find it helpful to assess the relevance of various aspects of the program after participants have applied (or attempted to apply) the skills and knowledge on the job. This feedback helps program designers identify

Progress with Objectives

This question is the first question from a sample questionnaire and is a good example of the type of question you may want to use to asses participants' progress with program objectives.

1. Listed below are the objectives of the training program. After reflecting on this course, please indicate the degree of success in meeting the objectives by checking the appropriate box for each item.

Objective	Very Little Success	Limited Success	Generally Successful	Completely Successful
To recognize that customer service is vital to the success of your organization.	☐	☐	☐	☐
To understand the terms of the human resources (HR) compact.	☐	☐	☐	☐
To recognize the links between corporate, organizational, and individual goals.	☐	☐	☐	☐
To demonstrate awareness of organizational career development and its benefits.	☐	☐	☐	☐
To understand the concept of "career resilience."	☐	☐	☐	☐
To identify tools, resources, and structures within your organization that support career development.	☐	☐	☐	☐
To clearly associate tools and resources with performance and the HR compact.	☐	☐	☐	☐
To develop a personal action plan that incorporates an individual development plan.	☐	☐	☐	☐

the parts of the program that were useful on the job. Question 2 in the sidebar on the next page shows the approach to this issue..

Use of program materials. If participants are provided with materials to use on the job, it may be helpful to determine the extent to which they have used these materials. A question that focuses on material use is particularly helpful when you have distributed and explained operating manuals, reference books, and job aids in the program and expected participants to use them on the job.

Knowledge or skill enhancement. One of the most important questions of your questionnaire should focus on the Level 3 data, job application. Notice how in the *Knowledge and Skills Enhance-*

ment sidebar on page 6 the designers simply state, "How has the program helped you to improve your ability to do your job?" To get responses on specific areas, the designers list skills and knowledge areas and ask if the participant has improved upon the application of these items since attending the program.

This is the recommended approach when there is no pre-program data. If you did collect pre-program data, make sure to use the same type of questions in both questionnaires for a more appropriate pre-program/post-program comparison.

Skills used As shown in question 4 of the sidebar on page 7, you may find it helpful to determine the most frequently used skills that link directly to the program. A more detailed variation of this question is to list each skill and indicate the frequency of use. For many skills, it is important for participants to experience frequent use quickly after acquiring the skills so that the skills become internalized.

Improvements linked with program. For this section of the questionnaire, you want to isolates the effects of training. Have participants indicate the percentage of improvement that they relate directly to the program. As an alternative, you can provide participants with a list of various factors that influence the results and ask them to allocate the percentages to each factor. The list may include items such as the following:

- leadership development program

- coaching, encouragement, or guidance by supervisor

- incentive compensation

- recognition for performance

- facilities (for example, work stations and environment)

- technical support (for example, improved information systems and communication systems)

- company/employee communication products (for example, newsletters and magazines)

Barriers. A variety of barriers can influence the successful application of the skills and knowledge learned in the training program. The sidebar on page 8 lists the barriers, and participants check all that apply. Still another variation is to list the barriers with a range of responses, indicating the extent to which the barrier inhibited the results.

Suggestions for improvement As a final wrap-up question, ask participants to provide suggestions for improving any part of the program or process. As illustrated in the question below, an open-ended structure will solicit qualitative responses you can use to make improvements:

What suggestions do you have for improving the training? Please specify.

Program Relevance

This question from our sample questionnaire exposes the portions of the program that participants found helpful once they returned to their jobs.

2. Please rate, on a scale of 1-5, the relevance of each of the program elements to your job, with 1 indicating no relevance and 5 indicating very relevant.

_____   Why an HR compact, and how does it impact us?
- The HR compact: Philosophy
- Mutual terms and commitments of the HR compact
- Element of superior performance

_____   *You* make a difference
- Corporate goals
- Organizational goals
- Individual goals

_____   Organizational career development
- Career resilient workforce
- What is organizational career development
- Twenty-first century career planning

_____   Self-Assessment
- Comparing personal values to organizational values
- Acting proactively to develop or improve processes
- Tools and resources for self-assessment and career planning

_____   Putting it all together
- Technical development resources
- Soft skills development resources
- Knowledge and skills assessment
- Performance assessment

_____   Action Plan
- Team action plan
- Personal action commitment

Follow-Up Interviews

Although not used as frequently as questionnaires, another helpful Level 3 data collection method is the interview. The training and development staff, the participant's supervisor, or an outside third party can conduct interviews. Interviews can secure data not available in performance records or data difficult to obtain through written

Knowledge and Skills Enhancement

Questions dealing with how participants apply what they learned on the job (Level 3 data) are very important. This sample question presents one method of guaranteeing responses on specific areas. To do this, the designers listed the skills and knowledge areas that most interest them.

3. How has the program helped you to improve your ability to do your job? Please use the following scale to respond to your frequency of job application of each skill or behavior and the extent to which the training helped to improve your job effectiveness.

Scale	1	2	3	4	5
Frequency of Application	Rarely (once a month)	Seldom (once every 2 weeks)	Occasionally (1-2 times per week)	Frequently (once per day)	Very frequently (several times per day)
Improved Job Effectiveness	Not much improvement	Somewhat improved	Moderately improved	Definitely improved	Significantly improved

	Frequency					Effectiveness				
Since attending the program, to what extent have you applied the following skills or behaviors in your job?	1	2	3	4	5	1	2	3	4	5
Customer focus	☐	☐	☐	☐	☐	☐	☐	☐	☐	☐
Empowerment	☐	☐	☐	☐	☐	☐	☐	☐	☐	☐
Continuous improvement	☐	☐	☐	☐	☐	☐	☐	☐	☐	☐
Involving everyone	☐	☐	☐	☐	☐	☐	☐	☐	☐	☐
Working to better integrate departments	☐	☐	☐	☐	☐	☐	☐	☐	☐	☐
Working to align all parts of the organization in service to customers	☐	☐	☐	☐	☐	☐	☐	☐	☐	☐
Acting responsive to changing demands	☐	☐	☐	☐	☐	☐	☐	☐	☐	☐
Taking a proactive role on your team to develop or improve processes	☐	☐	☐	☐	☐	☐	☐	☐	☐	☐
Making day-to-day job decisions to improve *departmental* performance that impacts organizational measures of availability, absenteeism, and time signed on	☐	☐	☐	☐	☐	☐	☐	☐	☐	☐
Making day-to-day decisions to improve *individual* performance that impacts organizational measures of availability, absenteeism, and time signed on	☐	☐	☐	☐	☐	☐	☐	☐	☐	☐

responses or observations. Also, interviews can uncover success stories that are useful in communicating evaluation results. Participants may be reluctant to described their results in a questionnaire but will volunteer the information to a skillful interviewer who uses probing techniques.

While the interview process uncovers changes in behavior, reaction, and results, it is primarily used with Level 3 data. A major disadvantage of the interview is that it is time-consuming. This method requires training for interviewers to ensure that the process is consistent.

Interviews usually fall into two basic types:

1. Structured.

2. Unstructured.

A structured interview is much like a questionnaire. Specific questions are asked with little room to deviate from the desired responses. The primary advantages of the structured interview over the questionnaire are that the interview process can ensure that participants complete the questionnaire and the interviewer understands the responses supplied by participants.

The unstructured interview allows probing for additional information. This type of interview uses a few general questions, which can lead into more detailed information as you uncover important data. The following examples of probing questions are typical:

- Can you explain that in more detail?
- Can you give me an example?
- Can you explain any difficulty?

Interview Guidelines

The design steps for interviews are similar to those of the questionnaire. A brief summary of key issues with interviews is presented here.

■ Develop Questions to be Asked
Once you decide about the type of interview, you need to develop specific questions. Questions should be brief, precise, and designed for easy response.

> ## Program Skills Used
>
> If you want to find out which skills participants are using most after training, consider a question such as the following as part of your questionnaire.
>
> 4. Using the list on the previous page, identify the three skills or abilities that you have used most as a result of the program you attended.
>
> A. _____
>
> B. _____
>
> C. _____

■ Try Out the Interview
Test the interview on a small number of participants. If possible, conduct the interviews as part of the trial run of the program. You should then analyze the responses and revise the interview.

■ Train the Interviewers
The interviewer should have appropriate skills, which include listening actively, asking probing questions, and collecting and summarizing information into a meaningful form.

■ Give Clear Instructions to the Participant
The participant should understand the purpose of the interview and know what will be done with the information. You should discuss expectations, conditions, and rules of the interview thoroughly. For example, participants should know if you will keep their statements confidential. If you notice that a participant is nervous during an interview and develops signs of anxiety, try to make him or her feel at ease.

■ Administer According to a Scheduled Plan
As with the other evaluation instruments, conduct interviews according to a predetermined plan. The timing of the interview, the person who conducts the interview, and the place of the interview are all issues that become relevant when developing an interview plan. For a large number of participants, a sampling plan may be necessary to save time and reduce the evaluation cost.

Barriers

This question from our sample questionnaire asks participants to identify barriers that affected the success of their application of skills and knowledge learned. Once you are aware of barriers, you can redesign the program to alleviate such problems.

13. What barriers, if any, have you encountered that have prevented you from using skills or knowledge gained in your training program? *Check all that apply. Please explain, if possible.*

☐ I have no opportunity to use the skills _____

_____.

☐ Not enough time _____

_____.

☐ My work environment does not support these skills ____

_____.

☐ My manager does not support this type of course _____

_____.

☐ This material does not apply to my job situation _____

_____.

☐ Other (please specify) _____

_____.

Follow-Up Focus Groups

Focus groups, as an extension of the interview, are particularly helpful when you need in-depth feedback for a Level 3 evaluation. The focus group involves a small group discussion conducted by an experienced facilitator. This process is designed to solicit qualitative judgments on a planned topic or issue. Group members are all required to provide their input, as individual input builds on group input.

When compared with questionnaires, surveys, tests, or interviews, the focus group strategy has several advantages. The basic premise of using focus groups is that when quality judgments are subjective, several individual judgments are better than one. The group process, where participants often motivate one another, is an effective method for generating new ideas and hypotheses. The process is inexpensive, and you can quickly plan and conduct a focus group. Its flexibility makes it possible to explore a training program's unexpected outcomes or applications.

Applications for Evaluation

The focus group is particularly helpful when you need qualitative information about the success of a training program. For example, the focus group can be used in the following situations:

- to evaluate the reactions to specific exercises, cases, simulations, or other components of a training program

- to assess the overall effectiveness of the program as perceived by the participants immediately following a program

- to assess the application of the program in a follow-up evaluation after the program is completed

Essentially, focus groups are helpful when you need evaluation information but you cannot collect it adequately with simple, quantitative methods.

Guidelines for Conducting Focus Groups

While there are no set rules on how to use focus groups for evaluation, the following guidelines should be helpful:

Ensure management buy-in. Because the process of using focus groups for evaluation is relatively new, it might be unknown to some management groups. By understanding the advantages of using focus groups, managers have more confidence in the information obtained from group sessions.

Plan topics, questions, and strategy carefully. As with any evaluation instrument, planning is the key. You must carefully plan and sequence the specific topics, questions, and issues you want to discuss. This enhances the comparison of results from one group to another and ensures that the group process is effective and stays on track.

Keep the group size small. While there is no magic group size, a range of 6 to 12 seems to be appropriate for most focus group applications. A group has to be large enough to ensure different points of view, but small enough to give every participant a chance to talk freely and exchange comments.

Use a representative sampling of the target population. For participants to represent the target population, you must stratify groups appropriately. The group should be homogeneous in experience, rank, and influence in the organization.

Use facilitators with appropriate expertise. The success of a focus group rests with the facilitator who must be skilled in the focus group process. Facilitators must know how to control aggressive members of the group and diffuse the input of those who want to dominate the group. Also, facilitators must create an environment in which participants feel comfortable in offering comments freely and openly. Because of this, some organizations use external facilitators.

For further reading on focus groups, refer to *Info-line* No. 9401, "Needs Assessment by Focus Group."

On-the-Job Observation

Observing participants on the job is an additional data collection method you can use to record any changes in participants' behavior on the job. The observer may be a member of the training and development staff, the participant's supervisor, a member of a peer group, or an outside third party. The most common observer, and probably the most practical, is a member of the training and development staff. Following is a brief description of various methods you can use to conduct on-the-job observation. You can choose between five different methods of observation, depending on the circumstances surrounding the type of information needed.

■ *Checklist*
Use a checklist to record the presence, absence, frequency, or duration of a participant's behavior

as it occurs. A variation of this approach involves coding behaviors on a form. This method is more time-consuming because you must enter the code that identifies a specific behavior.

■ *Delayed Report Method of Observation*
If using a delayed report method of observation, the observer does not use any forms or written materials during the observation. He or she either records the information after the observation is complete or at particular time intervals during the observation. The advantage to this approach is that the observer is not as noticeable and is less intrusive because there are no forms being completed or notes taken during the observation. The obvious disadvantage, however, is that when the observer does record observations, the information written may not be as accurate or reliable as information collected at the time it occurred.

The 360-degree feedback process is a variation of this approach and involves completing surveys on other individuals based on observations within a specific time frame. To learn more about 360-degree feedback, see *Info-line* No. 9508, "How to Build and Use a 360-Degree Feedback System."

■ *Video Recording*
The benefit of using video recording is that a video camera records every detail of the participant's behavior. This intrusion, however, may be awkward and cumbersome and may unnecessarily cause the participants to feel nervous or self-conscious. If the camera is concealed, the privacy of individual participants may be invaded. Because of this, video recording of on-the-job behavior is not often used.

■ *Audio Monitoring*
Use of audio assistance to monitor how effectively participants converse using the skills taught in the training program is an effective technique of observation. This approach is particularly useful for monitoring telemarketing sales. Because sales representatives are trained to sell by telephone, selectively or randomly monitoring telephone conversations is an effective tool for determining if they are using the skills properly. This approach may, however, stir some controversy.

■ *Computer Monitoring*
For employees who work regularly with a keyboard, computer monitoring is an effective way to "observe" participants as they perform job tasks.

The computer monitors the number of times an employee performed a certain task, the sequence of steps chosen, and other activities to determine if the participant is performing the work according to what he or she learned in the training program. Technology is a significant part of many jobs; thus, computer monitoring may hold the promise of monitoring actual applications on the job and be particularly helpful in securing Level 3 data.

Action Plans

One of the most useful tools for collecting data at Level 3 is the participant action plan. Sometimes labeled performance improvement plan, business application plan, and business improvement plan, participants develop this document in detail during the training and development program. Participants are usually informed of this requirement in advance, and you should develop specific guidelines for the plans. Discuss the action planning process in the program, and allocate time for participants to develop their plans. In addition, the facilitator often approves the plans. In a predetermined follow-up, the action plans provide evidence of actual on-the-job application.

Action planning is extremely versatile, and you can use it with almost any type of program. The actual detail on the document must meet several requirements. Typical requirements of the plans include that they be the following:

- specific
- measurable
- achievable
- retainable
- realistic
- time-based

The job aid at the back of this issue will help you design an action plan for Level 3 evaluation.

Program Follow-Up Session

In some situations you may want to redesign the program to allow for a follow-up session. At this session, you address evaluation along with additional education and training. For example, you can design a consecutive three-day program, such as an interactive selling skills program, as a two-day workshop to build skills followed by a one-day

session three weeks later. The follow-up session provides an opportunity for additional training and evaluation.

During the first part of a follow-up session, you collect Level 3 evaluation data using a focus group process. Have the groups discuss specific barriers and problems encountered in applying the skills. Devote the second half of the day to additional skill-building and refinement along with techniques to overcome particular barriers participants have had using the skills. Thus, the redesigned program has provided you with a mechanism for follow-up.

Selecting the Appropriate Method

You need to plan carefully if you hope to evaluate how well participants apply learning at the workplace successfully. Because acquisition of knowledge and skills from the training program is no guarantee that actual behavior change will occur, it is important to determine the extent to which behavior change has occurred. How participants of a training program apply the knowledge, skills, and attitudes learned reflects how well they have internalized the material taught. It is important that you select the appropriate method for data collection. Consider the following seven important issues before making a decision:

Participant Time

You should always minimize the amount of time required from participants in the data collection and evaluation systems, and position the method so that it is a value-added activity (that is, the participants perceive the activity as valuable so they will not resist). To do this, you can use sampling to keep the total participant time to a reasonable amount. Some methods (such as performance monitoring) require no participant time while others (such as interviews and focus groups) require a significant investment in time.

Supervisor's Time

You should minimize the time that a participant's direct supervisor must allocate to data collection. Some methods (such as the performance contracting) may require much involvement from the super-

Level 3 Evaluation Software

Software is available that allows for efficient creation of questionnaires and reports while simultaneously creating analytical reports that satisfy the most critical audiences. Most of the current software allows you to design questionnaires through pre-established templates of questions that you can alter to fit individual situations. Most of these questionnaires are graphic—allowing for easy rearranging and reformatting of questions. Four packages are explained below.

Survey Pro offers many features preferred by evaluation practitioners. Survey Pro is most useful in the evaluation of Level 3 data because of the ease in creating surveys and questionnaires that are used quite often to obtain Level 3 data. It effectively performs all survey functions, including questionnaires and reports. For an individual or organization needing electronic data entry or advanced statistical analysis, this package may not be the best choice. However, it is a useful program for anyone who designs and conducts surveys. The database lacks data sharing sophistication, but its flexibility in data analysis appears ample for most needs. Your biggest problem with Survey Pro may be that it generates too much data.

Survey Said may be the software of choice for those administering surveys via the Internet, intranet, diskette, touch screen entry, kiosk, and paper. Survey Said offers the most comprehensive graphic charting capabilities available for frequency survey analysis and can generate over 25 different graph types. The software is a networked application where it optimizes network performance to allow hundreds of users to access the same surveys concurrently. It does verbatim analysis and is flexible to allow

control of the parameters. It gives you options to pick and choose import and export formats (for data and questions) and offers qualifiers for data subset control.

Decisive Survey lets you collect data through e-mail or a Web site. This program is cleanly designed and relatively easy to use, but it is rather limited. Only four response types are supported, and you must enter numeric responses as text. The current version lacks the most rudimentary data-validation techniques. Although advertised as an e-mail program, this is the weakest part of the package. Respondents must manually copy a marker into their reply for the system. Decisive Technology plans to upgrade the program, but for now it is for only the simplest of surveys.

StatView is a Macintosh-based statistics package and is supported in the Windows environment. This product does not include a procedural macro language, but instead presents a series of analysis worksheets and templates for capturing manipulation, analysis, and plotting. These features make it relatively easy to use and learn. This program supports a variety of analytical procedures, including descriptive statistics and cross tabulation.

There are some limitations: The program requires a math coprocessor, which puts the program out of reach for users with older computers. It also lacks any Object Linking and Embedding (OLE) support. StatView's file import and export capacity is not exactly what it could be either. Support for spreadsheet formats are restricted to reading and writing Excel 3 and 4 worksheets. StatView is not industrial-strength; but for many users, it will come close enough.

visor prior to and after the program. Other methods (such as questionnaires administered directly to participants) may not require any supervisor time.

Disruption of Work Activities

One of the most critical issues when selecting the appropriate method, and perhaps the one that generates the most concern with managers, is the amount of disruption the data collection will create. Try to not interfere with routine work processes. Some data-collection techniques (such as performance monitoring) require very little time and distraction from normal activities. You

can have participants complete questionnaires in only a few minutes of time, or even after work, and not disrupt their work environment. Conversely, observations and interviews may be too disruptive for the work unit.

Costs

Some data collection methods are more expensive than others. For example, interviews and observations are very expensive. Surveys, questionnaires, and performance monitoring are usually inexpensive.

Accuracy of the Technique

Some data-collection methods are more accurate than others. For example, performance monitoring is usually very accurate, whereas surveys can be distorted and unreliable. If you must capture actual on-the-job behavior, unobtrusive observation is clearly the most accurate process.

Utility

Utility refers to the added value provided by the use of an additional data collection method. Because there are many different methods to collect data, it is tempting to use too many data collection methods. Multiple methods add to the time and costs of the evaluation and may result in very little additional value. When deciding whether or not to use an additional method, ask yourself this question: Does the value obtained from the additional data warrant the extra time and expense of the method? If the answer is "no," you should not implement the additional method.

Culture of the Organization

The culture or philosophy of the organization can dictate which data collection methods you use. For example, some organizations are accustomed to using questionnaires and find the process to fit well within their culture. Some organizations do not use observation because their culture does not support the potential "invasion of privacy" that is associated with the technique.

Credibility of Data

As previously indicated, many factors influence what data is collected. However, you must also consider the credibility of data to selected audiences. The following factors influence how much your target audience believes the data collected:

Reputation of data's source. This issue often causes the target audience to place more credibility on data obtained from those employees who are closest to the source of the actual improvement or change (such as participants or their direct supervisors).

Reputation of the study's source. The target audience will scrutinize the reputation of the individual, group, or organization presenting the data. They will ask questions such as the following:

- Do they have a history of providing accurate reports?

- Are they fair in their presentation?

- Are they unbiased in their analyses?

Motives of the evaluators. Individuals conducting the study or presenting data may have a personal vendetta against a particular group that could influence how they present results. They may have a personal interest in creating favorable or unfavorable results. The target audience will examine the motives of those involved in the study.

Methodology of the study. A major concern of the target audience is the methodology used to conduct the research. How were calculations made? What steps were followed? What processes were used? If you do not provide this information, the audience will be suspicious of the results. But more damaging is the possibility that the target audience will insert their own assumptions in the absence of a credible methodology.

Assumptions made in the analysis. The evaluation should include the assumptions you used to base calculations of the analysis. Highlight these assumptions. You should ask if the selected assumptions represent accepted practices within the organization. Include a comparison of current assumptions to previous studies, if available. When assumptions are omitted, the audience might substitute their assumptions, which can often be unfavorable.

Scope of the analysis. Evaluation sometimes includes many areas and employees within the organization. If you limit the evaluation to a small group, or a series of groups or employees, the process appears more accurate and results more believable.

Collectively, these factors influence the credibility of the evaluation studies and provide a framework from which to develop an evaluation study.

Using the Data Results

Level 3 evaluation data provides extremely valuable information when used properly and systematically. Following are the five distinct benefits possible for most organizations:

■ *Determining the Extent of Application*
By definition, a Level 3 evaluation provides important information to judge the success of the training program as participants apply it on the job in a real workplace setting.

■ *Improving Training Programs*
The information you collect at a Level 3 follow-up can be helpful in improving training programs. If the results are not what you expected, perhaps you should redesign or enhance the training program to increase its effectiveness. Inadequate results could mean that the training program is not relevant, useful, or helpful on the job.

■ *Improving Needs Assessment*
Level 3 data can provide evidence to determine whether or not the training program was actually needed. If participants do not identify any improvements or report changes on the job, it may mean that you did not need the training program.

■ *Identifying Barriers and Enablers*
Level 3 data identifies the barriers and obstacles to successful application of the training program on the job. Many barriers inhibit the extent of the actual benefits. You need to identify, report, and tackle these barriers so that they will not inhibit the overall application of the training program and the subsequent success of the effort. You also need to identify the enablers to the application so that you can enhance or replicate them in the future.

■ *Evaluating Instructors and Facilitators*
Level 3 evaluation data also provides additional input on the effectiveness of the facilitator. This moves the responsibility for the success of a training program to on-the-job applications. This is a key component of the results-based approach needed for the success of training programs and ultimately the transfer of skills to the workplace. The facilitators, whether internal staff or vendors, share some responsibility for the ultimate application of the solution (although the management team may share the primary responsibility).

Communication

Communicating results is as important as achieving results. Handling communication carefully and planning it thoroughly is extremely important. The best process will be ineffective if the communications are not productive, specific, and performance based. The skills required to communicate results effectively are almost as delicate and sophisticated as those required to obtain results. However, to ensure adequate results communications should be timely and targeted to specific audiences. The media used should be effective; the communication used should be unbiased and modest; and communication must be consistent with past practices.

When communicating with key client groups there are always concerns, for several reasons. Often communication will contain sensitive and confidential information. You must safe guard this information at all times, and it should be very clear as to how you will use the information and who will see the results. All communication should reflect a tone of using evaluation data and communication to be supportive, helpful, sincere, and timely.

You should carefully plan information presented to various groups around the needs of the targeted group. In some cases, your presentation should be brief and presented at a high level. In other cases, you should screen it for confidential and sensitive issues. Still other groups will need more detailed information. Keep communication with client groups performance based, focusing on specific issues, measures, behaviors, and additional items that reflect the nature of the training. Always, you should avoid unsupported claims and information.

Moving from Level 3

Level 3 evaluation is an important component of an overall evaluation strategy. It determines how much participants actually use—on the job—the skills taught in a training and development program. Observing if participants were able to transfer what they learned to job performance is a critical step. However, lack of transfer is equally critical. A Level 3 evaluation enables the training and development staff to determine the extent to which barriers exist so that they can removed these barriers.

References & Resources

Articles

Bassi, Laurie J., and Daniel P. McMurrer. "Training Investment Can Mean Financial Performance." *Training & Development,* May 1998, pp. 40-42.

Garavaglia, P.L. "Applying a Transfer Model to Training." *Performance and Instruction,* volume 35, number 4 (1997), pp. 4-8.

Kaufman, R., J. Keller, and R. Watkins. "What Works and What Doesn't: Evaluation Beyond Kirkpatrick." *Performance and Instruction,* volume 35, number 2 (1995), pp. 8-12.

Kirkpatrick, D.L. "Revisiting Kirkpatrick's Four-Level Model." *Training & Development,* January 1996, pp. 54-59.

Thornburg, Linda. "Investment in Training Technology Yields Good Returns." *HRMagazine,* January 1998, pp. 37-41.

Watson, Scott C. "Five Easy Pieces to Performance Measurement." *Training & Development,* May 1998, pp. 45-48.

"Why Go to Level 3 & 4 Evaluation? Gap Inc. Finds the Training Payoff." *Training Directors' Forum Newsletter,* July 1997, pp. 1-3.

Willyerd, Karie A. "Balancing Your Evaluation Act." *Training,* March 1997, pp. 52-58.

Books

Bassi, Laurie J., and Darlene Russ-Eft (eds.). *What Works: Assessment, Development, and Measurement.* Alexandria, VA: ASTD, 1997.

Broad, Mary L. (ed.). *Transferring Learning to the Workplace.* Alexandria, VA: ASTD, 1997.

Burnham, Byron R. *Evaluating Human Resources, Programs, and Organizations.* Malabar, FL: Krieger Publishing, 1995.

Dixon, Nancy M. *Evaluation: A Tool for Improving HRD Quality.* San Diego: University Associates, 1990.

Fink, Arlene. *The Survey Handbook.* Thousand Oaks, CA: Sage Publications, 1995.

———. *How to Analyze Survey Data.* Thousand Oaks, CA: Sage Publications, 1995.

———. *How to Ask Survey Questions.* Thousand Oaks, CA: Sage Publications, 1995.

———. *How to Report on Surveys.* Thousand Oaks, CA: Sage Publications, 1995.

Kirkpatrick, D.L. "Techniques for Evaluating Training Programs." In *Evaluating Training Programs.* Alexandria, VA: ASTD, 1975.

———. *Evaluating Training Programs: The Four Levels.* San Francisco: Berrett-Koehler, 1994.

Kraut, Allen I. (ed.) *Organizational Surveys: Tools for Assessment and Change.* San Francisco: Jossey-Bass, 1996.

Newby, A.C. *Training Evaluation Handbook.* San Diego: Pfeiffer, 1992.

Parry, Scott B. *Evaluating the Impact of Training.* Alexandria, VA: ASTD, 1997.

Phillips, Jack J. *Handbook of Training Evaluation and Measurement Methods.* 3rd edition. Houston: Gulf Publishing 1997.

———. *Measuring Return on Investment.* Vol. 2. Alexandria, VA: ASTD, 1997.

———. *Return on Investment in Training and Performance Improvement Programs.* Houston: Gulf Publishing, 1997.

Phillips, Jack J. (ed.) *Measuring Return on Investment.* Vol. 1. Alexandria, VA: ASTD, 1994.

Rea, Louis M., and Richard A. Parker. *Designing and Conducting Survey Research: A Comprehensive Guide.* (2nd edition.) San Francisco: Jossey-Bass, 1997.

Robinson, Dana Gaines, and James C. Robinson. *Training for Impact.* San Francisco: Jossey-Bass, 1989.

Schwarz, Norbert and Seymour Sudman (eds.) *Answering Questions.* San Francisco: Jossey-Bass, 1996.

Info-lines

Austin, Mary. "Needs Assessment by Focus Group." No. 9401.

Fisher, Sharon, et al. "Write Better Behavioral Objectives." No. 8505.

Phillips, Jack J., et al. "Level 1 Evaluation: Reaction and Planned Action." No. 9813.

———. "Level 2 Evaluation: Learning." No. 9814.

———. "Level 4 Evaluation: Business Results." No. 9816.

———. "Level 5 Evaluation: ROI." No. 9805.

Plattner, Francis. "Instructional Objectives." No. 9712.

Shaver, Warren, Jr. "How to Build and Use a 360-Degree Feedback System." No. 9508.

Level 3 Action Plan

In addition to being one of the most useful tools for collecting data, an action plan helps program participants keep track of how well they are applying learned skills and behavior. Use the action plan below as a guide when trying to design your own action plan.

Name _____ Instructor Signature _____ Manager Signature _____

Target Market_____ Evaluation Period _____ to _____

Part 1. Technicians Key Behavior and Skill

Use this list as a guide when attempting to improve your skills and change your work habits.

1. Be engaging and enthusiastic.

2. Take initiative, especially in negative situations.

3. Make time for the customer.

4. Make the customer feel unique.

5. Make clear and concise commitments and agreements —and keep them.

6. Turn negative messages into positive messages.

7. Speak at the same level as the customer—level up or down.

8. Listen actively and ask questions.

9. Be sociable, talk about other things.

10. Other: _____ .

Part 2. Technicians Check Point Action Steps

Work with program participants to help them write down the positive behaviors they need to continue doing, along with some behaviors or skills they can continue to work on.

Keep Doing This	Work on This
1. _____	1. _____
2. _____	2. _____
3. _____	3. _____
4. _____	4. _____
5. _____	5. _____
6. _____	6. _____
7. _____	7. _____
8. _____	8. _____
9. _____	9. _____
10. _____	10. _____

The material appearing on this page is not covered by copyright and may be reproduced at will.

Job Aid

Part 3. Behavior and Skill

Circle the appropriate answers under each key behavior or skill. Discuss the results with your team leader.

Legend: N = No   Y = Yes   NS = Not Sure

How did technician's behavior or skill influence customer satisfaction?	Be Engaging	Take Initiative	Make Time for Customer	Make Customer Feel Unique	Make Clear Agreements and Keep Them	Turn Negatives to Positives	Speak Level of Customer	Listen Actively and Ask Questions	Be Sociable
Influence customer's willingness to communicate with technician?	N Y NS	N Y NS	N Y NS	N Y NS	N Y NS	N Y NS	N Y NS	N Y NS	N Y NS
Influence customer's willingness to trust technician?	N Y NS	N Y NS	N Y NS	N Y NS	N Y NS	N Y NS	N Y NS	N Y NS	N Y NS
Influence customer's willingness to place his or her problem or concern in the hands of the technician?	N Y NS	N Y NS	N Y NS	N Y NS	N Y NS	N Y NS	N Y NS	N Y NS	N Y NS
Influence customer's belief that your organization keeps him or her informed of status while working on a solution?	N Y NS	N Y NS	N Y NS	N Y NS	N Y NS	N Y NS	N Y NS	N Y NS	N Y NS
Influence customer's belief that your organization excels at building good working relationships with customers?	N Y NS	N Y NS	N Y NS	N Y NS	N Y NS	N Y NS	N Y NS	N Y NS	N Y NS
Influence customer's belief that technician is service minded?	N Y NS	N Y NS	N Y NS	N Y NS	N Y NS	N Y NS	N Y NS	N Y NS	N Y NS
Influence customer's belief that your organization is proactive in informing customer about known problems and solutions?	N Y NS	N Y NS	N Y NS	N Y NS	N Y NS	N Y NS	N Y NS	N Y NS	N Y NS
Influence customer's belief that your organization's service is superior?	N Y NS	N Y NS	N Y NS	N Y NS	N Y NS	N Y NS	N Y NS	N Y NS	N Y NS

In my opinion, contact with customers that occurred during this reporting period resulted in (select one)

☐ no positive change in overall customer satisfaction

☐ some positive change in overall customer satisfaction

☐ significant positive change in overall customer satisfaction

The behavior or skill that has worked best for me this reporting period is _____ .

1st follow-up date: _____   3rd follow-up date: _____   5th follow-up date: _____

2nd follow-up date: _____   4th follow up date: _____   6th follow-up date: _____

Level 4 Evaluation: Business Results

Issue 9816

Level 4 Evaluation: Business Results

A U T H O R :

Jack Phillips, Ph.D.
Performance Resources
    Organization
P.O. Box 380637
Birmingham, AL 35238-0637
Tel.: 205.678.9700
Fax: 205.678.8070

Ronnie D. Stone
Performance Resources
    Organization
P.O. Box 380637
Birmingham, AL 35238-0637
Tel.: 205.678.9700
Fax: 205.678.8070

Daniel McLinden
Anderson Consulting
1405 North Fifth Ave.
St. Charles, IL 60174
Tel.: 630.444.5470
Fax: 630.377.2435

Editor
Cat Sharpe

Contributing Editor
Ann Bruen

Production Design
Anne Morgan

Why Evaluate Business Results?

In today's environment of global competition, the training and development function must demonstrate its contribution to the organization. When scarce resources are allocated to design, develop, and deliver training, there is an anticipation of results with measures that are easily understood, representing output, quality, cost, and time, as well as customer satisfaction. Several important influences account for this increased interest in examining business results and explain its sustained popularity as a level of evaluation.

First, there is persistent pressure on organizational departments (including training) to be lean and efficient, customer focused, and time responsive. Programs must also be linked to efficiency and effectiveness measures, which are reflected in operating and performance reports. Second, training and development have become more client focused. Clients need evidence of a contribution to business results.

Third, business impact data are needed to set priorities. Since business needs are the driving force for training and development, business results from programs provide a source for establishing priorities. Fourth, accountability for training has moved beyond the classroom—more organizations judge in terms of the success on the job, which is measured in terms of business impact.

Fifth, change initiatives, such as total quality management, business process reengineering, and balanced scorecard process, place increased pressure on the training function to show its contribution using the same measures. And last, the training function is being managed by a new breed of leaders who expect results that are reflected in operating reports, performance records, and budgets.

The Levels of Evaluation

The concept of different levels of evaluation is instructive in understanding the measurement and evaluation process. Donald Kirkpatrick created a four-level model of training evaluation that has been used for several decades:

1. Reaction and Planned Action.

2. Learning.

3. Application.

4. Business Impact.

These levels have been expanded to add a fifth level: measuring return-on-investment (ROI).

Although business results and ROI are desired, evaluation at the other levels is important. A chain of impact should occur through the levels as the skills and knowledge learned (Level 2) are applied on the job (Level 3) to produce business results (Level 4). If measurements are not taken at each level, it is difficult to conclude that a program actually caused the results.

This issue of *Info-line* will examine how to measure business results, or Level 4 evaluation. It is one of five issues relating to a specific level of evaluation. You may refer to the other issues: No. 9813, "Level 1 Evaluation: Reaction and Planned Action"; No. 9814, "Level 2 Evaluation: Learning"; No. 9815, "Level 3 Evaluation: Application"; and No. 9805, "Level 5 Evaluation: ROI", for more information.

Measuring Business Impact

The complete process for measuring the business impact, a Level 4 evaluation, is depicted below. This model covers the major steps involved in the Level 4 evaluation and follows a logical sequence to develop a thorough analysis that begins with exploring the feasibility for the evaluation and concludes with the important issue of communicating results (see "Model for Measuring Business Impact"). Steps 1 through 3 and 5 through 8 are the focus of this issue. Step 4 is covered in *Info-line*s No. 9813, "Level 1 Evaluation: Reaction and Planned Action," and No. 9814, "Level 2 Evaluation: Learning."

The last four steps in the model are completed after the program is conducted. Perhaps the most important part of the process is to collect Level 3 and Level 4 data and then prepare the data for additional analysis. While this *Info-line* focuses primarily on Level 4 data, in many cases, Level 3 data are collected at the same time.

Step 1: Feasibility of a Level 4 Evaluation

Not every program is a candidate for a Level 4 evaluation. The issue is often one of balance. Following are some questions to answer that can help you determine the feasibility of conducting a Level 4 evaluation:

■ *Is a Level 4 Evaluation Possible?*
After the evaluation effort, regardless of the outcome, conclusions must be clear and defensible. To achieve this, three questions must be answered before data are collected:

● Can data be obtained that stakeholders would regard as evidence of business results?

● Is the program capable of creating an impact on measurable results?

● Can the effects of the program be isolated?

■ *What Is the Scope of the Evaluation?*
When compared with other evaluation efforts, measuring business results usually has a larger project scope. As such, there is a trade-off between the need to obtain data (and isolate program effects) and the need to secure resources to complete the evaluation. Business results are measured when reasonable trade-offs can be made.

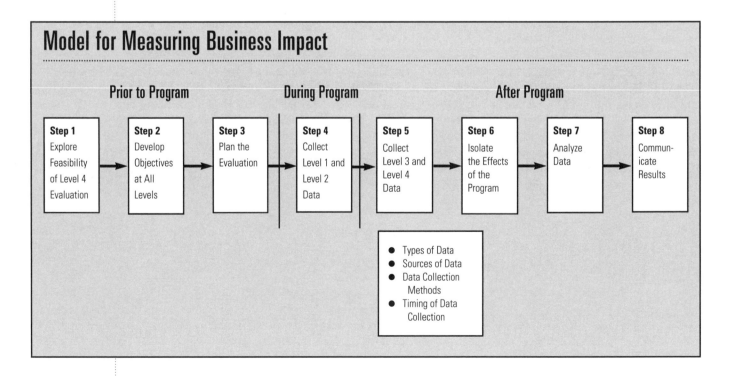

Model for Measuring Business Impact

Prior to Program			During Program		After Program		
Step 1 Explore Feasibility of Level 4 Evaluation	**Step 2** Develop Objectives at All Levels	**Step 3** Plan the Evaluation	**Step 4** Collect Level 1 and Level 2 Data	**Step 5** Collect Level 3 and Level 4 Data	**Step 6** Isolate the Effects of the Program	**Step 7** Analyze Data	**Step 8** Communicate Results

● Types of Data
● Sources of Data
● Data Collection Methods
● Timing of Data Collection

■ *Can Business Disruption Be Minimized?*
A certain amount of disruption to normal business occurs in a Level 4 evaluation. For example, the effects of training must be isolated from other factors, which may necessitate operating outside of normal procedures to determine who participates and when they do so.

■ *What Are the Measurable Results?*
Multiple stakeholders usually are interested in evaluation results. For the evaluator, the skills required to manage expectations of a diverse group of stakeholders are as important as the skills required for collecting and analyzing data. Business results should be measured when appropriate stakeholders have an interest in the outcome and understand the need for active participation. Stakeholders vary by organization, but typically they include participants, managers, sponsors, and top management.

Step 2: Develop Objectives

Determine if there has been, or will be, a link with a specific business need. This link should have been developed as part of the needs analysis. Ideally, the needs analysis should use the same framework of levels as the evaluation process, identifying needs at Levels 1, 2, 3, and 4. The objectives provide the link between the needs and the evaluation. They define precise expectations as the program is conducted and applied on the job, and they set up the evaluation process.

Use the following guide for objectives at the various levels:

Level 1 objectives define the expected reaction and planned action from participants.

Level 2 objectives identify the specific knowledge and skills that need improvement to enhance job performance.

Level 3 (application) objectives identify the performance expected on the job after the program is completed and participants apply what they have learned. These objectives are critical to measuring the use of skills and knowledge because they describe expected intermediate outcomes and the competent performance that should result from

training. Here are key questions to ask when developing application objectives.

- What new or improved knowledge will be applied on the job?

- What is the frequency of skill application?

- What new tasks will be performed?

- What new steps or action items will be implemented?

- What new procedures, process, or guidelines will be implemented or changed?

These objectives provide the basis for a follow-up evaluation while building the foundation for a Level 4 evaluation. Level 3 objectives must be met before Level 4 objectives are achieved (learning must be applied to produce a business impact).

Level 4 (impact) objectives describe expected outcomes and business unit performance that should be influenced by the training program. They may focus on output, quality, costs, time, customer service, and work climate.

The greatest challenge in developing objectives occurs when no previous Level 3 and Level 4 objectives exist. This usually can be accomplished by examining pertinent documentation related to the program, reviewing the program with developers, and interviewing a sample of participants to determine specifically how the program has been applied and what corresponding impact has been achieved.

Step 3: Plan the Evaluation

Planning should begin early, preferably during the needs analysis. Thorough planning helps identify the business measures that should be influenced by the training program and substantiate the need for the program. This is the time to review the Levels 2, 3, and 4 objectives for the training program, if they exist.

The principle tool for evaluation planning is the data collection plan. The data collection plan is quite simple. For each level (1 through 4), list objectives, the evaluation methods, when to evaluate, and who is responsible for conducting the

Using a Data Collection Plan

A training program, designed to improve customer satisfaction levels at auto dealerships, was pilot tested at 10 different sites. Consisting of three four-hour sessions, delivered one week apart, the program was targeted at all employees and managers. If successful, it would be implemented across North America at all the manufacturer's other dealerships.

Customer satisfaction surveys taken six months prior to the program indicated that dealerships were not customer friendly. Both customers and prospects were having unpleasant experiences as they visited dealerships to shop for vehicles, purchase parts, or to take advantage of repair or maintenance service. An analysis of trends indicated that lower customer satisfaction scores were likely contributing to a decrease in sales and a reduction in customer or prospect traffic patterns. Therefore, the program sought to achieve the following business impact objectives: 1) improve customer shopping and buying experience at retail stores; 2) increase customer satisfaction in the showroom and in the parts and service departments; and 3) increase sales of new vehicles as a result of improved customer care.

A comprehensive plan for evaluating the pilot training program was designed to determine business results and to serve as a guide for program designers and facilitators. Broad objectives were established before the actual program was designed and delivered, with specific details being developed later. Level 1 objectives included positive reactions to the training program and the participants' planned use of the skills. Level 2 objectives focused on measuring learning, and Level 3 objectives represented broad areas of application in the job setting. At Level 4, objectives focused on specific business impact measures.

The evaluation method selected was an existing customer feedback survey distributed at each dealership and administered and monitored by the manufacturer's North American headquarters. Sales increases were monitored at each of the locations for a period of six months. To measure customer satisfaction, evaluations were conducted three months after the training program. The results were then compared with satisfaction data obtained prior to the training.

evaluation. You can put this information on a matrix, which enables you to have a ready reference. The matrix could look something like this:

Level	Objectives	Method	Timing	Responsibilities
1				
2				
3				
4				

This matrix can expand to encompass any size program. See the sidebar at left for a case study.

In addition to collecting data, you also should address the issue of isolating the effects of the training. Select, plan, and implement the appropriate strategy or strategies in order to isolate the various influences that contribute to movement of performance measures. The data collection plan is also an excellent source document for evaluation at Level 5.

Step 4: Collect Level 1 and Level 2 Data

This data collection occurs at Levels 1 and 2. Please refer to *Info-lines* No. 9813, "Level 1 Evaluation: Reaction and Planned Action," and No. 9814, "Level 2 Evaluation: Learning," for this information.

Step 5: Collect Level 3 and Level 4 Data

A fundamental process in evaluation is to collect data directly related to the objectives of the program. Data needed to evaluate training are available and are usually being collected during previous evaluation levels. For more details see *Data Sources*.

To help focus on the desired measures, a distinction is made in two general categories—hard data and soft data. Preference for hard data does not mean soft data are not valuable. In practice, soft data are essential for a complete program evaluation. In some cases, a program's total success may rest on soft data measurements, such as customer satisfaction. Most program evaluations use a combination of hard and soft data items.

Hard Data

Hard data are the primary measurement of improvement, presented in rational undisputed facts, easily accumulated and converted to monetary values. The most desired types of data to measure the effectiveness of training and development, hard data include categories such as productivity, profitability, cost control, and quality control.

Hard data can be grouped into four categories: output, quality, cost, and time. These categories are typical performance measures in every organization.

Output can include:

- number of units produced
- number of tasks completed
- number of shipments
- inventory turnover

Quality can include:

- product defects/failures
- shortages
- scrap
- customer complaints

Cost can include:

- fixed costs
- variable costs
- penalties/fines
- unit costs

Time can include:

- training time
- processing time
- cycle time
- average delay time

The distinction between these groups of hard data is occasionally unclear, as some categories overlap. The categorization is not as important as an awareness of the vast number of measurements in these four areas.

Soft Data

Because changes in hard data may lag changes in behavior and attitudes, it is useful to supplement these measures with interim assessments of soft data, such as attitude, motivation, and satisfaction. Soft data are usually more difficult to collect and analyze, difficult to convert to monetary values, and are less credible as a performance measurement. Soft data are typically categorized into three areas: work habits, work climate, and satisfaction.

Work habits include:

- absenteeism
- tardiness
- violations of safety rules

Work climate includes:

- number of discrimination charges
- job satisfaction
- employee turnover

Satisfaction includes:

- customer or client satisfaction
- perceptions of job responsibilities
- perceived changes in performance

Level 4 Data Collection Methods

Reaching convincing conclusions about the impact of a program often rests on the adequacy and timing of data collection. Several methods are appropriate for Level 4 data; four of the most common are presented here.

Monitor Performance Records

The most common approach is to monitor hard performance data such as output, quality, cost, and time (refer to the hard data discussed above). These data are usually available in existing databases and reports. If not, additional record-keeping systems may have to be developed for measurement and analysis. You will need to determine the cost effectiveness of making this kind of decision. If the costs are greater than the expected return, then there is little point in developing the measures.

Data Sources

When considering possible sources of evaluation data, the following major categories are available:

■ *Organizational Performance Records*

The most useful and credible sources are the organization's records and reports. Whether individualized or group based, the reports reflect performance in a work unit, department, division, region, or company.

■ *Participants*

Participants are frequently asked to provide input on how new skills and knowledge have been applied on the job (Level 3), but sometimes they are asked to explain the impact of those actions (Level 4). Most participants are credible because they have effected the performance improvement and are cognizant of other influences.

■ *Participants' Supervisors*

This group often has a vested interest since they have probably approved participants' attendance. In many cases, they also observed participants using their newly acquired knowledge and skills.

■ *Direct Reports*

In situations where supervisors and managers are being trained, their direct reports can provide information about changes in behavior that have occurred since the program was conducted.

■ *Team or Peer Group*

Here, peer group members provide input on improvements after the program.

■ *Internal or External Groups*

Internal or external groups can be customers, mystery shoppers, staff specialists, or external consultants who provide input regarding improvements resulting from the application of new skills.

Performance measures should directly relate to the objectives of the program. As an example, the efficiency of a production unit can be measured in a variety of ways:

- number of units produced per hour
- percent utilization of the equipment
- percent of equipment downtime
- labor cost per unit of production
- total unit cost

Action Planning

The action plan approach is a straightforward, easy-to-use method for determining how participants will achieve success with training. In this approach, participants develop action plans with detailed steps to accomplish specific objectives related to the program. Plans are typically prepared on printed customized forms and show what is to be done, when, and who is responsible. Specific improvement steps are identified and tied to results and measures of success. This approach also produces data that answer such questions as:

- What on-the-job improvements have been realized since the program was conducted?

- Are the improvements linked to the program?

- What may have prevented participants from accomplishing specific action items?

Developing an action plan requires two tasks: determining the areas for action and writing the action items. Both tasks should be completed during the program. The area for action should originate from the content of the program and at the same time be related to on-the-job activities.

It is usually more difficult to write specific action items than it is to identify action areas. Most important is that the item is written so that everyone knows when it will occur. Use specific verbs, have a date for completion, and indicate other individuals or resources needed for completion. Action plans, as used in this context, do not require prior approval or input from the participant's manager, although they may be helpful.

To gain maximum effectiveness from action plans and collect data for a Level 4 evaluation, take the following steps:

- Communicate the action plan requirement early.

- Describe action planning at the beginning of the program.

- Teach action planning during the program.

- Allow time to develop the plan, preferably during the program.

- Have the facilitator approve the action plans.

- Require participants to identify a unit of measure for improvement.

- Require participants to develop a monetary value for the unit of measure.

- Ask participants to indicate the amount of improvement directly related to the program.

- Ask participants to provide a confidence level for estimates.

- Require action plans to be presented to the group, if possible.

- Explain the follow-up process.

- Collect action plans at the predetermined follow-up time.

- Summarize the data.

Performance Contracts

This is a slight variation on action planning. Based on the principle of mutual goal setting, a performance contract is a written agreement between participant and instructor. The participant agrees to improve performance in a specific area with set goals related to the content and objectives of the program.

Follow-Up Questionnaires

These are among the most versatile data collection instruments. Typically used to capture reaction, learning, and application data, they are also suited to Level 4 data collection. Specific questions focus on accomplishments and improvement after training, including a link between the program and business impact measures. This process is simple when business measures are known in advance. For example, in a program designed to improve sales, participants may be asked to provide sales data. In situations where business measures vary by participant, questions focus on individual accomplishments. Participants show the chain of impact (or chain of evidence) as application has driven improvements in a business measure.

As another variation, lists of specific business measures may be included and participants asked to indicate the extent to which the program has influenced these measures. Where influence has been noted, a question about the specific amount of the improvements is presented next. Designing follow-up questionnaires is presented in *Info-line* No. 9815, "Level 3 Evaluation: Application."

Timing of Data Collection

This is a critical decision and requires careful attention during pre-program planning and post-program analysis. Several issues influence timing. First, after a program is completed, you need an elapsed period of time for business measures to change and a clear pattern of improvement to emerge. For example, if sustained program impact requires six months, data collection should span this time period. Program impact changes usually do not occur dramatically. Therefore, data should be collected at reasonable intervals, such as monthly. On the other hand, if measurable effects are expected immediately after training, then daily or weekly data collection may be appropriate. This approach provides an opportunity to observe trends in business results while identifying application and transfer problems so they may be corrected.

Second, the availability and consistency of the data may drive timing. In some cases, the data might be available only quarterly, or every six months. Where data are available more frequently, collection can be accomplished earlier. Other factors to consider are the possible cyclical features of the data, such as seasonality and economic variation.

Third, the convenience of data collection is another consideration. When data are collected directly from participants using a questionnaire or action plan, it may be helpful to obtain data at a convenient follow-up session. Fourth, specific management constraints may require that data be collected for a shorter period of time than the ideal. A final consideration is that data collection at multiple intervals can provide management with interim reports. Key clients are very interested in results, even if preliminary. In addition to keeping stakeholders informed, this approach provides an opportunity to expose any barriers to program implementation that may require management intervention.

Step 6: Isolate Program Effects

This step is often overlooked, but it allows you to pinpoint the amount of improvement directly related to the program, thereby increasing the accuracy and credibility of the evaluation. This is important because a number of factors influence performance data after training. The following techniques will provide you with a comprehensive set of tools to isolate the effects of training:

■ *Control Group*

This allows you to isolate training impact. In this method, one group receives training while another group does not. The performance difference between the two groups is directly attributed to training.

■ *Trend Line Analysis*

Trend line analysis projects the value of specific output variables if training had not occurred. You can compare the projection to the actual data after training; the difference represents an estimate of the impact of training. This strategy can be an accurate way to isolate the effectiveness of training when no new factors have influenced the output measure during the evaluation period (see the figure opposite).

■ *Forecasting Models*

When the mathematical relationship between input and output variables is known, you can use a forecasting model to isolate the effects of training. To estimate the impact of training, compare the actual performance of the variable after the training with the forecasted value.

■ *Impact Estimates*

This allows you to estimate the impact of training on the output variables by gathering input from one or more of the following groups:

Participants estimate the amount of improvement related to training. Provide participants with the total amount of improvement, on a pre- and post-program basis, and ask them to indicate the percent of the improvement that is actually related to the training program.

Supervisors of participants estimate the impact of training on the output variables. Present supervisors with the total amount of improvement, and ask them to indicate the percent related to training.

Senior managers estimate the impact of training by providing an estimate or adjustment to reflect the portion of the improvement related to the training program. While this approach is sometimes inaccurate, having senior management involved in this process develops ownership of the value and buy-in for the process.

Customers sometimes provide input on the extent to which training has influenced their decision to use a product or service. Although this approach has limited applications, it can be quite useful in customer service and sales training.

Step 7: Analyzing Your Data

Here are a few general guidelines for analyzing evaluation data.

Review data for consistency and accuracy. While this may be obvious, additional checks are necessary to ensure the accuracy and consistency of the data. Incorrect, insufficient, or extreme data items should be eliminated.

Use all relevant data. Improvement is not always possible in an evaluation, and some data will be both positive and negative. Although it may be tempting to eliminate data that does not support the desired outcome, all relevant data should be used.

Treat individual data confidentially. When analyzing and interpreting data and reporting results, the confidentiality of the sources should be paramount unless conditions warrant their exposure. The same atmosphere of confidentiality used in collecting data should be used in the analysis and reporting phases.

Use the simplest statistics possible. There are many ways to analyze data and a variety of statistical techniques are available to compare performance variations, but the analysis should be as simple as possible and limited to what is absolutely necessary to draw the required conclusions from the data. Additional analyses that serve little or no benefit should be avoided.

Statistics

Statistics should be used to report the results of evaluations because they provide a concrete means by which results can be analyzed. The use of statistics in evaluation has three main functions.

■ *Information Summary*

Probably the most practical use of statistics is in summarizing large amounts of information, with two basic measures. One is the measure of *central tendency*, or *average*, which is the mean, median, and mode. This measure presents, in a single number, a summary of the characteristics of an entire group, such as the average absenteeism rate for a group of employees. The other category is *dispersion*, or *variance*, and the most useful measure of dispersion is the standard deviation. This reveals how much the individual items in the group are dispersed. For example, a large standard deviation for an average attendance means that there is a wide variation among the absenteeism records for the group of employees.

■ *Relationships Between Items*

Statistics allow you to determine the relationship between two or more items that may be important in analyzing data. The term used for this relationship is *correlation*, representing the degree to which the items are related; it is expressed in terms of a coefficient. A positive correlation between two items means that as one item increases, the other increases. For example, a high score on a knowledge test might correlate with a high level of performance on the job. There can also be a negative correlation between items where one decreases as the other increases.

■ *Comparisons Between Groups*

Statistics are useful when comparing differences in performance between two groups. If performance improves after a program, a likely question is: Did the improvement occur because of the program, or would it have occurred anyway? In other words, without the program, would the same results have been achieved? And, how accurately can the conclusions be drawn? Statistical analyses give credibility to differences in groups of data. Normally, conclusions are based on a 95 percent confidence level.

Trend Line Analysis

This example of a trend line analysis is taken from the production department of a large manufacturing company. The percentage reflects the level of actual production availability of the assembly line robotics apparatus except for robotics downtime for routine maintenance. Data are presented before and after the Robotics Troubleshooting training program.

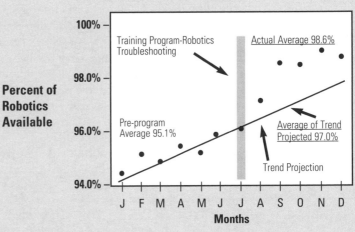

(Note: The trend line analysis is essentially a correlational analysis. The projected trend is developed from the pre-program data. On a practical basis, this can be developed with several spreadsheet packages.)

Determining Sample Size

Sampling is an important part of the Level 4 evaluation. Often, a specific group is identified for the evaluation, and there is some concern whether or not that group can represent an entire population. Sometimes, a sample is taken within a group, and there is some concern that the sample size might not be large enough to make an inference about that group. In other situations, individuals respond to a data collection method, and there is a question whether or not the total response represents an appropriate sample of that group.

In all of these instances, there are two major concerns: the makeup of the sample and the size of the sample. In some cases, a convenience process is used when only a certain group of participants is available or only a particular group can be surveyed. In these situations, the statistical significance of the outcome may be circumvented by the practical problems of a realistic work environment. When this is not the case, charts available in many statistical textbooks can provide a sample size needed for a particular population when a desired level of accuracy or confidence is required. References listed at the end of this *Info-line* will provide you with more detail.

Adjustments

Strategies used to isolate the effects of the training play a role in directing the data analysis. For example, if data are collected from participants using follow-up questionnaires and participants also provide estimates to isolate the effects of the training, then additional steps must be followed to develop a conservative approach to analysis. Here are suggestions for adjustments.

- For participants who do not provide improvement data, assume that they had little or no improvement to report; therefore, no analysis is required for these individuals.

- Each estimate of improvement should be reviewed for realism, usability, and feasibility. Discard and omit extreme claims or unsubstantiated claims from the analysis.

- Usable data items should be adjusted by the percentage of improvement directly related to the program being evaluated (this is one of the isolation strategies).

- The net performance improvement resulting from these adjustments should then be adjusted for the level of confidence that the participants place on their estimate of performance improvement.

For example, if participants estimate that they have improved sales by 30 percent as a result of the training, they are asked about their confidence in that estimate on a 0 to 100 percent scale. Participants responding with 80 percent confidence with the process are reflecting a 20 percent error possibility, suggesting that the value could be plus or minus 20 percent. Because a conservative approach is recommended, the minus 20 percent is used, which is achieved by multiplying the value by 80 percent. Thus, the sales improvement of 30 percent is adjusted by 80 percent resulting in a 24 percent improvement in sales.

The analysis of data at Level 4 is limited to the extent of improvement influenced by the training program. Level 4 analysis does not consider the value of the improvement, nor does it factor in the cost of the improvement. A Level 5 (ROI) analysis is required to compare costs with benefits.

Step 8: Communicate Results

Although evaluation is typically associated with the technical tasks of collecting and analyzing data, the role of communication is critical to project success. Notice the term *communication* rather than *reporting*. While reporting is important, it is only one of the tasks that occur throughout the life of a project. Communication should be thought of as managing the tasks associated with the following issues: purpose, audience, timing, and reporting format.

Purpose

The purposes for communicating program results depend on the specific program, the setting, and unique needs. The most common are:

- to secure approval for programs and allocate resources of time and money

- to gain support for the training and development department and its mission

- to build credibility for the department's strategies, approaches, techniques, and finished products

- to obtain a commitment for a participant to attend a program

- to create a desire to attend a specific program

- to enhance reinforcement of the training and development process

- to show the importance of measuring program results

- to stimulate interest in the department's products and services

Because there may be other reasons for communicating results, the list should be tailored to the organization.

Audience

When approaching a particular audience, the following questions should be asked about each potential group:

- Are they interested in the subject?

- Do they really want to receive the information?

- Is the timing right for this audience?

- Are they familiar with the department's products and services?

- How do they prefer to have results communicated?

- Are they likely to find the results threatening?

- Which medium will be most convincing to this group?

For each target audience, understand the audience and find out what information is needed and why. Try to understand audience bias. With this understanding, communications can be tailored to each group. This is especially critical when the potential exists for the audience to react negatively to the results.

Timing

Start laying the groundwork for communication before program implementation. Avoid delivering a message, particularly if the message is negative, to an audience unprepared to hear the story and unaware of the methods that generated the results. Communication is not an event, but a process; developing a summary of results and conclusions and stating them either in presentation or on paper is often insufficient. Surprising results are difficult to communicate effectively, particularly if the news is negative. If stakeholders are apprised of progress, alerted to barriers to success, and kept informed about progress toward business results, however, the potential for surprises is minimized.

The final report of a Level 4 impact study is usually communicated to selected target audiences as soon as the report is completed. Swift action may be needed if changes are required. It is also important to communicate to all audiences within a narrow time frame.

Reporting Format

The type of formal evaluation report depends on how much detailed information is presented to target audiences. Brief summaries of program results with appropriate charts may be sufficient for some communication efforts. In other cases, particularly those with programs requiring significant funding, the amount of detail in the evaluation report is more crucial. A full evaluation report may be necessary. This report can then be used as the basis for the information for the specific audiences and various media. The report may contain the following sections:

Management or Executive Summary, a brief overview of the entire report, explaining the basis for the evaluation and significant conclusions and recommendations.

Background Information, including a general description of the program.

Evaluation Strategy or Methodology, including all the components that make up the total evaluation process.

Data Collection and Analysis, which explains the methods used to collect and analyze data and presents program results at Levels 3 and 4, with charts, diagrams, tables, and other visual aids.

Moving Toward Level 5 Evaluation

This *Info-line* provides the basic steps in conducting a Level 4 evaluation as well as examples to show how the process can actually work. While Level 4 provides much-needed information concerning the payoff of training, in some cases the return-on-investment is needed, which is represented in Level 5. *Info-line* No. 9805, "Level 5 Evaluation: ROI," completely describes how the ROI is developed. In addition, when a Level 4 evaluation is conducted, information collected at Levels 1, 2, and 3 as a chain of impact, or chain of evidence, is developed.

References & Resources

Articles

Bassi, Laurie J., and Daniel P. McMurrer. "Training Investment Can Mean Financial Performance." *Training & Development*, May 1998, pp. 40-42.

Benabou, Charles. "Assessing the Impact of Training Programs on the Bottom Line." *National Productivity Review*, Summer 1996, pp. 91-99.

Bramley, P., and B. Kitson. "Evaluating Training Against Business Criteria." *Journal of European Industrial Training*, volume 18, number 1 (1994), pp. 10-14.

Heideman, James, and Bruce Sanderson. "Zooming In On Training Goals." *Technical & Skills Training*, July 1997, pp. 26-28.

Kaufman, R., J. Keller, and R. Watkins. "What Works and What Doesn't: Evaluation Beyond Kirkpatrick." *Performance and Instruction*, volume 35, number 2 (1995), pp. 8-12.

Kidder, Pamela J., and Janice Z. Rouiller. "Evaluating the Success of a Large-Scale Training Effort." *National Productivity Review*, Spring 1997, pp. 79-89.

Kirkpatrick, D.L. "Revisiting Kirkpatrick's Four-Level Model." *Training & Development*, January 1996, pp. 54-59.

Shelton, Sandra, and George Alliger. "Who's Afraid of Level 4 Evaluation? A Practical Approach." *Training & Development*, June 1993, pp. 43-36.

Thornburg, Linda. "Investment in Training Technology Yields Good Returns." *HRMagazine*, January 1998, pp. 37-41.

Watson, Scott C. "Five Easy Pieces to Performance Measurement." *Training & Development*, May 1998, pp. 45-48.

"Why Go to Level 3 & 4 Evaluation? Gap Inc. Finds the Training Payoff." *Training Directors' Forum Newsletter*, July 1997, pp. 1-3.

Willyerd, Karie A. "Balancing Your Evaluation Act." *Training*, March 1997, pp. 52-58.

Books

Basarab, David J. Sr., and Darrell K. Root. *The Training Evaluation Process*. Norwell, MA: Academic Publishers, 1992.

Bassi, Laurie J., and Darlene Russ-Eft (eds.). *What Works: Assessment, Development, and Measurement*. Alexandria, VA: ASTD, 1997.

Bramley, Peter. *Evaluating Training Effectiveness*. London: McGraw-Hill, 1996.

Burnham, Byron R. *Evaluating Human Resources, Programs, and Organizations*. Malabar, FL: Krieger Publishing, 1995.

Dixon, Nancy M. *Evaluation: A Tool for Improving HRD Quality*. San Diego: University Associates, 1990.

Hubbard, Edward E. *Measuring Diversity Results*. Petaluma, CA: Global Insights Publishing, 1997.

Kirkpatrick, D.L. "Techniques for Evaluating Training Programs." In *Evaluating Training Programs*. Alexandria, VA: ASTD, 1975.

———. *Evaluating Training Programs: The Four Levels*. San Francisco: Berrett-Koehler, 1994.

Newby, A.C. *Training Evaluation Handbook*. San Diego: Pfeiffer, 1992.

Parry, Scott B. *Evaluating the Impact of Training*. Alexandria, VA: ASTD, 1997.

Phillips, Jack J. *Handbook of Training Evaluation and Measurement Methods*. (3d edition). Houston: Gulf Publishing 1997.

———. *Measuring Return on Investment*. Vol. 2. Alexandria, VA: ASTD, 1997.

———. *Return on Investment in Training and Performance Improvement Programs*. Houston: Gulf Publishing, 1997.

Phillips, Jack J. (ed.). *Measuring Return on Investment*. Vol. 1. Alexandria, VA: ASTD, 1994.

Robinson, Dana Gaines, and James C. Robinson. *Training for Impact*. San Francisco: Jossey-Bass, 1989.

Info-lines

Callahan, Madelyn R. "The Role of the Performance Evaluator." No. 9803.

Callahan, Madelyn R. (ed.). "Be a Better Needs Analyst." No. 8502 (revised 1998).

Falletta, Sal, and Wendy Combs. "Evaluating Technical Training." No. 9709.

Phillips, Jack J., et al. "Level 1 Evaluation: Reaction and Planned Action." No. 9813.

———. "Level 2 Evaluation: Learning." No. 9814.

———. "Level 3 Evaluation: Application." No. 9815.

———. "Level 5 Evaluation: ROI." No. 9805.

Sparhawk, Sally, and Marian Schickling. "Strategic Needs Analysis." No. 9408 (revised 1999).

Waagen, Alice. "Essentials for Evaluation." No. 9705.

Level 5 Evaluation: ROI

Issue 9805

Level 5 Evaluation: ROI

AUTHORS:

Jack Phillips, Ph.D.
Performance Resources
    Organization (PRO)
P.O. Box 380637
Birmingham, AL 35238-0637
Tel: 205.678.9700
Fax: 205.678.8070
E-mail: roipro@wwisp.com

Patricia F. Pulliam
Performance Resources
    Organization (PRO)
P.O. Box 380637
Birmingham, AL 35238-0637
Tel: 205.678.9700
Fax: 205.678.8070
E-mail: roipro@wwisp.com

Editor
Cat Sharpe

Associate Editor
Sabrina E. Hicks

Designer
Steven M. Blackwood

ASTD Internal Consultant
Phil Anderson

Why ROI?

Forty years ago, Donald Kirkpatrick developed the four levels of evaluation that have become the preferred framework for practitioners: reaction, learning, behavior, and results. Today's human resource development (HRD) staff must conduct, in addition to the established evaluations, an additional measurement: return on investment (ROI). The issue of ROI in training and development has become a critical challenge for HRD personnel. In the last decade, the interest in ROI has mushroomed, leaving most major organizations scrambling for ways to tackle the issue.

ROI has become a hot topic for some good reasons. First, in most industrialized nations, HRD budgets have continued to grow year after year, and, as expenditures grow, accountability becomes a more critical issue. An increasing budget draws the attention of internal critics, often forcing the development of the ROI.

Second, total quality management and continuous process improvement have focused increased attention on measurement issues. Organizations now measure processes and outputs that previously were not measured, monitored, and reported. This measurement focus has placed increased pressure on the training and HRD function to develop measures of its output and successes.

Third, the reengineering and restructuring experience and the threat of outsourcing has caused many HRD executives to focus directly on bottom-line issues. Because of this scrutiny, many training and development functions have been reengineered to link programs to business needs and to enhance efficiencies. Change processes have caused HRD executives to examine evaluation issues and measure the contribution of specific programs. The threat of outsourcing has forced some HRD managers to more closely align programs to organizational objectives and success measures so that management can understand the contribution of HRD.

Fourth, the business management mindset of current training and HRD managers leads them to place more emphasis on economic issues within the training function. Today's training manager is more aware of the bottom-line issues in the organization and is more knowledgeable of the operational and financial areas. This new "enlightened" manager often takes a business approach to training and development, and the ROI issue is a part of this process.

Fifth, accountability has been a persistent trend for all functions in organizations. Each support function is attempting to show its worth by capturing the value that it adds to the organization. From an accountability perspective, the HRD function should be no different than the other functions: It must show its contribution.

Finally, top executives are now demanding ROI calculations in organizations where they were not required previously. For years, training and HRD personnel have convinced top executives that training cannot be measured, at least to the level desired by executives. Yet, many executives are now finding out that training *can* and *is* measured in many organizations, thanks in part to articles in publications aimed at top executives. Now aware that evaluation can be done, top executives are subsequently demanding the same accountability from their HRD departments. In some extremes, these executives are asking their HRD departments to show the return or face significant budget cuts; others are just asking for results.

This issue is one of five *Info-line*s covering the different levels of evaluation (see below for a more complete explanation of the different levels). One issue will be devoted to each evaluation level.

The Levels of Evaluation

The concept of different levels of evaluation is both helpful and instructive in understanding the measurement and evaluation process. The following text describes the five-level framework used in this series, which expands upon Kirkpatrick's original four levels (reaction, learning, behavior, and results) and adds a fifth level for ROI.

■ *Level 1: Reaction and Planned Action*

Measurements focus on satisfaction from program participants, along with a listing of how they plan to apply what they have learned. Almost all organizations evaluate at Level 1, usually with a generic, end-of-program questionnaire.

■ *Level 2: Learning*

Measurements (determined by tests, skill practices, role plays, simulations, group evaluations, and other assessment tools) focus on what participants learned during the program. A learning check is helpful to ensure that participants have absorbed and know how to use the material.

■ *Level 3: Application*

Measurements focus on the actual program application. A variety of follow-up methods are available to determine if participants applied their new knowledge to their jobs. The frequency and use of skills, with input on barriers and enablers, are important measures at Level 3.

■ *Level 4: Business Impact*

Measurements focus on the actual results (i.e., business impact) achieved by program participants as they successfully apply the program material. Typical Level 4 measures include output, quality, costs, time, and customer satisfaction.

■ *Level 5: ROI*

Measurement compares the monetary benefits of the program with the program costs. While ROI can be expressed in several ways, it is usually presented as a percent or benefit and cost ratio (BCR).

Almost all HRD practitioners conduct evaluations to measure satisfaction; very few actually conduct evaluations at the ROI level. Perhaps the best explanation for this situation is that HRD managers often characterize ROI evaluation as a difficult and expensive process. Although business results and ROI are desired, evaluation at the other levels is important. A chain of impact should occur through the levels as the skills and knowledge learned (Level 2) are applied on the job (Level 3) to produce business results (Level 4). If measurements are not taken at each level, it is difficult to conclude that the HRD program actually caused the results.

Recognizing the complexity of moving up the chain of evaluation levels, some organizations attempt to manage the process by setting goals or targets for each level of evaluation. Repeat sessions of the same program are counted in the total to arrive at the target percentage.

Establishing evaluation targets has two major advantages. First, the process provides objectives for the HRD staff to clearly measure evaluation progress for all programs or any segment of the HRD process. Second, adopting targets also focuses more attention on the accountability process, communicating a strong message about the extent of the commitment to measurement and evaluation.

Characteristics of Evaluation Levels

Level	Measures
1. Reaction and Planned Action	Participant's reaction to the program and outlines specific plans for implementation.
2. Learning	Skills, knowledge, or attitude changes.
3. Application	Changes in behavior on-the-job and specific application of the training material.
4. Business Impact	Business impact of the program.
5. ROI	Monetary value of the results and costs for the program, usually expressed as a percentage.

At *Level 1—Reaction and Planned Action,* a high level of activity is achieved, usually 100 percent, because it is easy to measure reaction. *Level 2—Learning* is another relatively easy area to measure, and the target is also high, usually in the 40–70 percent range. At *Level 3—Application,* the percentage drops because of the time and expense of conducting follow-up evaluations. Targets in the range of 30–50 percent are common.

Targets for *Level 4—Business Impact* and *Level 5—ROI* are relatively small, reflecting the challenge of a comprehensive evaluation process. Common targets are 10 percent for Level 4 and 5 percent for Level 5. The box at right provides an example of evaluation targets.

An Effective ROI Process

For an ROI process to be useful, it must balance issues such as feasibility, simplicity, credibility, and soundness. In addition, the following three major audiences (i.e., HRD practitioners; senior managers, sponsors, and clients; and researchers) must be willing to accept a particular ROI process in order to use it.

HRD Practitioners

For years, HRD practitioners have assumed that ROI could not be measured. When they examined a typical process, they found long formulas, complicated equations, and complex models that made the ROI process appear to be too complex. This resulted in HRD managers visualizing the tremendous efforts required for data collection and analysis, and, more important, the increased cost associated with making the process work.

Because of these concerns, HRD practitioners seek an ROI process that contains the following qualities:

● is simple and easy to understand
● implements the steps and strategies easily
● does not take a long time
● does not take away staff time
● is not expensive

In summary, the ROI process, from the perspective of the HRD practitioner, must be user friendly and time and cost efficient.

Evaluation Targets

Below is an example of evaluation targets established for a large telecommunications company. In this example, half of the *Level 4* evaluations are taken to *Level 5.*

Level		Percent of Courses
Level 1	Participant Satisfaction	100
Level 2	Learning	50
Level 3	Application	30
Level 4	Results	20
Level 5	ROI	10

Senior Managers, Sponsors, Clients

Managers who must approve HRD budgets or request HRD programs and live with the results have a strong interest in developing ROI. They want an ROI process that provides quantifiable results using a method similar to the ROI formula applied to other types of investments. Senior managers have a never-ending desire to have it all come down to an ROI calculation, reflected as a percentage.

Like HRD practitioners, senior managers want a process that is simple and easy to understand. The assumptions made in the calculations and the methodology used in the process should reflect their points of reference, backgrounds, and levels of understanding. They do not want or need a string of formulas, charts, and complicated models. Instead, they need a process that they can explain to others, if necessary. More important, they need a process with which they can identify; one that is sound and realistic enough to earn their confidence.

Internal ROI Network at NCR Corporation

One way to integrate the needs of HRD practitioners, senior managers, and researchers for an effective ROI evaluation process is through an internal ROI network. The experience with networks—in a handful of organizations where the idea has been tried—shows that these communities of practice are powerful tools for both accelerating evaluation skill development and cultivating a new culture of accountability.

The concept of a network is simplicity itself. The idea is to bring people throughout the organization who are interested in ROI together to work under the guidance of trained ROI evaluators. Typically, advocates within the HRD department see both the need for beginning networks and the potential of ROI evaluation to change how the department does its work. Interested network members learn by designing and executing real evaluation plans. This process generates commitment for accountability as a new way of doing business for the HRD department.

To begin, have the HRD group attend an ROI awareness session. Next, train one or more department members thoroughly in ROI methods so that they can serve as consultants to the rest of the developing network. Researchers are good choices for these roles.

Form project teams to develop and execute evaluation designs for key programs. Teams should share their progress and learnings periodically with the rest of the network through meetings or through Web pages.

When the network has results to demonstrate, it's time to share these with senior management. The reception by senior management is usually positive and enthusiastic; someone has finally figured out how to show them the benefits of learning activities in terms they understand. The final stage of network development is to secure a formal charter and sponsorship for the network from a senior management member.

Researchers

Finally, researchers will only support a process that measures up to their close examination. Researchers usually insist that models, formulas, assumptions, and theories are sound and based on commonly accepted practices. Also, they want a process that produces accurate values and consistent outcomes.

If estimates are necessary, researchers want a process that provides the most accuracy within the constraints of the situation, recognizing that adjustments need to be made when there is uncertainty in the process. The challenge is to develop acceptable requirements for an ROI process that will satisfy researchers and, at the same time, please practitioners and senior managers. Sound impossible? Maybe not.

Specific Criteria

To satisfy the needs of the three audiences above, the ROI process must meet several specific requirements. The following list contains the 10 essential criteria for an effective ROI process.

1. Simple.
The ROI process must be simple, void of complex formulas, lengthy equations, and complicated methodologies. Most ROI models have failed with this requirement. In an attempt to obtain statistical perfection and use too many theories, several ROI models and processes have become too complex to understand and use. Consequently, they have not been implemented.

2. Economical.
The ROI process must be economical and easily implemented. The process should become a routine part of training and development without requiring significant additional resources. Sampling for ROI calculations and early planning for ROI are often necessary to make progress with this concept without adding new staff.

3. Credible.

The assumptions, methodology, and techniques must be credible. Logical, methodical steps are needed to earn the respect of practitioners and senior managers. This requires a very practical approach for the process.

4. Theoretically Sound.

From a research perspective, the ROI process must be theoretically sound and based on generally accepted practices. Unfortunately, this requirement can lead to an extensive, complicated process. Ideally, the process must strike a balance between maintaining a practical and sensible approach and a theoretical basis for the process. Finding this balance is perhaps one of the greatest challenges to those who have developed models for the ROI process.

5. Account for Other Factors.

An ROI process must account for other factors that have influenced output variables. One of the most often overlooked issues—isolating the influence of the HRD program—is necessary to build credibility and accuracy. The ROI process should pinpoint the amount of contribution from the program when compared to other influences.

6. Appropriate.

The ROI process must be appropriate with a variety of programs. Some models apply to only a small number of programs, such as sales or productivity training. Ideally, the process must be applicable to all types of training, HRD programs (e.g., career development and organization development), performance improvement, and change initiatives.

7. Flexible.

The ROI process must have the flexibility to be applied on a pre-program basis as well as a post-program basis. In some situations, an estimate of the ROI is required before the actual program is developed. Ideally, the process should be able to adjust to a range of potential time frames.

8. Applicable.

The ROI process must be applicable with all types of data, including hard data (such as sales, productivity, rejects, and cycle time) and soft data (such as job satisfaction, customer satisfaction, grievances, and complaints).

9. Costs.

The ROI process must include the costs of the program. The ultimate level of evaluation is a comparison of benefits with costs. Although the term ROI has been loosely used to express any benefit of training, an acceptable ROI formula must include costs. Omitting costs will present only half of the equation. Underestimating costs will destroy the credibility of ROI values.

10. Successful Track Record.

The ROI process must have a successful track record in a variety of applications. In too many situations, models are created but never successfully applied. An effective ROI process should withstand the wear and tear of implementation and obtain the results expected.

Because these criteria are considered essential, an ROI process should meet the vast majority, if not all, of the criteria. The following ROI process model meets all the criteria.

The ROI Process Model

The calculation of ROI in HRD begins with the basic model (below), where sequential steps simplify a potentially complicated process. The ROI process model provides a systematic approach to ROI calculations.

The step-by-step approach keeps the process manageable so that users can tackle one issue at a time. The model also emphasizes that this is a logical process that flows from one step to another. Applying the model from one ROI calculation to another provides consistency, understanding, and credibility. Each step of the model is briefly described on the following pages.

Collecting Post-Program Data

Data collection is central to the ROI process and is the starting point of the ROI process. As illustrated in the graphic, items in the circles are issues that must be addressed when determining the specific data collection method. Although the ROI analysis is (or should be) planned early in the training and development cycle, the actual ROI calculation begins with data collection. (Additional information on planning for the ROI analysis is presented later under "Essential Planning Steps.")

The HRD staff should collect both hard data (representing output, quality, cost, and time) and soft data (including work habits, work climate, and attitudes). Collect Level 4 data using a variety of the methods described on the next page.

ROI Model

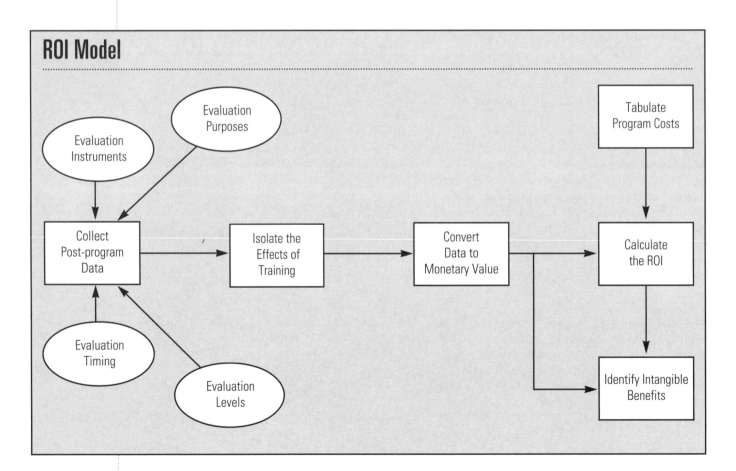

■ *Follow-up Questionnaires*

Administer follow-up questionnaires to uncover specific applications of training. Participants provide responses to a variety of types of open-ended and forced response questions.

Use questionnaires to capture both Level 3 and Level 4 data. The sidebar on the next page shows a series of Level 4 impact questions contained in a follow-up questionnaire for evaluating an automotive manufacturer's sales training program in Europe. With appropriate responses, HRD practitioners can use the data in an ROI analysis. When combined with other questions, the instrument becomes a versatile tool for ROI evaluations.

■ *Program Assignments*

Program assignments are useful for simple, short-term projects. Participants complete the assignment on the job, using the skills or knowledge learned in the program. Report completed assignments as evaluation information, which often contain Level 3/Level 4 data. Convert Level 4 data to monetary values and compare the data to costs to develop the ROI.

■ *Action Plans*

Developed in training and development programs, action plans on the job should be implemented after the program is completed. A follow-up of the plans provides evaluation information. Level 3/Level 4 data are collected with action plans, and the HRD staff can develop the ROI from the Level 4 data.

■ *Performance Contracts*

Developed prior to conducting the program and when the participant, the participant's supervisor, and the instructor all agree on planned specific outcomes from the training, performance contracts outline how the program will be implemented. Performance contracts usually collect both Level 3/ and Level 4 data and are designed and analyzed in the same way as action plans.

■ *Performance Monitoring*

As the most beneficial method to collect Level 4 data, performance monitoring is useful when HRD personnel examine various business performance records and operational data for improvement.

The important challenge in this step is to select the data collection method or methods that are appropriate for both the setting and the specific program and the time and budget constraints.

Isolating the Effects of Training

Isolating the effects of training is an often overlooked issue in evaluations. In this step of the ROI process, explore specific techniques to determine the amount of output performance directly related to the program. This step is essential because many factors influence performance data after training. The specific techniques of this step will pinpoint the amount of improvement directly related to the program, increasing the accuracy and credibility of the ROI calculation. Collectively, the following techniques provide a comprehensive set of tools to tackle the important and critical issue of isolating the effects of training.

■ *Control Group*

Use a control group arrangement to isolate training impact. With this technique, one group receives training while another, similar, group does not receive training. The difference in the performance of the two groups is attributed to the training program. When properly set up and implemented, control group arrangement is the most effective way to isolate the effects of training.

Impact of Skills Example

1. Please identify specific accomplishments/improvements in your performance that you can link to what you have learned (e.g., job performance, sales closings, etc.)

2. Indicate the extent to which you think this program has influenced the following measures in your work.

	Very Much Influence	Significant Influence	Moderate Influence	Some Influence	No Influence
Sales Volume	☐	☐	☐	☐	☐
Customer Satisfaction	☐	☐	☐	☐	☐
Profit Margin	☐	☐	☐	☐	☐
Conversion Ratio	☐	☐	☐	☐	☐

3. Estimate your contribution to increased sales in annual dollars . . . . $_____

Please explain the basis for your estimate:

_____

_____

_____

_____

_____

_____

What percentage of this estimate is linked to this program? . . . . _____%

What is your level of confidence in these values? (100% = Certainty to 0% = No confidence) . . _____%

What percentage of this estimate is linked to this program? . . . . _____%

What is your level of confidence in these values? (100% = Certainty to 0% = No confidence) . . _____%

4. Estimate your contribution to increase profit margin in annual dollars . . . . $_____

Please explain the basis for your estimate:

_____

_____

_____

_____

5. Do you think the Sales Training Program was a good investment? . . . . ☐ Yes ☐ No

Please explain:

_____

_____

_____

■ *Trend Line Analysis*

Use trend line analysis to project the value of specific output variables if training had not occurred. Compare the projection to the actual data after training; the difference represents the estimate of the impact of training. Under certain conditions, this strategy can be an accurate way to isolate the impact of training.

The figure shown at right provides an example of a trend line analysis that was taken from a shipping department of a large distribution company. The marked percentages reflect the level of actual shipments compared to scheduled shipments. Data are presented before and after a team training program that was conducted in July. As shown in the figure, an upward trend existed on the data prior to conducting the training program. Using pre- and post-program differences, the program apparently had a significant effect on shipment productivity (7 percent). However, the trend projection line shows that improvement would have continued anyway, based on the trend that had been previous established. The impact of the program is estimated to be 2.1 percent: the difference in the actual average and the projected average.

■ *Forecasting Models*

When mathematical relationships between input and output variables are known, use a forecasting model to isolate the effects of training. With this approach, the output variable is predicted using the forecasting model with the assumption that no training is conducted. Next, compare the actual performance of the variable after the training to the forecasted value to estimate the impact of training.

■ *Impact Estimates*

When the previous approaches are not feasible, estimating the impact of training on the output variables is another approach and can be accomplished on the following four levels.

1. Participants estimate the amount of improvement related to training. In this approach, provide participants with the total amount of improvement, on a pre- and post-program basis, and ask them to indicate the percent of the improvement that is actually related to the training program.

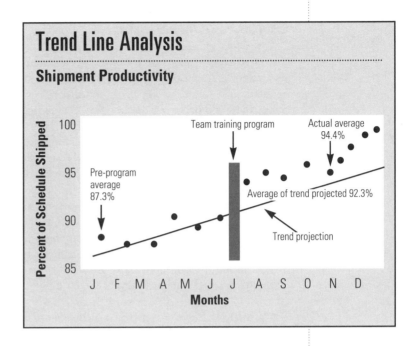

Trend Line Analysis

Shipment Productivity

2. Supervisors of participants estimate the impact of training on the output variables. Present supervisors with the total amount of improvement, and ask them to indicate the percent related to training.

3. Senior managers estimate the impact of training by providing an estimate or *adjustment* to reflect the portion of the improvement related to the training program. While perhaps inaccurate, having senior management involved in this process develops ownership of the value and buy-in for the process.

4. Experts estimate the impact of training on the performance variable. Because these estimates are based on previous experience, experts must be familiar with the type of training and the specific situation.

Customers sometimes provide input on the extent to which training has influenced their decision to use a product or service. Although this approach has limited applications, it can be quite useful in customer service and sales training.

Converting Data to Monetary Values

To calculate ROI, convert Level 4 data to monetary values and compare with program costs. This requires placing a value on each unit of data connected with the program. A number of techniques are available to convert data to monetary values; the selection depends on the type of data and the situation.

- Convert output data to profit contribution or cost savings. With this technique, output increases are converted to monetary value based on their unit contribution to profit or the unit of cost reduction. These values are readily available in most organizations and are seen as generally accepted standard values.

- Calculate the cost of quality, and convert quality improvements directly to cost savings. This standard value is available in many organizations for the most common quality measures (such as rejects, rework, and scrap).

- Use the participants' wages and employee benefits as the value for time in programs where employee time is saved. Because a variety of programs focus on improving the time required to complete projects, processes, or daily activities, the value of time becomes an important and necessary issue. The use of total compensation per hour provides a conservative estimate for the value of time.

- Use historical costs when they are available for a specific variable. In this case, use organizational cost data to establish the specific value of an improvement.

- Use internal and external experts, when available, to estimate a value for an improvement. In this situation, the credibility of the estimate hinges on the expertise and reputation of the individual.

- Use external databases, when available, to estimate the value or cost of data items. Research, government, and industry databases can provide important information for these values. The difficulty lies in finding a specific database related to the situation.

- Ask participants to estimate the value of the data item. For this approach to be effective, participants must understand the process and be capable of providing a value for the improvement.

- Require supervisors and managers to provide estimates when they are willing and capable of assigning values to the improvement. This approach is especially useful when participants are not fully capable of providing this input or in situations where supervisors or managers need to confirm or adjust the participant's estimate.

Converting data to monetary value is very important in the ROI model and is absolutely necessary to determine the monetary benefits from a training program. The process is challenging, particularly with the conversion of soft data, but can be methodically accomplished using one or more of the above techniques.

Tabulating Program Costs

The other part of the equation in a cost/benefit analysis is the cost of the program. Tabulating the costs involves monitoring or developing all of the related costs of the program targeted for the ROI calculation. Include the following items among the cost components:

- cost to design and develop the program, possibly prorated over the expected life of the program

- cost of all program materials provided to each participant

- cost for the instructor/facilitator, including preparation time as well as delivery time

- cost of the facilities for the training program

ROI Calculation: Sexual Harassment Prevention

Target Group
All supervisors and managers (655) in a regional hospital chain. Subsequent meetings were conducted with all employees (6,844).

Impact Objectives
Reduce internal complaints of sexual harassment.
Reduce employee turnover related to sexual harassment.

Collection Methods
- Level 3 Data: Self-assessment Questionnaire (six months after program)
- Level 3 Data: Employee Survey—25 percent sample (six months after program)
- Level 4 Data: Complaint and Turnover Records (12 months after program)

Isolating the Effects of the Program
- complaints
- trend line analysis
- turnover
- forecasting

Converting Data to Monetary Values
- complaints—historical costs and input from internal EEO/AA staff
- turnover—external studies within industry

Program Costs
- fully loaded to include needs assessment, development, coordination, participant salaries and benefits, and evaluation
- total program costs = $277,987

Intangible Benefits
- increased job satisfaction
- less absenteeism
- reduced stress
- enhanced community image
- better recruiting

ROI Calculation
Monetary benefits from complaint reduction
- value of one internal complaint = $24,343
- annual improvement related to program = 14.8 complaints
- benefits = $24,343 x 14.8 = $360,276

Monetary benefits from turnover reduction
- value of one turnover statistic = $20,887
- annual improvement related to program = 136 turnovers (prevented)
- benefits = $20,887 x 136 = $2,840,632

$$BCR = \frac{\text{Total Benefits}}{\text{Program Costs}} = \frac{\$3,200,908}{\$\ 277,987} = 11.51$$

$$ROI = \frac{\text{Total Benefits} - \text{Program Costs}}{\text{Program Costs}} = \frac{\$3,200,908 - \$277,987}{\$277,987} \times 100 = 1051\%$$

Interpretation

This program produced a tremendous ROI. For every dollar invested, $11.51 was returned, as reflected in the BCR. In terms of the ROI calculation, for every dollar invested, the dollar was recovered and another $10.51 was produced. This value was based on actual calculations and was accepted by the management team. This case illustrates the potential impact of programs when they are needed. While extremely large, this calculation still follows conservative approaches.

Adapted from In Action: Measuring Return on Investment, *ASTD, 1997, pp. 17–35.*

- cost of travel, lodging, and meals for the participants, if applicable

- salaries, plus employee benefits, of the participants to attend the training

- administrative and overhead costs of the training function, allocated in some convenient way

In addition, specific costs related to the needs assessment and evaluation should be included, if appropriate. The conservative approach is to include all of these costs so that the total is fully loaded.

Calculating the ROI

Calculate the ROI using the program benefits and costs. The BCR is the program benefits divided by cost:

$$BCR = \frac{Program\ Benefits}{Program\ Costs}$$

(Sometimes this ratio is stated as a cost/benefit ratio, although the formula is the same as BCR.)

The net benefits are the program benefits minus the costs:

$$Net\ Benefits = Program\ Benefits - Program\ Costs$$

The ROI uses the net benefits divided by program costs:

$$ROI\ (\%) = \frac{Net\ Benefits}{Program\ Costs \times 100}$$

Use the same basic formula in evaluating other investments where the ROI is traditionally reported as earnings divided by investment. The ROI from some training programs is high. For example, in sales training, supervisory training, and managerial training, the ROI can be quite large, frequently over 100 percent, while the ROI value for technical and operator training may be lower.

Identifying Intangible Benefits

In addition to tangible, monetary benefits, most training programs will have intangible, non-monetary benefits. The ROI calculation should be based on converting both hard and soft data to monetary values. Intangible benefits include the following items:

- increased job satisfaction
- increased organizational commitment
- improved teamwork
- improved customer service
- reduced complaints
- reduced conflicts

During data analysis, make every attempt to convert all data to monetary values, including all hard data (such as output, quality, and time). Attempt to convert soft data for each data item; however, if the process used for conversion is too subjective or inaccurate and the resulting values lose credibility in the process, list the measure as an intangible benefit with the appropriate explanation. For some programs, intangible, non-monetary benefits are extremely valuable, often wielding as much influence as the hard data items.

Selecting Programs for ROI Analysis

Selecting programs for ROI analysis is an important and critical task. Only specific types of programs should be selected for the comprehensive, detailed analysis, and criteria for identifying programs should be developed. Candidates for analysis are programs that include the following features:

- involve large target audiences
- expect to have a long life cycle
- are important to strategic objectives
- link to operational goals and issues
- are expensive
- take a significant investment of time
- have high visibility
- have a comprehensive needs assessment
- have the interest of top executives

Using these or similar criteria, the staff must select the appropriate programs to consider for an ROI project. Ideally, management should concur with, or approve, the criteria.

The next major step is to determine how many projects to undertake initially and in which particular areas. Start with a small number of initial projects, perhaps two or three programs. The targeted programs may represent the functional areas of the business (such as operations, sales, finance, engineering, and information systems). Another approach is to select programs representing functional areas of training and development (e.g., sales training, management, development, supervisor training, Web-based training, and technical training). Selecting a manageable number is important to ensure that the process will be implemented. As presented earlier, eventually a prescribed percentage of programs (usually 5 percent) will be targeted for an ROI analysis.

Essential Planning Steps

An important ingredient to the success of the ROI process is to properly plan for the ROI early in the training and development cycle. Appropriate, up-front attention will save time later when data are actually collected and analyzed, thus improving the accuracy and reducing the cost of the ROI process. Planning properly also avoids any confusion surrounding what will be accomplished, who will accomplish it, and when it will be accomplished. Two planning documents are the key to the up-front analysis and should be completed before designing or developing the program. An example of each document is provided as a job aid.

The *Data Collection Plan* on the following page shows a completed form depicting an interactive sales skills program. The three-day training program was designed for retail sales associates in the electronics department of a major store chain. An ROI calculation was planned for a pilot of three groups. This document provides a place for the major elements and issues regarding collecting data for the four evaluation levels. (At Level 5 evaluation, Level 4 data develops ROI.)

Broad program objectives are appropriate for planning. Specific, detailed objectives are developed later, before the staff designs an actual program. The objectives for Level 1 include positive reactions to the training program. If it is a new program, as in this example, another category, *suggested improvements,* may be included.

Level 2 evaluation focuses on the measures of learning. The specific objectives include those areas where the instructor expects the participants to change knowledge, skills, or attitudes. The data collection method is the specific way in which learning is assessed, whether as a test, simulation, skill practice, or facilitator assessment. The timing for Level 2 evaluation is usually during or at the end of the program, and the responsibility usually rests with the instructor or facilitator.

For Level 3 evaluation, the objectives represent broad areas of program application, including significant on-the-job activities that should follow application. The data collection (i.e., evaluation) method includes one of the post-program methods described earlier and usually is conducted within a matter of weeks or months after program completion. A Level 3 evaluation often precedes a Level 4 evaluation. Because several groups often share responsibilities (including the training and development staff, division trainers, or local managers), it is important to clarify this issue early in the process.

For Level 4 evaluation, objectives focus on business impact variables influenced by the program. The objectives may include the way in which each item is measured. For example, if one of the objectives is to improve quality, a specific measure would indicate how that quality is actually measured (such as defects per thousand units produced). While the preferred evaluation method is performance monitoring, other methods (such as action planning) may be appropriate. The timing depends on how quickly participants can generate a sustained business impact, which is usually a matter of months after training. The participants, supervisors, division training coordinators, or perhaps an external evaluator may be responsible for Level 4 data collection.

Data Collection Plan

Program: __Interactive Sales Skills__   Responsibility: _____   Date: _____

Level	Broad Program Objective(s)	Data Collection Method	Timing of Data Collection	Responsibilities for Data Collection
1. Reaction, Satisfaction, and Planned Actions	☐ Positive Reaction ☐ Suggested Improvements ☐ Action Items	☐ Reaction Questionnaire	☐ End of 2nd Day ☐ End of 3rd Day	☐ Facilitator
2. Learning	☐ Acquisition of Skills ☐ Selection of Skills	☐ Skill Practice	☐ During the Program	☐ Facilitator
3. Application	☐ Use of Skills ☐ Frequency of Skills ☐ Barriers	☐ Questionnaire ☐ Follow-up Session	☐ 3-months After Program ☐ 3-weeks After the First Two Days	☐ Training Coordinator ☐ Facilitator
4. Business Impact	☐ Sales Increase	☐ Performance Monitoring	☐ 3-months After Program	☐ Training Coordinator

The data collection plan is an important part of the evaluation strategy and should be completed prior to moving forward with the training program. For existing training programs, the plan is completed before pursuing the ROI evaluation. The plan provides a clear direction of what type of data will be collected, how it will be collected, when it will be collected, and who will collect it.

The *ROI Analysis Plan* on the following page shows a completed ROI analysis plan for the interactive sales skills program described above. This planning document is the continuation of the data collection plan and captures information on several key items that are necessary to develop the actual ROI calculation.

In the first column, significant Level 4 data items are listed. These items will be used in the ROI analysis. The second column lists next to each data item the method used to isolate the effect of training. For most cases the method will be the same for each data item, but there could be variations. For example, if no historical data are available for one data item, trend line analysis is not possible for that item, although it may be appropriate for other items.

The third column includes the method of converting data to monetary values, using one of the 10 strategies outlined earlier. The fourth column outlines the cost categories that will be captured for the training program. Instructions about how certain costs should be prorated would be noted here. Normally, the cost categories will be consistent from one program to another. However, a specific cost that is unique to the program would also be noted.

The fifth column outlines the intangible benefits expected from this program. Discussions about the program with sponsors and subject matter experts generate the items on this list.

The sixth column would highlight other issues or events that might influence program implementation. Typical items include the capability of participants, the degree of access to data sources, and unique data analysis issues. Finally, the last column outlines communication targets. Although many groups should receive the information, four target groups are always recommended:

- senior management group
- supervisors of participants
- program participants
- training and HRD staff

The ROI analysis plan, when combined with the data collection plan, provides detailed information on calculating the ROI and, thus, illustrates how the process will develop from beginning to end. When thoroughly completed, these two plans provide the direction necessary for ROI evaluation.

Barriers to ROI Implementation

Although progress has been made in the implementation of ROI, significant barriers inhibit the implementation of the concept. Some of these barriers are realistic; others are actually myths based on false perceptions. Each barrier is briefly described in the following section.

■ Costs and Time
The ROI process will add costs and time to the evaluation of programs, although the amount will not be excessive. A comprehensive ROI process will probably not cost more than 4–5 percent of the overall training and HRD budget. The additional investment in ROI would perhaps be offset by the additional results achieved from these programs and the elimination of unproductive or unprofitable programs. This barrier alone stops many ROI implementations early in the process.

ROI Analysis Plan

Program: <u>Interactive Sales Skills</u>   Responsibility: _____ Date: _____

Data Items	Methods of Isolating Effects of Program	Methods of Converting Data	Cost Categories	Intangible Benefits	Other Influences/ Issues	Communi- cation Targets
☐ Weekly sales per employee	☐ Control group analysis	☐ Direct conversion using profit contribution	☐ Facilitation fees ☐ Program materials ☐ Meals/ refreshments ☐ Facilities ☐ Participant salaries/ benefits ☐ Cost of coordination/ evaluation	☐ Customer satisfaction ☐ Employee satisfaction	☐ Must have job coverage during training ☐ No commu- nication with control group ☐ Season fluctuations should be avoided	☐ Program participants ☐ Electronics department managers— targeted stores ☐ Store managers— targeted stores ☐ Senior store executives, district, regional, headquarters ☐ Training staff: instructors, coordinators, designers, and managers

■ *Lack of Skills and Orientation for Staff*

Many training staff members neither understand ROI nor have the basic skills necessary to apply the process within their scope of responsibilities. The typical training and development program does not focus on results; it focuses more on learning outcomes. Consequently, a tremendous barrier to implementation is the change needed for the overall orientation, attitude, and skills of the HRD staff. As once said, "We have met the enemy and he is us."

■ *Faulty Needs Assessment*

Many of the current training and HRD programs do not have an adequate needs assessment. Some of these programs have been implemented for the wrong reasons (such as an effort to chase a popular fad or trend in the industry). If the program is not needed, there will probably not be sufficient or economic benefits from the program to offset the costs. Thus, an ROI calculation for an unnecessary program will likely yield a negative value. This is a realistic barrier for many programs.

■ *Fear*

Some HRD departments do not pursue ROI because of fear of failure or fear of the unknown. A concern may exist about the consequence of negative ROI. Some HRD staff members may feel threatened. Ideally, the ROI process should be considered a learning and improvement tool. The ROI process also stirs up the traditional fear of change. This fear is often based on unrealistic assumptions and a lack of knowledge of the process and is so strong that it becomes a realistic barrier to many ROI implementations.

■ *Discipline and Planning*

A successful ROI implementation requires much planning and a disciplined approach to keep the process on track. Implementation schedules, evaluation targets, ROI analysis plans, measurement and evaluation policies, and follow-up schedules are required. The HRD staff may not have enough discipline and determination to stay on course. This becomes a barrier, particularly when there are no immediate pressures to measure the return. If the current senior management group is not requiring ROI, the HRD staff may not allocate time for planning and coordination. Also, other pressures and priorities will often consume precious time necessary for ROI implementation. Only a carefully planned implementation will be successful.

■ *False Assumptions*

Many HRD staff members have false assumptions about the ROI process, which keep them from attempting ROI. The following list contains examples of typical faulty assumptions:

- Managers do not want to see the results of training and development expressed in monetary values.

- If the CEO does not ask for the ROI, he or she is not expecting it.

- As manager of HRD, I have a professional, competent staff; therefore, I do not have to justify the effectiveness of our programs.

- The training and development process is a complex, but necessary, activity; consequently, it should not be subjected to an accountability process.

These false assumptions form realistic barriers that impede the progress of ROI implementation.

Benefits of ROI

Although the benefits of adopting the ROI evaluation may appear to be obvious, the following six distinct and important benefits can be derived from the implementation of ROI in an organization.

■ *Measure the Contribution*
The HRD staff will know the specific contribution from a select number of programs. The ROI will determine if the benefits of the program, expressed in monetary values, have outweighed the costs. The ROI will also determine if the program made a contribution to the organization and if it was indeed a good investment.

■ *Develop Priorities for Programs*
Calculating ROIs in different areas will determine which programs contribute the most to the organization, allowing priorities to be established for high-impact training.

■ *Improve Programs*
As with any evaluation process, an ROI impact study provides a variety of data to make adjustments/changes with the program. Because data are collected at other levels, six types of data are usually available:

- reaction/satisfaction
- learning
- application
- impact
- ROI
- intangible benefits

This allows for a complete analysis of problems and opportunities to lead to redesigning, retargeting, or eliminating the program.

■ *Focus on Results*
The ROI process is a results-based process that focuses on results with all programs, even for those not targeted for an ROI calculation. The process requires instructional designers, facilitators, participants, and support groups to concentrate on measurable objectives (i.e., what the program is attempting to accomplish). Thus, this process has the added benefit of improving the effectiveness of all training programs.

■ *Build Management Support*
The ROI process, when applied consistently and comprehensively, can convince the management group that training is an investment and not an expense. Managers will see training as making a viable contribution to their objectives, thus increasing the respect and support for the function. The ROI process is an important step in building a partnership with management and increasing commitment for training and development.

■ *Alter Perceptions of Training*
Routine ROI impact data, when communicated to a variety of target audiences, will alter perceptions of training. Participants, supervisors, and management will view training and development as an integral part of the organization, adding value to work units, departments, and divisions. They will have a better understanding of the connection between training and results.

These key benefits, inherent with almost any type of impact evaluation process, make the ROI process an attractive challenge for the HRD function.

References & Resources

Articles

Alliger, George M., et al. "A Meta-Analysis of the Relations Among Training Criteria." *Personnel Psychology,* Summer 1997, pp. 341-358.

Benabou, Charles. "Assessing the Impact of Training Programs on the Bottom Line." *National Productivity Review,* Summer 1996, pp. 91-99.

Barron, Tom. "Is There An ROI In ROI?" *Technical & Skills Training,* January 1997, pp. 21-26.

Chase, Nancy. "Raise Your Training ROI." *Quality,* September 1997, pp. 28-41.

Heideman, James, and Bruce Sanderson. "Zooming In On Training Goals." *Technical & Skills Training,* July 1997, pp. 26-28.

Kidder, Pamela J., and Janice Z. Rouiller. "Evaluating the Success of a Large-Scale Training Effort." *National Productivity Review,* Spring 1997, pp. 79-89.

Kirkpatrick, D.L. "Techniques for Evaluating Training Programs." *Evaluating Training Programs,* Alexandria, Virginia: American Society for Training & Development, 1975, pp. 1-17.

Lowther, Nancy. "Asset or Liability?" *American Printer,* August 1997, pp. 56-58.

Parry, Scott B. "Measuring Training's ROI." *Training & Development,* May 1996, pp. 72-77.

Parsons, Jennifer Gail. "Values as a Vital Supplement to the Use of Financial Analysis in HRD." *Human Resource Development Quarterly,* Spring 1997, pp. 5-13.

Phillips, Jack J. "How Much is the Training Worth?" *Training and Development,* April 1996, pp. 20-24.

——— . "Measuring Training's ROI: It Can Be Done." *William & Mary Business Review,* Summer 1995, pp. 6-10.

——— . "The ROI Process: Issues and Trends." *Educational Technology,* March-April 1998.

——— . "ROI: The Search for Best Practices." *Training and Development,* February 1996, pp. 42-47.

——— . "Was It the Training?" *Training and Development,* March 1996, pp. 28-32.

Thornburg, Linda. "Investment in Training Technology Yields Good Returns." *HRMagazine,* January 1998, pp. 37-41.

Solomon, Matt. "Employee Training." *Credit Union Magazine,* August 1997, pp. 46-50.

"Why Go to Level 3 & 4 Evaluation? Gap Inc. Finds the Training Payoff." *Training Directors' Forum Newsletter,* July 1997, pp. 1-3.

Willyerd, Karie A. "Balancing Your Evaluation Act." *Training,* March 1997, pp. 52-58.

Books

Bartel, Ann P. "Return-on-Investment." *What Works: Assessment, Development, and Measurement.* Eds. Laurie J. Bassi and Darlene Russ-Eft. Alexandria, Virginia: American Society for Training & Development, 1997, pp. 151-184.

Hubbard, Edward E. *Measuring Diversity Results.* Petaluma, California: Global Insights Publishing, 1997.

Parry, Scott B. *Evaluating the Impact of Training.* Alexandria, Virginia: American Society for Training & Development, 1997.

Phillips, Jack J. *Handbook of Training Evaluation and Measurement Methods.* (3rd edition.) Houston, Texas: Gulf Publishing, 1997.

——— . *Return On Investment In Training And Performance Improvement Programs.* Houston, Texas: Gulf Publishing, 1997.

Phillips, Jack J. (ed.) *Measuring Return on Investment.* Vol. 1. Alexandria, Virginia: American Society for Training & Development, 1994.

——— . *Measuring Return on Investment.* Vol. 2. Alexandria, Virginia: American Society for Training & Development, 1997.

Info-lines

Cheney, Scott. "Benchmarking." No. 9801.

Falletta, Sal, and Wendy Combs. "Evaluating Technical Training." No. 9709.

Hodell, Chuck. "Basics of Instructional Systems Development." No. 9706.

O'Neill, Mary. "How to Focus Training Evaluation." No. 9605.

Robinson, Dana Gaines. "Tracking Operational Results." No. 9112.

Robinson, Dana Gaines, and James C. Robinson. "Measuring Affective and Behavioral Change." No. 9110 (revised 1997).

Waagen, Alice K. "Essentials for Evaluation." No. 9705.

Job Aid

Data Collection Plan

Fill in the objectives, methods, timing, and responsibilities of the data collection as a means to improve the accuracy and reduction of ROI cost. You can use the example on page 14 as a sample for your work. Then use the ROI Analysis Plan below to complete the collection.

Program: _____ Responsibility: _____ Date: _____

Level	Broad Program Objective(s)	Data Collection Method	Timing of Data Collection	Responsibilities for Data Collection
1. Reaction and Planned Action				
2. Learning				
3. Application				
4. Business Impact				

ROI Analysis Plan

Data Items	Methods of Isolating Effects of Program	Methods of Converting Data	Cost Categories	Intangible Benefits	Other Influences/ Issues	Communication Targets

Evaluating Technical Training:
A Functional Approach

Issue 9709

Evaluating Technical Training: A Functional Approach

AUTHORS:

Salvatore V. Falletta
360 Communications
    Training & Development
    Regional Manager
4000 Regency Pkwy., Suite 400
Cary, NC 27511
Tel.: 919.573.4828
Fax: 919.573.4992
E-mail: Salvatore.Falletta@360.com

Wendy L. Combs
Technical Manager
Nortel Process Improvement
    Manager
4307 Emperor Blvd.
Durham, NC 27703
Tel.: 919.992.8702
Fax. 919.992.6265
E-mail: wcombs@nortel.com

Editor
Cat Sharpe

ASTD Internal Consultant
Dr. Walter Gray

Evaluation of Technical Training

Technical training is a primary strategy for addressing performance needs in business and industry. With the emergence of alternative performance improvement strategies—job aids, online technical documentation, and measurement and feedback systems—the technical training enterprise must provide evidence of its value and worth by measuring the impact of training. In an era of continuous quality improvement, it must also improve its training products and services to meet present and future demands. By planning and conducting targeted and purpose-driven training evaluations, these demands can be satisfied.

Evaluation can tell you many things about training. Designers may be interested in knowing whether the course instructional design has been effective; technical trainers may want to know how much of the course's content participants learned; supervisors may want to know whether learners can perform the acquired skills on-the-job; and senior management is most likely interested in overall job performance as well as the training's impact on the organization's bottom line.

A Functional Approach

There is no single evaluation effort that can answer all of these questions at one time. To get these answers, your evaluation needs to have a purpose or objective, and to help you accomplish this task, you will need to target your questions and identify the functional dimensions you want evaluated. At its most basic level, a functional evaluation *evaluates by purpose*—it targets the questions being asked and identifies the relevant functions being evaluated.

Targeting Questions

In the early stages of planning, a list of important evaluation questions is typically developed. These questions are often based on curiosity and tend to be rather broad in nature. For example, just answering "yes" or "no" to the question, "Can the instructional design be improved?" does not provide specific enough details to help designers improve the course. By conducting working sessions with stakeholders, these broad kinds of questions can be replaced with narrower, more focused questions. The following questions demonstrate more specificity:

- Are the learning objectives of the training clear, specific, and measurable?

- To what extent does the instructional design provide for practice and feedback to assure mastery of the learning objectives?

- To what extent does the instructional design define learner training preparation before, during, and following training?

These targeted evaluation questions are all related to a particular function and the function of interest is instructional design.

It is important to revise broad evaluation questions as they are posed. During working sessions, the technical training practitioner or evaluation specialist should facilitate the process of targeting evaluation questions. By including stakeholders in the session, you get immediate feedback; by modeling the process, stakeholders will become more proficient in targeting their own questions in the future. (See "Targeting Evaluation Questions" on page 114.)

Sometimes, targeted evaluation questions are so specific that they automatically lend themselves to measurement with a specific tool (see the "Matrix of Common Evaluation Tools" on page 122). But more importantly, targeted evaluation questions allow you to identify the specific function of interest in an evaluation.

Identifying Functions

As an example, if the following two targeted questions are identified, "To what extent do learners feel the training is relevant to their jobs?" and, "To what extent do supervisors feel the training is relevant to learners' jobs?" the purpose of the evaluation becomes clear—it's to determine whether the training is relevant on the job. Therefore, the function of interest is "training relevancy."

Different functions often represent dimensions that are commonly addressed while evaluating technical training. There is, of course, some overlap in these functions, but they serve to highlight specific functions of interest in any given evaluation. The functional dimension brings issues of importance into sharper focus. See the box on the next page for other examples of functions of interest.

Functional Dimensions

The different functions represented in this diagram depict dimensions commonly addressed in technical training evaluations. There are some obvious overlaps between dimensions, but they serve to highlight the specific function of interest for any given evaluation. Functional dimensions bring issues of importance into sharper focus.

Stakeholders may pose targeted evaluation questions that serve multiple functions. For example, the following targeted evaluation questions address the functional dimensions of "strategic performance planning" and "learner motivation":

1. To what extent is the training linked to the strategic performance needs of the organization?

2. To what extent are learners reinforced or rewarded for applying new skills on the job?

The first question addresses the functional dimension of "strategic performance planning." The second question addresses the dimension "learner motivation" because rewards for skill performance are presumed to affect employee motivation. Usually, multiple-targeted evaluation questions are needed to adequately address a particular functional dimension. Additionally, several dimensions may be of interest in a given evaluation.

Examples of Functional Dimensions Within The Context of Training

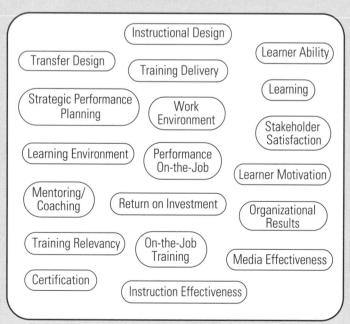

The most important indicator of success is stakeholders' perceptions of the usefulness of the evaluation data. If the data does not meet stakeholders' information needs, the evaluation will not succeed. Rather than wonder why evaluations fail, technical trainers and evaluation specialists should focus their time and energy on clarifying the questions the evaluation will address.

In summary, the time spent in the development of targeted evaluation questions and the clarification of specific evaluation functions is vital to successful training evaluation.

Conducting Working Sessions

Planning a functional training evaluation requires that you devote time and energy to working sessions. These sessions serve the purpose of fostering collaboration and maintaining communication with stakeholders. The successful evaluation is in reality an ongoing process and the results will meet the information requirements of the stakeholders.

Targeting evaluation questions and identifying the function(s) of interest typically require several working sessions. Since the development of targeted questions is an iterative process, stakeholders may wish to gather information and meet in two or more sessions. This information may include:

- documentation on the training design (including front-end analysis)

- information on previous trainees

- any critical incident logs available

- previous course feedback data

Collection of this type of data allows stakeholders to understand the background and context of the training.

During all working sessions, an agenda with the purpose and desired outcomes should be developed to facilitate the process. A facilitator should provide advance notice of the meeting (e.g., date, time, location, duration, agenda) and he or she should also be prepared for the session. Stakeholders prefer sessions that are focused and productive, and do not waste their limited time. For more

Contingency Flowchart for a Functional Training Evaluation

Technical Aspects

Stakeholder-Collaborative Aspects

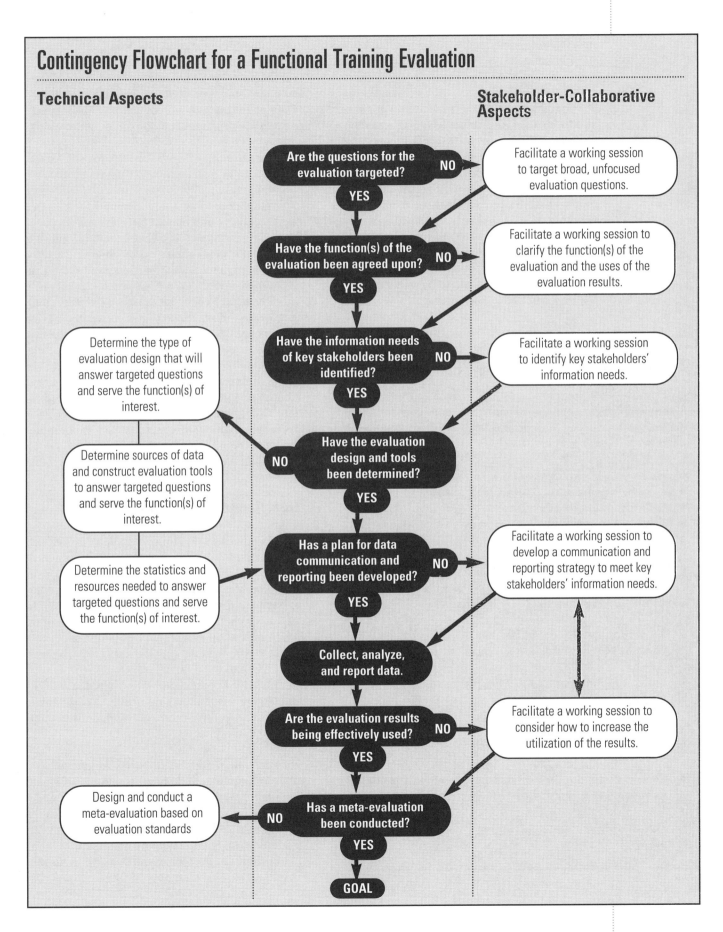

Are the questions for the evaluation targeted?
NO — Facilitate a working session to target broad, unfocused evaluation questions.
YES

Have the function(s) of the evaluation been agreed upon?
NO — Facilitate a working session to clarify the function(s) of the evaluation and the uses of the evaluation results.
YES

Determine the type of evaluation design that will answer targeted questions and serve the function(s) of interest.

Have the information needs of key stakeholders been identified?
NO — Facilitate a working session to identify key stakeholders' information needs.
YES

Determine sources of data and construct evaluation tools to answer targeted questions and serve the function(s) of interest.

Have the evaluation design and tools been determined?
NO
YES

Determine the statistics and resources needed to answer targeted questions and serve the function(s) of interest.

Has a plan for data communication and reporting been developed?
NO — Facilitate a working session to develop a communication and reporting strategy to meet key stakeholders' information needs.
YES

Collect, analyze, and report data.

Are the evaluation results being effectively used?
NO — Facilitate a working session to consider how to increase the utilization of the results.
YES

Design and conduct a meta-evaluation based on evaluation standards

Has a meta-evaluation been conducted?
NO
YES

GOAL

information on working sessions and facilitation, see *Info-lines* No. 8710, "More Productive Meetings," and No. 9406, "How to Facilitate."

The intended use of the evaluation data should also be introduced at this point to make certain all critical questions have been asked. Identifying the intended uses is a natural follow-up to determining functions—after all, much of the work has already been accomplished once the evaluation questions were targeted. Once the targeted evaluation questions have been developed and agreed upon, the functional dimensions can be identified. Identifying the functional dimensions stimulates the exploration of additional targeted questions that are important and add to the evaluation. (See the flowchart on the previous page.)

Targeting Evaluation Questions

Stakeholders tend to pose broad, unfocused questions during initial evaluation planning sessions. Following are some examples of these types of questions:

- Do learners have the prerequisite knowledge and skill?
- Does the training meet strategic performance plans?
- Is the course length appropriate?
- Do participants have the resources to perform on the job?
- Are learners motivated to perform new skills on the job?

Writing targeted evaluation questions takes some time and practice, but is worth the effort. See the examples below for how the above listed questions can be better targeted:

- To what extent do learners feel they have adequate prerequisite knowledge and skills to succeed in the training?

- To what extent is the training linked to the strategic performance needs of the organization?

- What percentage of participants (or trainers) feel the course length is too long? Too short?

- To what extent are the tools and equipment available to perform newly acquired skills on the job?

- To what extent are learners reinforced or rewarded for applying new skills on the job?

Evaluation Tools

Once the informational needs of the key stakeholders have been identified, the technical trainer can begin to determine which evaluation tool or tools and what type of design should be employed. Data collection and analysis constitute the technical aspects of the evaluation process. After all the data is presented to stakeholders, the practitioner will want to ensure that the results are used for the evaluation's original purpose.

The evaluation tools commonly used for measuring the effects of technical training include questionnaires or surveys, knowledge and performance assessments, observations, focus groups, and telephone interviews. Use the "Matrix of Common Evaluation Tools," located on pages 122-125, as a quick-reference check for assessing the most commonly used measurement tools. Other tools such as work logs, face-to-face interviews, action plans, role plays, and simulations can also be used. The particular tool or tools used in any evaluation depends on the targeted questions and the function or functions of interest. If a tool is created internally, you will need to use the appropriate methodology to assure its effectiveness. In other words, it should be constructed based on sound assessment and measurement practices.

Questionnaires and Surveys

Questionnaires and surveys are used to collect standardized information from a wide range of individuals. The term "standardized" means that everyone receives the exact same survey in order to compare responses. Whether the format used is paper, scannable form, or an online document, a written version of the survey is initially constructed. Use the following steps to build a survey:

1. Identify the items of interest based on the targeted evaluation questions. These items are the questions and statements you want asked in the survey.

2. Write questions in everyday language; use short, simple, and clear sentences. To make sure questions are easily understood, each question should only refer to a single idea or thought and be as specific as possible. Don't use terms such as "most of the time." Say instead, "90 percent of the time." If available,

you can modify a pre-existing survey. Keep the reading level fairly basic—an 8th-10th grade level is about right.

3. Review, revise, or omit items with questionable language, duplication, or ambiguity.

4. Determine the type of responses you will use for the survey—not all questions can be answered the same way. The different response alternatives typically used in training evaluations are:

- open-ended or short answer
- Likert-type scale
- semantic differential
- multiple choice
- binary (yes/no, true/false)
- matching
- ranking
- checklist response alternatives

5. Prepare and write clear instructions on how to fill out the survey and explain when and where to return it. Spell out the purpose of the survey and assure participants that all responses will be held in confidence. All of this information should appear on the first page of the survey document.

6. Review the overall sequence of the survey. Items should flow from general to specific within categories; group items together based on similar content and types of response alternatives; demographic items should appear last on surveys (research studies have found that participants are more likely to complete and return a survey if personal questions are asked at the end).

7. Layout the survey in an easy-to-read typeface and straightforward design. The layout depends, of course, on what type of media will deliver the survey (CBT, paper, e-mail, and so on). Fonts should be large and attractive in size and shape. Use underlining, italics, and bold face to make distinctions between items. Borders may also highlight certain sections or simplify the format of the survey.

8. Conduct a trial run or pilot test of the survey to identify any problems or shortcomings.

Likert-Type Scales

These scales are frequently used on questionnaires in technical training evaluations. Examples of several Likert-type scales follow:

- Strongly Agree, Agree, Disagree, Strongly Disagree
- Very Satisfied, Satisfied, Dissatisfied, Very Dissatisfied
- Too Long, Just Right, Too Short
- Increase, Remain the Same, Decrease

Notice that the response alternatives on each side of the scale are equivalent (e.g., Strongly Agree is parallel to Strongly Disagree). The more lengthy the scale (e.g., a 7 or 9-point Likert-type scale), the broader the range of information obtained. An even numbered scale forces the participant to select one side of the scale or the other, rather than the middle. If an odd numbered scale is used, avoid the use of "neutral" because participants often misinterpret its meaning (that is, does "neutral" mean "no opinion" or "not applicable"?). Instead, use "neither agree nor disagree," "neither satisfied nor dissatisfied," or a similar phrase.

Regardless of the type of response alternatives used with items, it is important to:

- List all relevant response alternatives for each item.

- Alert the participant to the number of responses which are applicable for each item.

- Ensure the response alternatives match the items.

If you do not identify and list all relevant response alternatives, participants will either not complete the item or will incorrectly mark the response alternative nearest in meaning to their intended response. For example, if an item asks participants to identify their "professional position" from a list, the list should include all professional positions relevant to the audience.

Second, some items may call for two or more possible responses (e.g., "Check all that apply") and should be labeled as such. If participants do not fully complete these items, data will be missing. Finally, if response alternatives do not match their respective items, participants will be confused. A common mistake is to use the wrong scale with an item (e.g., asking the extent to which the participant "agrees or disagrees" with a statement and using a "satisfaction" scale).

Assessments

Two types of assessments or tests can be used as training evaluation tools. These are: knowledge assessments, which measure knowledge or learning, and performance assessments, which measure skill. Both measure the trainees' mastery of the learning objectives and either one can be constructed internally.

■ *Knowledge Assessment*

The knowledge assessment should contain items that represent the training content and that are fair and objective. Like a survey, it is essential to pilot the assessment and analyze the responses in order to identify those items that should be revised or omitted.

To construct an assessment tool, the training designer, developer, or subject matter expert (SME) prepares and writes a knowledge assessment based on the critical learning objectives. These should be written in simple and concise language; meanings should be clear without having to read response alternatives. Use the Assessments sidebar on the next page as a guide for preparing this tool.

Typical response alternatives on knowledge assessments are:

- multiple choice
- true/false
- matching

There should be only one correct response per item and the correct answers should be randomly placed—that is, not all answers should be "B" if multiple choice, or follow a pattern such as "True, True, False, False."

Depending on the evaluation design, pre-and post-assessments can be administered as part of the evaluation process to measure any gain in learning. If employed, the same assessment should be administered on both occasions. Even though an equivalent assessment can be created, it must have the exact number of easy, moderate, and difficult items, and has to correlate to the first assessment.

■ *Performance Assessment*

To construct this tool, the designer, developer, or SME must use his or her understanding of the training content. First, a list of the most significant skills to be mastered is prepared based on the learning objectives. The tasks comprising each skill are identified and arranged in a logical sequence. Then, the criterion or standard for performance is identified for each skill.

If skills are observed in classrooms or labs, the trainer or a peer can serve as the observer and rater. In the classroom, the learner may be asked to *role play* the solution to a problem that requires applying recently acquired skills. In a *simulation*, an attempt is made to replicate the condition, that is problem, equipment failure, and so on that are likely to appear on the job.

If the assessment is conducted in the workplace, learners' performance can be observed and rated by supervisors. The procedures for observing job performance follow.

Structured Observations

This is a useful tool for observing an activity or product and then recording key behaviors or features on a checklist or rating form. Structured observation can be used to examine work samples as well as the actual performance of a skill. First, identify the specific behaviors of interest or various features to be evaluated. Typically, a checklist or rating scale is used—it includes the performance goal or work sample to be observed, instructions for the rater, and the criteria or standards against which the performance should be judged.

Checklists allow observers to record whether the objective has been met. In contrast, rating scales allow the observer to record performance or characteristics on a continuous scale. For example:

Meets all *standards, meets* most *standards, meets* some *standards, meets* a few *standards, meets* no *standards.*

When using continuous scales, key definitions must be provided for ambiguous terms. That is, "meets all" standards must mean that 100 percent of the standards have been met. Checklists are the preferred choice for simple objects, while rating scales are the better selection for evaluating complex skills. In an ideal scenario, observations are comprised of both checklists and ratings scales, depending on the skill being observed.

Assessments

	YES	NO
Knowledge or Cognitive-based Assessments		
1. Are items based on the learning objectives of the training?	☐	☐
2. Are items written in simple and concise language?	☐	☐
3. Are items arranged from easy to difficult?	☐	☐
4. Is the meaning of items clear without have to read the response alternatives?	☐	☐
5. Have ambiguous terms been eliminated from items and response alternatives?	☐	☐
6. Have double negatives been eliminated from items and response alternatives?	☐	☐
7. Are the response alternatives similar in length?	☐	☐
8. Is the order of answers randomized across items?	☐	☐
9. Are the incorrect response alternatives plausible?	☐	☐
10. Is *"All of the Above"* and *"None of the Above"* avoided?	☐	☐
11. Are items with the same type of response alternatives grouped together?	☐	☐
12. Is the assessment representative of the training content?	☐	☐
13. Does the assessment discriminate among participants?	☐	☐
14. Is the assessment fair and objective?	☐	☐
15. Are the directions for completing the assessment obvious, direct, and explicit?	☐	☐

Performance or Skill-based Assessments		
1. Are the skills to be performed based on the learning objectives of the training?	☐	☐
2. Are the skills to be performed limited to those that are most important?	☐	☐
3. Are the skills to be performed arranged in a logical sequence?	☐	☐
4. Are the instructions to the rater obvious, direct, and explicit?	☐	☐
5. Is the standard of performance clearly specified?	☐	☐
6. Is the standard of performance realistic?	☐	☐
7. Is the assessment fair and objective?	☐	☐

Let individuals know in advance the purpose and timing of these observations. Allow sufficient time to ensure accuracy and completeness. The rater should never provide directions, answers, nonverbal cues, or help during the observation. Raters must be objective in their observations, so training is usually required. Otherwise, some subjective bias may enter into the process. Using more than one individual to conduct observations allows the reliability or percent agreement between two observers to be easily calculated.

As a final note, observation is not always necessary in performance assessment. For example, learners can rate their own ability to perform various skills related to training. This can be useful if there are a large number of participants and limited resources.

Focus Groups

The focus group is a structured group process designed to explore a topic in-depth with a group of six to 12 participants. Focus groups may be used for any number of purposes, including gathering impressions of training effectiveness or diagnosing problems related to training. Participants discuss their ideas and react to and build upon the ideas of others.

Synergism and snowball effects, which aid in the process, occur when participants are interested in and engaged in the focus group activity. With synergism, the combined effect of participants' interaction and discussion is greater than the sum of their individual contributions. Similarly, the snowball effect means that one idea stimulates others. The main benefit of focus groups is the depth of inquiry made possible and the potential for clarification and elaboration.

A trained moderator is needed to structure and facilitate the focus group. The topics and/or questions of interest are developed in advance and should allow for in-depth exploration of ideas. Only a few questions can be sufficiently addressed in a typical two hour session. Since participants should be grouped together based on similarities, several different sessions may be needed. To capture the ideas generated, chart paper and audio or video recording can be used. The ideas can be written in transcript form and later analyzed for themes.

Telephone Interviews

Telephone interviewing is a useful tool that allows interviewers to engage in a dialogue with interviewees. Over the telephone, the interviewer is able to ask questions and to probe or clarify interviewees' responses. The interviewer should be trained in telephone interviewing techniques.

The actual interview script is primarily conversational in tone. The questions and response alternatives must be simple enough for an interviewer to read to a respondent without the respondent getting lost or forgetting parts of the questions. A special recording form is often created to record the respondent's answers. Highlighting or color-coding the script helps the interviewer remain on track, or quickly find his or her place.

Because respondents cannot see the transcript, success depends on the interviewer's ability to present the items and response alternatives in a clear and complete manner. Standard probes such as "Tell me more about that" and "How do you mean that?" should be employed to clarify incomplete or ambiguous responses. It is also helpful if these probes are included on the interview script to prompt the interviewer.

Interviewers may inadvertently introduce bias into the conversation through voice intonation or other commentary. Interviewers must use a neutral tone and record interview responses verbatim. Telephone interviews are time consuming and often numerous attempts at contacting individuals have to be made. The best approach for setting up an interview is to contact the individual beforehand and set aside a date and time that will work for the respondent.

Alternatively, in-person, or face-to-face, interviews can also be conducted. Physical appearance, verbal and nonverbal cues are potential sources of bias. Since the data obtained through in-person interviews can usually be collected through telephone interviews, which are quicker and less costly, telephone interviews are the better choice.

Learner Profiles

This is a data collection tool that can be designed to include demographic items, work history, and prior training experience (that is, professional experience and time in present position). The information collected on a learner profile is background data and therefore, does not measure the results of training. By using student identification numbers, learner profiles can be linked to other evaluation tools—questionnaires and assessments.

Learner profiles are generally mailed to participants prior to training and once returned, forwarded to the evaluation department. The use of this evaluation tool has many advantages. It allows you for example, to reduce the length of other tools used in the evaluation if demographic and other items can be collected on the learner profile. Since the learner does not have to complete redundant items on different tools, the learner may be less defensive when asked to complete evaluation tools.

Sources of Information

All of the tools discussed above can be used as methods of collecting information. This information can come from a host of individuals—learners, trainers, developers, designers, SMEs, supervisors, peers, and customers—especially those people directly involved with the technical training process. As a general rule, those who have the most knowledge, experience, and opportunity to observe the issues in question, are those individuals who can provide the most valuable information.

Following are some of the people you can use as sources of information:

Instructional designers and developers can provide information on the adequacy of the front-end analysis, course design, and media used in the training.

Senior management can provide information on the extent to which training addresses strategic performance planning.

Subject matter experts (SMEs) can provide information on the accuracy and completeness of the training content once a course has been in use for some time.

Learners can provide information on the frequency with which they perform the acquired skills on the job. This usually occurs two to four months after the training to allow time for learners to perform the new skills.

Existing Documentation

Some technical training practitioners recommend using existing documents as sources of information for training evaluations but these documents were not originally designed for this purpose. Because of this, they tend to be insensitive sources of information, not directly related to the purposes of the evaluation. If existing documentation is used, the information contained therein should be relevant to the targeted evaluation questions and the functional dimension(s) of interest.

Interpretation

Interpreting outcomes related to technical training depends upon the evaluation design itself. The design allows you to compare the outcome data to data collected earlier or to a comparison group. Without a basis for comparison, data interpretations are limited to only descriptive statements. These statements simply report what is occurring at a given point in time. More complex interpretations of data can be made when comparison data is available.

More powerful evaluation designs employ a comparison group and multiple measurement tools and sources. The design most commonly used is the *one-group pre- and post-design*. It involves administering the same assessment tool twice—once before the training and once after.

A different design, the *pre- and post-comparison group design* includes a comparison group and is frequently used in training evaluation as well. In this design, assessments are administered before and after the training, and to a group of individuals who will not attend the training. This way, comparisons between training participants and nonparticipants can be made. A sampling strategy can be used to limit the number of participants.

Following is a list of training evaluation designs as well as their limitations:

■ *One-Group Post Only Design*
This design involves a single group that receives training and is evaluated once after the training is completed. The data collected under this design can only be described; this design has no point of comparison and is the least useful.

■ *One-Group Pre- and Post-Design*
This design consists of two assessments—one conducted before training and one after. It does, however, have a *practice effect*, which means individuals are likely to score higher on the second administration of the assessment because they have already taken the assessment once. Constructing an equivalent assessment minimizes this problem.

■ *Pre- and Post-Comparison Group Design*
A comparison group, composed of individuals not attending the training and a group of actual training participants complete before and after assessments. Comparisons can be made between learners' and non-learners' pre-assessment scores as well as between their post-assessment scores; interpretations can be made from this design. As a cautionary note, both groups should be composed of individuals with similar characteristics, that is: knowledge base, professional position, and so on, in order to make legitimate comparisons.

■ *Time Series Design*
This design is similar to the *one-group pre- and post-design* except that more than two assessments are made. The design allows for measuring the long-term effects of training and the points of comparison in this design are the multiple administrations of the assessment. Again, practice effects cannot be ruled out.

■ *Pre- and Post-Control Group Design*
This design is rarely used. It involves the random assignment of individuals who are interested in training into two groups—one receives training and the other group has to wait to receive training. The latter group serves as a comparison, much the way the *pre- and post-comparison group design* works. Since the decision of who receives the training first is randomly determined, systematic differences between the two groups are unlikely.

Statistical Analysis

Once the evaluation tools and design have been identified, the statistics and resources needed to answer the targeted evaluation questions must be identified. Statistical analyses may be conducted internally or contracted out to a statistical consultant. Depending on how complex the evaluation design is, how much data collection is required, or what the organizational reporting requirements are, the statistical analyses may be calculated and stored on a standard spreadsheet application or relational database.

Participants' responses on any of the tools can be coded and entered into a spreadsheet. The way in which participants' responses are entered depends on the response alternatives for each item. For example, the different response alternatives can be coded as follows:

> True/False: True = 1, False = 2
> Multiple choice: A = 1, B = 2, C = 3, D = 4, E = 5
> Check all that apply: A = 1, unmarked A = 0 (coded in one column)
> B = 1, unmarked B = 0 (coded in the next column)
> C = 1, unmarked C = 0 (coded in the next column)

For any demographic item, assign consecutive numbers to each response alternative as they appear under the item on the questionnaire and follow the same coding procedure.

Before any calculations are performed, it is imperative to check the data for errors. That is, ensure that all numbers are in the correct columns after coding. This can be done simply by printing the spreadsheet of data, highlighting every other column with a marker, and systematically examining the columns.

Simple calculations that are most useful and can be easily computed by a spreadsheet application include:

- frequency
- percentage
- mean
- mode
- median
- range
- variance
- standard deviation

Some spreadsheet applications have advanced statistical functions including t-tests and correlations. Consult your software manual for specific commands related to these functions. There are certain assumptions regarding the level of the data that must be met when performing statistical analyses—be sure these assumptions have been met before applying statistics (for example, some statistics require a minimum number of participants to be valid). Otherwise, the results will be inaccurate.

Powerful relational databases may also be used in the storage, analysis, and reporting of evaluation data. The practicality of using a database depends on the extent of data collection, the size of the training enterprise, and stakeholders' information needs.

Summarizing the Data

After the design and tools have been developed, it is once again useful to involve stakeholders. Since you now know what stakeholders' needs are, you'll want to confirm the format of the information they receive, the frequency of reporting, and how the material is presented. That is, do they prefer presentation slides, bound reports, statistical summaries, and so on. You will want the presentation and reporting strategies to portray the evaluation results accurately.

Bar charts, pie charts, and tables that summarize evaluation results are usually depicted in reports, presentations, and informal communications. Tables allow a large amount of information to be presented in an orderly fashion on a single page. It is helpful to include the number of participants or sample size with the percentages.

Charts and tables may need titles, headings, labels, keys, and footnotes to be self-explanatory. Be careful when creating bar charts—they can easily misrepresent data if the axes are truncated; for example, if the vertical axis is shortened, a percentage of 62 percent will appear higher than it actually is if presented on a scale that only extends to 70 percent. Standard spreadsheet applications can be used to create bar and pie charts to summarize evaluation data.

Data from open-ended responses are typically typed verbatim into a table. The responses can then be categorized based on themes and if not too long, the table can be included in the body of the report. If longer than one page, create an appendix to the report. Verbatim comments should never be included in published reports if you can in any way identify the individuals who made the comments.

Next Steps

The evaluation process is not complete once the data has been reported and used for its intended purpose. For example, the evaluation reporting process is ongoing when more than one course is being evaluated. Additionally, stakeholders often request more information as they discover it helps the decision-making process.

For these reasons, it is prudent for the technical training practitioner to evaluate the training evaluation process and outcomes so as to improve subsequent training evaluations. Conducting a postmortem of the training evaluation process itself also provides closure. See the References & Resources section for more detailed sources on evaluating training evaluations

Matrix of Common Evaluation Tools

TOOL	PURPOSE	REQUIREMENTS
Questionnaires and Surveys	To collect standardized data from a large number of participants	• Construction of survey • Explicit verbal and/or written instructions • If not proctored, follow-up contact to increase return rate
Knowledge Assessments	To assess participants' knowledge acquired through training or in the work environment	• Construction of assessment test • Assessment must have content validity and reliability • Must use exact test or an equivalent test for pre- and postassessment
Performance Assessments	To assess participants' application of skills acquired through training or in the work environment	• Construction of assessment (checklist, rating form) • Tasks or skills to be performed must be identified • Criteria or standards of performance must be specified and realistic • Assessment must have content validity and reliability

ADVANTAGES	DISADVANTAGES
• Paper, scannable forms, CBT embedded surveys, e-mail, intranet, or Internet can be used	• If not proctored, participants cannot ask for clarification or instructions
• Variety of response alternatives can be used (Likert-type scales, multiple choice, open-ended)	• Participants may choose more than one response or give invalid responses
• Questions can be direct or indirect, general or specific	• Open-ended responses may be grammatically incorrect or ambiguous
• Easy and efficient to administer	• Participants may skip items
	• Response rate may be low, if not proctored
• Paper, scannable forms, CBT embedded tests, e-mail, intranet, or Internet can be used	• If a pretest is used, participants may score higher on the posttest due to familiarity
• Easy to administer pre-and postassessments	• Some participants may experience test anxiety and may not perform optimally
• Paper, scannable forms, and interactive multimedia embedded tests can be used	• Potential rater bias
• Performance can be rated by instructor, participant, peer, team, or supervisors	• Equipment and tools may not be available in the classroom
• Provides direct evidence or application of learning	• If obtrusive, the observation and rating may affect performance due to nervousness or anxiety
• Can be obtrusive or unobtrusive	• May not have time to measure all critical skills
	• Pretest may not be practical given time constraints

Matrix of Common Evaluation Tools, continued

TOOL	PURPOSE	REQUIREMENTS
Structured Observations	To watch an activity and record what is seen or, to examine a product (for example, a work sample)	• Construction of checklist or rating form • Explicit directions for the observer • Observer must be objective • Observer should not give directions, answers, or nonverbal cues when observing performance • Consistent use of the checklist • Percentage agreement between observers should be calculated
Focus Groups	To explore a topic in-depth with a small number of participants	• Development of session questions • Trained moderator • Limited number of participants (6-12) • Different sessions for different groups of participants
Telephone Interviews	To collect standardized reporting data over the telephone	• Creation of interview transcript and recording form • Trained interviewers • Multiple contact attempts

ADVANTAGES	DISADVANTAGES
• Objective of interest (for example, learner, designer, instructor, work sample) can be observed by a senior trainer, subject matter expert, designer/developer, evaluation specialist, supervisor, or manager • Observation of performance can be obtrusive or unobtrusive (if unobtrusive, observation can be naturalistic)	• Potential observer bias • If obtrusive, observation of behavior may affect performance due to nervousness or anxiety
• Depth of inquiry possible • Opportunity for clarification • Synergistic and snowball effects	• Potential group bias • Potential moderator bias • A few participants may dominate • Results are not representative given the limited number of participants
• Probing of incomplete answers is possible • Clarification of misunderstandings is possible • Interviewer has greater control over data collection	• Potential interview bias • Participants may give socially desirable answers • Questions and response alternatives must be simple because participants are unable to see the questionnaire • Participants may be difficult to contact

Glossary of Evaluation Terms

Closed-ended—a type of response alternative that is limited to those alternatives that are listed (e.g., yes or no; true or false).

Coding—the translation of information into numerical values for tabulation and statistical analysis.

Critical incident log—a form that is used to document a common process (e.g., the delivery of training) or a procedure.

Demographic items—questions that pertain to personal characteristics, work history, and training experience (e.g., professional position, prior training experience).

Evaluation design—a plan specifying the groups involved in the evaluation and the timing of data collection activities.

Front-end analysis—the first stage of the instructional systems development process; it involves needs assessment, task analysis, and performance analysis.

Functional dimension—a particular area within the training context that is the focus of an evaluation (e.g., instructional design, learner motivation).

Instructional delivery—the presentation of course content and material, and the facilitation of structured learning activities.

Items—the questions or statements to be answered on questionnaires and assessments and in interviews.

Likert-type scale—a popular response alternative developed by Rensis Likert that includes a range of possible closed-ended responses. (See sidebar on page 5.)

Open-ended—a type of response alternative that allows the respondent to generate the answer on his or her own; often lines and space follow the item, which allows respondents to write in their answer.

Pilot—a trial run that provides information to improve or revise a product (e.g., data collection tool) or process.

Practice effort—the fact that taking a test with the same items will result in improvement in performance even if no training has occurred between the two assessments.

Probe—a statement used by an interviewer to clarify a response.

Proctored—administered and collected on-site by a designated individual.

Response alternatives—the options for answering a question.

Sampling strategy—a method that is used to decide the characteristics and size of the group(s) of individuals who will participate in an evaluation.

Stakeholder—anyone interested in, or affected by training, including: technical trainers, training participants, designers/developers, senior managers, executives, supervisors, and customers.

Targeted evaluation questions—specific questions identified by stakeholders that have been revised for evaluation purposes.

References & Resources

Articles

Alliger, G.M., and E.A. Janak. "Kirkpatrick's Levels of Training Criteria: Thirty Years Later." *Personnel Psychology,* 42, 1989, pp. 331-340.

Basarab, D.J., Sr. "Assessing the Quality of Training Evaluation Studies." *Performance & Instruction,* March 1994, pp.19-22.

Berardinelli, P., et al. "Management Training: An Impact Theory." *Human Resource Development Quarterly,* 1995, 6 (1), pp. 79-90.

Bernthal, P.R. "Evaluation that Goes the Distance." *Training & Development,* September 1995, pp. 41-37.

Bushnell, D.S. "Input, Process, Output: A Model for Evaluating Training." *Training & Development Journal,* March 1990, pp. 41-43.

Dick, W., and D. King. "Formative Evaluation in the Performance Context." *Performance and Instruction,* October 1994, pp. 3-7.

Dionne, P. "The Evaluation of Training Activities: A Complex Issue Involving Different Stakes." *Human Resource Development Quarterly,* 7 (3), 1996, pp. 279-286.

Garavaglia, P.L. "How To Ensure the Transfer of Training." *Training & Development,* October 1993, pp. 63-68.

Holton, E.F., III. "The Flawed Four-Level Evaluation Model." *Human Resource Development Quarterly,* 7 (1), 1996, pp. 5-29.

Jedrziewski, D. "Putting Methods to the Madness of Evaluating Training Effectiveness." *Performance and Instruction,* January 1995, pp. 23-31.

Kaufman, R., and J.M. Keller. "Levels of Evaluation: Beyond Kirkpatrick." *Human Resource Development Quarterly,* 5 (4), 1994, pp. 371-380.

Marshall, V. "Using Evaluation to Improve Performance." *Technical & Skills Training,* January 1994, pp. 6-9.

Martelli, J.T. "Using Statistics in HRD." *Training and Development,* February, 1997, pp. 62-63.

Mavis, M. "Painless Performance Evaluations." *Training & Development,* October 1994, pp. 40-44.

Mitchell, D.B. "Performance Testing for Maintenance Technicians." *Technical & Skills Training,* November/December 1995, pp. 14-17.

O'Donnell, J.M. "Focus Groups: A Habit-forming Evaluation Technique." *Training & Development Journal,* July 1988.

Reynolds, A. "The Basics: Formative Evaluation." *Technical & Skills Training,* November/December 1995, pp. 8-9.

Sullivan, R.L., and M.J. Elenburg. "Writing Knowledge-Based Tests." *Technical & Skills Training,* April 1991. pp. 25-30.

Willyerd, K.A. "Balancing Your Evaluation Act." *Training,* March, 1997, pp. 53-58.

Zemke, R., and J. Armstrong. "Evaluating Multimedia." *Training,* August 1996, pp. 48-52.

Books

Alkin, M.C. *Debates on Evaluation.* Newbury Park, California: Sage Publications, 1990.

Basarab, D.J. and D.K. Root. *The Training Evaluation Process.* Boston, Massachusetts: Kluwer Academic Publishers, 1992.

Brinkerhoff, R.O. *Achieving Results from Training.* San Francisco: Jossey-Bass Publishers, 1987.

Broad, M.L. and J.W. Newstrom. *Transfer of Training.* Reading Massachusetts: Addison-Wesley Publishing, 1992.

Campbell, D.T. and J.C. Stanley. *Experimental and Quasi-Experimental Designs for Research.* Dallas, Texas: Houghton Mifflin Company, 1963.

Chelimsky, E. and W.R. Shadish. *Evaluation for the 21st Century.* Newbury Park, California: Sage Publications, 1997.

Fink, A. *How to Analyze Survey Data: The Survey Kit.* Vol. 8. Newbury Park, California: Sage Publications, 1995.

——. *How to Design Surveys: The Survey Kit.* Vol. 5. Newbury Park, California: Sage Publications, 1995.

Fitz-Gibbon, C.T. and L.L. Morris. *How to Design a Program Evaluation.* Newbury Park, California: Sage Publications, 1987.

Fowler, F.J. *Survey Research Methods.* 2nd ed. Newbury Park, California: Sage Publications, 1993.

References & Resources

Fowler, F.J., and T.W. Mangione *Standardized Survey Interviewing: Minimizing Interviewer-related Error.* Thousand Oaks, California: Sage Publications, 1990.

Herman, J.L. et al. *Evaluator's Handbook.* Newbury Park, California: Sage Publications, 1987.

Holloway, J. et al. (eds.). *Performance Measurement and Evaluation.* Thousand Oaks, California: Sage Publications, 1995.

Joint Committee on Standards. *Program Evaluation Standards.* 2nd ed. Newbury Park, California: Sage Publications, 1994.

Kanji, G. *100 Statistical Tests.* Newbury Park, California: Sage Publications, 1993.

Kelly, L. *The ASTD Technical and Skills Training Handbook.* New York: McGraw-Hill, 1995.

Kirkpatrick, D.L. *Evaluating Training Programs: The Four Levels.* San Francisco: Berrett-Koehler, 1994.

Love, A.J. *Internal Evaluation: Building Organizations From Within.* Newbury Park, California: Sage Publications, 1991.

Mager, R.F. *Preparing Instructional Objectives.* 2nd ed. Belmont, California: Fearon Publishers, 1975.

Morris, L., et al. *How to Measure Performance and Use Tests.* Newbury Park, California: Sage Publications, 1987.

Newman, D.L., and R.D. Brown. *Applied Ethics for Program Evaluation.* Thousand Oaks, California: Sage Publications, 1996.

Nowakowski, J., et al. *A Handbook of Educational Variables.* Boston, Massachusetts: Kluwer Academic Publishers, 1985.

Phillips, J.J. *Handbook of Training Evaluation and Measurement Methods.* Houston, Texas: Gulf Publishing Company, 1991.

Phillips, J.J. (ed.). *Measuring Return on Investment: Eighteen Case Studies from the Real World of Training.* Alexandria, Virginia: American Society for Training & Development, 1994.

Rosenfeld, P., et al. (eds.). *Improving Organizational Surveys: New Directions, Methods, and Applications.* Newbury Park, California: Sage Publications, 1993.

Rossi, P.H., and H.E. Freeman. *Evaluation: A Systematic Approach.* Newbury Park, California: Sage Publications, 1993.

Rothwell, W.J., and H.J. Sredl. *The ASTD Reference Guide to Professional Human Resource Development Roles and Competencies.* 2nd ed. Amherst, Massachusetts: HRD Press, 1992.

Schmitt, N., and R. Klimoski. *Research Methods in Human Resources Management.* Cincinnati, Ohio: South-Western Publishing Co., 1991.

Schouborg, G. *FLEX: A Flexible Tool for Continuously Improving Your Evaluation of Training Effectiveness.* Amherst, Massachusetts: Human Resource Development Press, 1993.

Scriven, M. *Evaluation Thesaurus.* 4th ed. Newbury Park, California: Sage Publications, 1991.

Shrock, S.A., and W.C. Coscarelli. *Criterion-Referenced Test Development: Technical and Legal Guidelines for Corporate Training.* Reading, Massachusetts: Addison-Wesley Publishing Company, 1989.

Stecher, B., and W. Davis. *How to Focus an Evaluation.* Newbury Park, California: Sage Publications, 1987.

Stewart, D.W., and P.N. Shamdasani. *Focus Groups: Theory and Practice.* Newbury Park, California: Sage Publications, 1990.

Torres, R.T., et al. *Evaluation Strategies for Communicating and Reporting: Enhancing Learning in Organizations.* Newbury Park, California: Sage Publications, 1996.

Vella, J., et al. *How Do They Know? Evaluating Adult Learning.* San Francisco: Jossey-Bass Publishers, 1997.

Wallgren, A., et al. *Graphing Statistics and Data: Creating Better Charts.* Newbury Park, California: Sage Publications, 1996.

Wholey, J.S., et al. (eds.). *Handbook of Practical Program Evaluation.* San Francisco: Jossey-Bass Publishers, 1994.

Witkin, B.R., and J.W. Altschuld. *Planning and Conducting Needs Assessments: A Practical Guide.* Newbury Park, California: Sage Publications, 1995.

References & Resources

Info-lines

Darraugh, Barbara (ed). "How to Facilitate." No. 9406 (revised 1999).

———. "Legal Liability & HRD: Implications for Trainers." No. 9309.

Garavaglia, P. "Transfer of Training: Making Training Stick." No. 9512.

Gill, S. J. "Linking Training to Performance Goals." No. 9606 (revised 1998).

Hodell, Chuck. "Basics of Instructional Systems Development." No. 9706.

Long, Lori. "Surveys from Start to Finish." No. 8612 (revised 1998).

O'Neill, M. "How to Focus a Training Evaluation." No. 9604.

Sharpe, Cat (ed.). "More Productive Meetings." No. 8710 (revised 1997).

Waagen, Alice. "Essentials of Evaluation." No. 9705.

Internet Sites

American Society for Training & Development (ASTD)
http://www.astd.org/

American Educational Research Association (AERA)
http://aera.net/

American Evaluation Association (AEA)
http://www.eval.org/

ERIC Clearinghouse on Assessment and Evaluation (ERIC/AE)
http://ericae2.educ.cua.edu/

Job Aid

Planning a Functional Training Evaluation

I. Training To Be Evaluated:

_____

II. Targeted Evaluation Questions:

A. _____

B. _____

C. _____

D. _____

E. _____

III. Functional Dimension(s) of Interest:

A. _____

B. _____

C. _____

D. _____

IV. Intended Use for Each Functional Dimension:

A. _____

B. _____

C. _____

D. _____

V. Have the information needs of the stakeholders been identified?

☐ Yes ☐ No

VI. Evaluation Tools (check all that apply):

☐ Questionnaire/Survey

☐ Knowledge Assessment

☐ Performance Assessment

☐ Structured Observation

☐ Focus Group

☐ Telephone Interview

☐ Other: _____

VII. Evaluation Design (check all that apply):

☐ One-Group Post Only

☐ One-Group Pre- and Postdesign

☐ Pre- and Postcomparison Group

☐ Time Series (Time interval: _____)

☐ Pre- and Postcontrol Group

☐ Other: _____

VIII. Will a sampling strategy be employed?

☐ Yes ☐ No

IX. Is there a plan for data communication and reporting?

☐ Yes ☐ No

X. Data Collection (check all that apply):

☐ Paper

☐ Scannable Technology

☐ CBT Diskette

☐ Intranet/Internet

☐ E-mail

☐ Interactive Multimedia

XI. Data Analysis (check all that apply):

☐ Computerized Spreadsheet

☐ Scannable Technology with Scoring Software

☐ Statistical Software

☐ Relational Database

☐ Statistician

☐ Other: _____

The material appearing on this page is not covered by copyright and may be reproduced at will.

How to Collect Data

How to Collect Data

**R E V I S I O N
C O N S U L T A N T :**

Malcolm J. Conway
IBM Education & Training
Hamilton Square, New Jersey
  08690-2812
Tel: 609.890.7772
Fax: 609.890.7762
e-mail: mconway44@aol.com

Editorial Staff for 9008

Author
Jerry W. Gilley, Ph.D.

Editor
Barbara Darraugh

Revised 1998

Editor
Cat Sharpe

Contributing Editor
Ann Bruen

Internal ASTD Consultant
Scott Cheney

Why Collect Data?

The need for accurate information is critical in the human resource and performance training areas to accomplish the following things:

1. Determine the current local level of training in particular skills.

2. Identify optimal performance levels and gaps compared with current levels.

3. Conduct needs and training requirements analyses.

4. Determine whether courses provide the required learning.

Human resource and development (HRD) personnel have research requirements in other areas: statistics to comply with federal and state employment regulations, salary surveys, levels of employee benefits, and statistics on labor availability and unemployment rates. Much of this information must be researched.

Before collecting data within his or her organization, the human resource, training, or performance specialist needs to determine whether any external definitions and standards exist for a particular question. For example, local unemployment figures may list clerical help as "typists," "stenographers," and "secretaries," while the HRD specialist's organization uses titles like "word processor," "secretary," and "administrative assistant." Is there a difference in definition that can skew the analysis of the data collected?

Where does a performance, training, or human resource specialist go to find this information and to generate company-specific data? How can these professionals ensure that the information they receive is both what they want and valid to the research they are conducting? This *Info-line* provides instructions on the development of various data collection methodologies and outlines numerous sources of national and local information. For purposes of this *Info-line* the term *researcher* is being applied to anyone who needs to compile data for an organization.

A Model for Data Collection

Models are useful in guiding practice. They help provide a focus for tasks—bounding the tasks to be performed and integrating work effort. A practical research model developed by Greg Kearsley of The George Washington University comprises five steps (see "Steps in Data Collection"). The "most important thing about research," Kearsley asserts, is that "it is a repeating cycle rather than a one-shot effort." To develop a comprehensive solution or report, the researcher "will need to go back for additional data a number of times, possibly using different data collection methods and tools." Here are the steps that make up Kearsley's model:

Step 1: Identify Data Needs

The initial step in any applied (versus theoretical) research project is to identify the data that need to be collected. This can be a policy statement to be examined or a hypothesis to be tested. When listing the data requirements, the researcher also should note the unit definitions to be examined and possible sources of information.

Step 2: Identify Data Collection Methods

Training, performance, and HRD professionals commonly use the following methods of data collection:

Analyses of written sources of information provide quick, reliable information. Sources outside the organization include government publications, books, periodicals, newspaper articles, and so forth. In-house sources include financial, marketing, production, or personnel records.

Questionnaires are a very common way of collecting data because they are often the least expensive. The development of effective questionnaires will be addressed below.

Interviews are used when the data are considered sensitive, when the data need to be acquired quickly, or the purpose is to *prove* opinions or attitudes as opposed to quantifying opinions. Interviews are also used when little or nothing is known about the topic of interest. Usually, interviews are conducted face-to-face (or one-on-one), by telephone, or in focus groups. Interviewing costs more

Steps in Data Collection

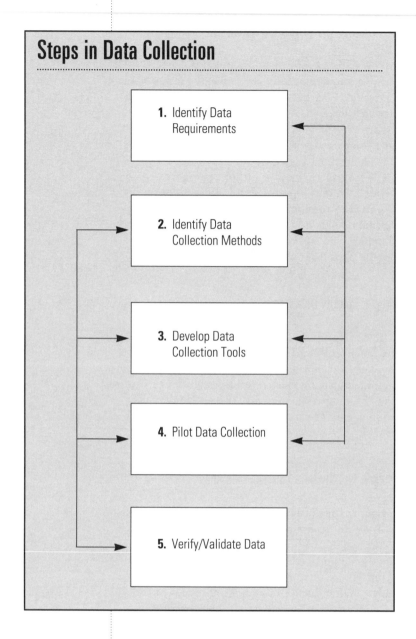

1. Identify Data Requirements

2. Identify Data Collection Methods

3. Develop Data Collection Tools

4. Pilot Data Collection

5. Verify/Validate Data

training or in making a comparison between one training program and another.

Step 3: Design Data Collection Instruments

One of the outcomes of the first two steps is the determination of the appropriate instruments to collect the data. This issue of *Info-line* will briefly discuss different techniques.

Step 4: Collect Preliminary Data

When the instruments are designed, a test run should be scheduled to ensure that the design collects the information desired. There are three possible outcomes of this pilot:

1. The data collected are exactly correct. This outcome is unlikely.

or,

2. The information collected does not support the hypothesis or policy. This outcome is also unlikely.

or,

3. The data desired are not quite what was expected or are more difficult to collect than anticipated.

In any of the above cases, the researcher would refine the data collection requirements, methods, or tools.

Step 5: Validate the Data

"Scientific" research requires corroboration. The researcher needs to find two or more independent sources for each data item collected. To determine the average length of a training session, for example, the researcher may interview several practitioners and observe some actual training sessions.

The focus of this *Info-line* will be on Step 2, identifying data collection methods, as well as on ways to develop the various instruments available to the researcher.

than questionnaires, but may be more reliable. For more information on interviewing skills, see *Info-line* No. 8612, "Surveys from Start to Finish."

Observation of trainees or jobholders is especially useful to determine skill deficiencies or to set performance standards. On the training side, observation may provide valuable data on average course completion time or the average utilization of training equipment.

Experiments may be hard to adapt to a training or personnel setting, but the experimental approach can be helpful in determining the effectiveness of

Types and Sources of Research

Before collecting data, it is important to first understand the type of research the data supports. We are all too busy to be collecting information only to discover that the data are incompatible for the purpose at hand. For example, if you design an experimental study, gathering data through a survey would not be an appropriate method of collecting the necessary information. Instead, you would want to directly observe the participants or conditions in question, and record scientifically reliable data. On the other hand, survey research could be very appropriate for conducting either "after the fact" or "descriptive research." The table on the following pages summarizes some common types of research and their purpose, adding examples, strengths, and weaknesses for each.

Research conducted by training, performance, and HRD professionals can be divided into two categories: **primary,** or internal, and **secondary,** or external. Internal research is conducted within an organization, while external research often tries to quantify the environment in which an organization operates.

Company documents are the primary source for internal data collection. They contain useful historical information: personnel, productivity, and financial records; planning, audit, budget, and program reports; program evaluations; quality control documents; career development materials; and exit interviews.

Employees are one of the best sources of internal data. There are several ways to gather information from them: questionnaires, inventories or checklists, observation, and interviews. In addition, critical incident reports, records of questions asked during training, and user comments about training courses are useful sources of data. Secondary data usually is gleaned from public sources such as libraries and, more recently, the Internet.

Questionnaires

A questionnaire is an internal research tool and is one means of eliciting the thoughts, feelings, beliefs, experiences, and attitudes of a sample group of individuals. It is a concise, preplanned set of questions designed to yield specific information about a particular topic from one or more groups of people.

Questionnaires should be used only after all other sources of information on the topic have been thoroughly researched, and the researcher has specific areas to explore. Questionnaires succeed or fail based on the questions they ask: the more specific the questions, the more valuable the answer. Prior to developing a questionnaire, the researcher should consider using an interview to understand the topic of interest and the range of opinions if little or nothing is known about it. For specific formats to use, see the box "Structuring Questionnaires" that follows.

Characteristics of a Good Questionnaire

Effective questionnaires have many common features. A good questionnaire:

- Deals with a significant topic—a topic that individuals in the sample recognize as important enough to warrant the time required for completing the questionnaire. The significance should be clearly stated on the questionnaire or in an accompanying cover letter.

- Seeks only that information that cannot be obtained from other sources.

- Should be as short as possible.

- Should be attractive in appearance, neatly and logically arranged, clearly printed, and easy to answer.

- Contains clear and complete directions and definitions of necessary terms; is concise.

- Is objective with no leading questions, that is, questions that signal the response desired.

- Is logical and proceeds from general to specific responses.

- Is easy to tabulate and interpret. Tabulation sheets should be preconstructed, showing how the data will be handled *before* the final form of the questionnaire is determined.

Types of Research

Type	Purpose	Example
EXPERIMENTAL	To investigate possible cause-and-effect relationships by exposing experimental group(s) to treatment condition(s) and comparing the results to control group(s) not receiving the treatment. All variables of concern are held constant except the single treatment variable, which is deliberately varied.	Test the effectiveness of a new computer software program to teach budgeting to managers under controlled conditions using random assignments to groups and pre- and posttesting.
QUASI-EXPERIMENTAL	To approximate the condition of the true experiment in a real or natural setting that does not allow for the control or manipulation of *all* relevant variables.	Investigate the effectiveness of three different techniques for teaching performance appraisal to managers where control or manipulation is not feasible.
AFTER THE FACT	To investigate possible relationships and interactions, in a real or natural setting, by observing existing dependent variables and searching back through data for plausible independent factors that are related to or have effects on the dependent variables.	Investigate factors related to turnover in a specific job classification over a specific period of time.
DESCRIPTIVE	To systematically describe the characteristics, background, current status, and environmental interactions of an identified social unit, group, institution, organization, or community.	Study the characteristics, roles, and responsibilities of corporate HRD managers of the *Fortune* 500.
THEORETICAL MODEL BUILDING	To develop a conceptual theoretical framework that postulates the relationships of concepts.	Develop a theoretical model of organizational structures that predicts which factors affect worker morale, productivity, and profits.

Strengths	Weaknesses
• Clearly defined hypotheses. • Can answer how strong a relationship is. • Uses control group as baseline for comparisons. • Controls all relevant variables. • Controls extraneous variables. • Uses pretest or posttest comparisons. • Random selection of subjects to groups. • Good for testing alternative procedures.	• Artificial setting—not real world. • Hard to generalize beyond the single experiment. • Cannot always control all variables. • Cannot always have completely random assignment.
• Real setting. • Can control some, but not all, relevant variables. • Can study complex social influences, processes, and changes in real settings. • Can test broad hypotheses.	• Cannot control all relevant variables. • Cannot manipulate all independent variables. • Practicality of setting. • Cannot randomly assign to groups. • Lack of precision—systematic and random "noise." • Extraneous variables abound.
• Realistic. • Data is collected after events of interest have taken place. • Looks back for relations, causes, and meanings. • Socially significant. • Many relations and interesting hypotheses emerge as the data is examined.	• Great deal of "noise." • Cannot always have random samples. • Cannot manipulate independent variables. • Cause-and-effect determination often difficult to assess. • Risk of improper interpretation. • Precision of measurement lacking.
• Describes existing situations and phenomena. • Examines totality or selected factors of the unit. • Identifies problems for further study. • Identifies key variables, processes, and interactions for planning purposes. • Answers questions about the unit or group.	• Difficult to test hypotheses. • Difficult to make predictions. • Often narrow focus. • Sampling is often not random.
• Serves as practical guide for action. • Serves as foundation for testing and evaluating new procedures and actions. • Helps to explain concepts and make them easier to understand.	• Often too abstract. • Often ignores important information for the sake of the model. • Often goes untested and can provide an erroneous view of a set of relationships.

Structuring Questionnaires

Questionnaires can use one or more of the following formats:

■ *Multiple-Choice*

Multiple-choice questions contain two or more mutually exclusive answers. The respondent is asked to pick one of them. Multiple-choice questions are used when all the responses to a question can be included, when exclusivity can be constructed, and when bias resulting from the forced selection is insignificant. Advantages of multiple-choice questions include easy tabulation and interpretation, and little time is required for completion.

Example: What is your income?

☐ $19,999 or less   ☐ $20,000–$49,999
☐ $50,000–$69,999   ☐ More than $70,000

■ *Multiple-Answer*

The multiple-answer format is similar to the multiple-choice format, except that the respondent is allowed to choose more than one statement. Unlike multiple-choice, multiple-answer responses are not exclusive. Multiple-answer questions are used to help respondents remember and to ensure that they consider all viable options. Researchers may list only those answers of special interest and provide a space for respondents to write in other answers.

Example: Which television news programs do you watch each week?

☐ *Nightline*   ☐ *48 Hours*
☐ *60 Minutes*   ☐ *Other (specify)* _____

■ *Ranking Questions*

Ranking questions ask respondents to indicate, in order, their personal preferences and reveal the relative importance of the answers. The respondents may be asked to mark their first choice or rank some or all of the responses.

Example: Which of the following news programs do you like best? (Place the number 1 in the space provided to indicate your first choice, the number 2 for your second choice, and so forth. Be sure to rank all four items)

_____ *Nightline*   _____ *48 Hours*
_____ *60 Minutes*   _____ *Date Line*

■ *Open Ended*

Open-ended questions allow respondents to answer without prompting in their own words as compared with closed questions, such as multiple-choice questions, which ask the respondent to select an answer from among the options given. Open-ended questions usually begin with who, what, when, where, why, or how. Open-ended questions are used when the individual response is important, when the range of responses cannot be predicted, or when free expression is needed to clarify a multiple-choice answer.

Example: What suggestions do you have for improving this training program? _____

_____
_____
_____
_____
_____

or,

Example: Do you have any suggestions for improving this training program?
☐ Yes   ☐ No
(If yes, please write your suggestions in the space below.)

_____
_____
_____
_____
_____
_____

■ Scaled Questions

Scaled questions are used to determine opinions or attitudes. A scaled question measures direction (negative to positive) and intensity (strongly negative to strongly positive). There are three commonly used types of scales:

Semantic-differential scales allow respondents to indicate how they feel about a specific item by selecting a position on a bipolar (agree/disagree, good/bad) scale.

Example: Place a check [✔] at the appropriate point on the scale below to indicate how you feel about the length of this training session.

Too Long ____ ____ ____ ___ ____ Too Short

Diagrammatic or graphic scales are grids or diagrams on which respondents indicate their position with respect to a statement. Words or numbers usually are not included on the grid, with the scale expressed by a diagram or graphic.

Likert or agreement scales provide a standard set of words and ask respondents to indicate agreement or disagreement with a particular statement. Possible answers are assigned weights that are used to compute individual and group ratings.

Example: Women should be paid at the same rate as men for work of comparable value.

- ☐ Strongly disagree
- ☐ Disagree
- ☐ Neutral
- ☐ Agree
- ☐ Strongly agree

Construction Tips for Questionnaires

Wording in a questionnaire is extremely important, since the success of a questionnaire depends on words alone. Questions that are "open for interpretation" may invalidate months of hard work. Following is a list of rules for constructing a questionnaire properly:

1. Define or qualify terms that could be easily misunderstood or misinterpreted. Questions about monthly salaries, for example, may be hard to determine for those who are earning wages on a no-work, no-pay basis.

2. Be careful of descriptive adjectives and adverbs that have no agreed-upon meaning, such as "frequently," "occasionally," and "rarely." Different respondents will define these relative terms differently.

3. Beware of double negatives. A respondent must study these carefully to answer properly. (Example: "Are you opposed to not requiring students to take showers after gym classes?")

4. Provide adequate alternatives. "Yes" or "No" responses to the question "Are you married?" do not allow for possibilities such as "widowed," "divorced," or "separated."

5. Use gender-neutral wording, for example, "he or she." Also avoid stereotypical terms like "housewife."

6. Define all acronyms, for example, "IRA." This may mean Individual Retirement Account, Irish Republican Army, or the International Reading Association.

7. For questions with scales, such as agreement questions, place the scale points in negative-to-positive order, for example, "Strongly Disagree," through "Strongly Agree." This will overcome the "positive response bias," that is, respondents' tendency to be more lenient in rating than their true opinion.

8. Avoid double-barreled questions, such as "Should trainees be placed in separate groups for instructional purposes and assigned to different classrooms?" These questions actually ask for two pieces of information, and the respondent may be in favor of one part and opposed to the other.

9. <u>Underline</u> or *italicize* or **bold** a word if you want to emphasize it.

10. Give a point of reference when asking for a rating.

11. Avoid questions that assume knowledge or experience that the respondent may not have.

12. Phrase questions so that they are appropriate for all respondents.

13. Design questions that give complete possibilities for comprehensive responses, for example, start an age question from 0.

14. Write questions with non-overlapping response scales, for example, "Which of the following categories indicates your age: 0-9, 10-19, 20-29, 30-39, 40 and above?" and not "0-10, 10-20, 20-30, …"

15. Avoid jargon. Define any technical terms even if your questionnaire is going to a very focused audience. Someone new to the audience may not be familiar with the term.

16. Include between 5 and 9 response scale categories. Beyond 9, the respondent cannot meaningful remember and compare all the items.

17. Avoid leading questions, that is, questions that suggest that certain negative conditions existed before an event and may continue to exist and, therefore, lead the respondent.

18. Present questions in good psychological order, putting questions that are easy or that create "warm fuzzies" before proceeding to questions that may be sensitive. Avoid annoying or embarrassing questions.

19. Group similar types of questions together.

Choose the sample carefully. Send questionnaires only to those who have the desired information and who are likely to be sufficiently interested to respond conscientiously and objectively. Consider anonymous responses if the requested information is sensitive. If the respondent's identity is needed for classification purposes, ensure confidentiality. Get a sponsor, if possible; recipients are more likely to answer a questionnaire if a prestigious person, organization, or institution endorses the project.

Points to Remember

To make the process simple and easy to carry out, every questionnaire should provide complete directions. These should always be located at the beginning of the questionnaire. You should also include a cover letter that provides answer to the following questions:

- Who is sponsoring the questionnaire?

- How was the respondent chosen?

- Is there any incentive for completing the survey?

- Whom should the respondent contact if he or she has questions while completing the questionnaire?

- How will the data be used?

- Are the responses confidential, or is the survey anonymous, that is, no name is needed?

- What is the approximate time needed to complete the survey? (This information is gleaned from the pilot test, described below.)

- How can the respondent get a summary of the results? (Offering this can motivate some respondents to complete the questionnaire.)

Pilot-Testing Questionnaires

Just as software developers and manufacturers never produce software or a manufactured product without first extensively testing it to get the bugs out, so, too, the researcher should pilot-test a draft questionnaire before mailing it. Prominent survey experts and authors Seymour Sudman and Norman Bradburn caution not to send the survey out unless it is tested.

Follow these guidelines when you are pilot-testing questionnaires:

- Have people familiar with the topic—subject matter experts (SMEs)—review the content of the draft questionnaire and provide feedback to improve it.

- Use a 6- to 12-person focus group as the target audience. Ask the group to indicate start and finish times so you can estimate the time required to complete the survey.

- As participants complete the questionnaire, request that they circle or mark any unclear directions, confusing wording, unclear scales, and other problems. Then lead a discussion with the participants incorporating their comments.

- Have other people review the questionnaire as appropriate. These include an editor to pick up spelling errors, a graphic artist for formatting, a diversity management specialist to screen for unintentional bias (for example, stereotypic wording), or a data analyst or person with statistical training to give input on how best to format questions to facilitate statistical analysis.

Electronic Questionnaires

With the advent of e-mail, the Internet, and company Web sites on the Internet, the possibilities of designing and administering questionnaires and interviews using these technologies has opened up exciting new possibilities for data collection. Surveys conducted via the Internet, the worldwide system of **inter**connected computer **net**works, for example, promise speed and efficiency. Questionnaires can be created and distributed quickly, and the data returned, analyzed, and reported quickly,

too. This technology eliminates the printing and mailing of written questionnaires and telephone or in-person interviews.

As with any new technology, however, there are some drawbacks. For example, Internet and other forms of electronic surveys work well for questionnaires sent within a company or business where employees have and use e-mail, and access the Internet regularly (there are estimates that 80 to 90 percent of U.S. business people have Internet access). Such questionnaires have been shown to be able to produce response rates comparable to and even higher than traditional written questionnaires. For the general population, they are not a good fit, though, since a small number of U.S. households regularly use Internet services. Coupled with this is the reluctance to use computers and fear of the Internet among some segments of the population.

It should also be noted that while e-mail questionnaires are declining in popularity due to being limited to plain text, the inability to check the data until after the questionnaire is returned, and so forth, Web-based questionnaires are growing dramatically in popularity. Multimedia—graphics, video, audio—are possible, attractive formatting is possible, checks for validity can be done, and respondents can be prompted to correct their responses because these forms are interactive. See the box on the next page for guidelines to follow when using electronic questionnaires.

Observation

Researchers and practitioners who collect data by watching one or more persons performing a series of skills are using *observation* as their research method—another source of primary, or internal, information. Use this data collection method when detailed information is required or when acquired skills need to be measured in terms of accuracy and effectiveness. Observation is perhaps most useful in determining or setting standards for job tasks, but it also can measure personal traits, such as self-control, cooperativeness, truthfulness, and honesty. Observation is appropriate only when job activities are observable, detailed information is required, and the employee cannot supply the information.

There are two types of observations:

Structured—those in which the observed performance has been predetermined. Usually, researchers in structured observations use checklists to determine that the activity has been completed correctly. The checklist notes each task in the order in which it is performed to complete the activity. The results are used to show which tasks are performed correctly and which involve errors.

Unstructured—those that do not involve predetermined activities and result in descriptions of tasks performed. The descriptions can include opinions and general information about the performance and the performer. Most of the "evidence" is anecdotal.

If researchers or practitioners choose observation as their research method, they need to do the following things:

- identify the persons to be observed
- select the best time for observation
- prepare the checklist, if one is used
- compare performance with existing standards

The researcher or practitioner and the person under observation usually should not interact during the exercise. The researcher needs to be familiar enough with the task to recognize if the performance meets existing standards. If possible, the observer should be impartial. Sources of observers include course developers, instructors, SMEs, immediate supervisors, end-user personnel, or internal or external consultants.

For specific steps to follow in observation, see the box "Observation System" opposite.

When making observations, the researcher must do the following things:

1. Identify the person being watched and what his or her job function is.

2. Describe the procedures being studied in sufficient detail to allow persons with no knowledge of the activity to follow the resulting instruction.

3. Outline the order in which the task is completed.

4. List any forms or other job aids used in accomplishing the task.

5. Identify decision points and develop a decision tree showing any alternatives resulting from those decisions.

6. Pinpoint the circumstances under which the task takes place.

Using Electronic Surveys

When collecting data by means of electronic questionnaires, there are a number of suggestions you should follow:

- Make sure that your audience has access to, or actually uses, e-mail, the Internet, or intranet before you consider using an electronic questionnaire.

- Check that the required skills and expertise, in addition to questionnaire construction, are available. Required skills include **programming,** using HTML, JavaScript, Visual Basic, or similar languages, or Web survey systems or construction languages; **human factors** or user interface skills to design the computer screens so they are easy to fill out and navigate between; and **computer networking** or information technology (IT) skills to manage the survey administration over the network used.

- Generally, electronic-based questionnaires should use fewer words and simpler directions because of the limitations of the technology. For example, there is a limit to the number of words that can fit on a computer screen and be easily read and understood. It is also very tiresome to scroll through screen after screen of directions before starting to answer the questions.

- In administering electronic questionnaires, you need to check the reliability of the hardware (PC or workstation), the software, telecommunications, and the computer networks over which the questionnaire is administered.

Observation Guidelines

When conducting observations, it is important to follow these rules:

- Use a checklist or rating scale, log, or diary. Such structure can improve the reliability or consistency of observation.

- Make sure the person(s) being observed know that the observation is being done. This is an ethical as well as a practical suggestion.

- Use multiple observers. Because even trained observers tend to "drift" in their observations, using multiple observers improves the chances of consistent, accurate observation.

- Conduct multiple observations. Such "moving pictures" of behavior are preferable to just doing a single "slice" or observation.

- Validate observation data with data from other collection methods. For example, in addition to asking people on a written questionnaire to rate how skillful they are on a particular task, observe them actually doing the task on the job and determine if their self-assessment and the observation data agree.

Other Internal Data Collection Methods

Listed below are other research methods that may be used by training, performance, and HRD specialists for specific needs.

■ Critical or Significant Incidents

A critical or significant incident report records an example of extreme behavior or performance and the responses of individuals who observed or were otherwise involved in the event. This method is used to identify problems, to evaluate field trials, and as a prerequisite to remedial action. To qualify as significant incident, the event must:

- involve performance that actually took place on the job

- have a clear purpose and identifiable consequences

- have firsthand witnesses

Observation System

Since an observer cannot see everything that happens, a system for observing behavior needs to be developed. The five steps below outline one systematic model.

Step 1: Select an aspect of behavior that can be observed. The first behavior aspect is the one on which the observer should focus.

Step 2: Define the behaviors that fall within a specific category. Know in advance what makes up the observed behavior.

Step 3: Determine if you need to count the number of times the behavior is displayed or whether it is just present or absent.

Step 4: Train the observers for uniformity of interpretation and standard application of the observation categories.

Step 5: Monitor the observers to ensure they are consistently using the observation categories. Retrain if necessary.

This extremely subjective data collection method has the advantage of considering past performance and providing a "frame of reference" for performance.

■ Record of Questions

A record of questions chronicles all questions asked about a job or training activity during a specific period of time. Most frequently, training or performance specialists keep these records during field tests to guide course revisions, but supervisors also can use the method during probation periods or other on-the-job training situations. The result of this method is a pattern of questions that can be analyzed to determine areas that need clarification or revision.

■ User Comments

Training or performance specialists often use this method of data collection after the completion of a training course. Comments may be obtained from course participants on course materials, facilities, training, knowledge, applicability, and the "happiness quotient." Remember that responses may be strongly influenced by the respondents' anonymity.

Secondary Research

Traditionally, the first place to look for this information has been the local public and college or university library. Among the helpful resources most libraries provide are the following:

- Almanacs and yearbooks that provide current statistics and information on events, progress, and conditions.

- Monthly catalogs of government publications that list federal government publications by department and subject.

- Doctoral dissertation and master's degree abstracts that provide summaries of graduate research.

Once general information is gleaned from these public sources, training, performance, or HRD specialists need to specify the data that pertain to their own situations. National figures for average salaries, for example, may not apply to areas where a labor shortage of overage exists.

Local personnel associations, chambers of commerce, and commerce or industry groups usually compile employment statistics. Other sources for personnel statistics include state or municipal departments of labor or unemployment assistance and the federal Department of Commerce, Department of Labor, the Bureau of Labor Statistics, and the Census Bureau. Organized labor unions or associations also may provide information on employment levels in their fields.

Membership associations and technical and scientific associations may conduct periodic member surveys and provide the public with "state of the profession" information. Check the *Encyclopedia of Associations and National Trade and Professional Associations of the United States* (available in the public library) for descriptions of these organizations. Nonstatistical data and answers to policy or practice questions also can be researched through the library. Review of current literature on a particular topic is often the first place training,

performance, or HRD professionals begin their research. Following are some resources of local libraries that should prove helpful:

- Directories that list names and addresses of persons, periodicals, publishers, and corporations.

- Bibliographic sources that list sources on given topics. Many of these sources are available through libraries as computerized databases that make searching for topics faster and more efficient than using printed tools.

- Education indexes that catalog articles from most educational journals and other educational sources, such as dissertations.

- *The Reader's Guide to Periodical Literature* that provides a subject and author index of articles in more than 30 general-interest magazines.

- *New York Times Index* that classifies articles appearing in that newspaper by subject, personality, and organization.

- *Review of Educational Research* that provides an overview of educational research in 11 subcategories.

- Psychological, sociological, and educational abstracts that summarize journal articles from several fields.

- *Resources in Education (RIE)* that supplies abstracts of documents in the 16 ERIC (an educational information retrieval and dissemination system) clearinghouses.

- *Business Periodicals Index* that provides an index to magazine articles of interest to business people.

Many business and membership organizations also will conduct research for their members. Among these organizations are:

- American Management Association (AMA), New York

- American Society for Training & Development (ASTD), Alexandria, Virginia

- International Society for Performance Improvement (ISPI), Washington, D.C.

- Society for Human Resource Management (SHRM), Alexandria, Virginia

- Conference Board, New York

- Industry-specific organizations, such as the National Restaurant Association or the American Bankers Association

More recently, the use of the Internet has expanded rapidly. Many of the physical resources mentioned above are now accessible on the researcher's own personal computer or desktop. To access these resources online, contact the resources directly or use the search capacity provided by various Internet services.

Final Research Report

After gathering all the pertinent data, the researcher prepares a final report. These reports are the result of a repetitive process, in which the various elements may be repeated as the subject under investigation becomes more sharply defined. The elements of a research project include the following: a problem statement, a review of the literature, a question statement, and a discussion of the data collection procedures used. For further discussion of this final report, see the box to the right.

A Good Research Study Final Report

Good research studies have several common elements that should be reflected in the final report. They include the following:

■ Problem Statement
The problem statement should present a clear problem or dilemma. It should be detailed enough to describe the purpose of the study.

■ Review of the Literature
A complete research study should include a summary of relevant, current literature that is linked to the study.

■ Question Statement
A specific, concrete list of hypotheses or questions should flow from the problem statement and review of the literature. This statement of questions to be answered by the study should cover the testability or answerability of the questions.

■ Discussion of Procedures
The procedures to investigate the questions should be discussed in detail. Among the elements to be addressed are these:

Design. A section should review how the study was done: type of research, methods of data collection, variables introduced, sequence of steps followed.

Sample. A description of the population studied must be included in the report. The description should cover the population's characteristics, sample, size, type of sampling, and identification of control and experimental groups.

Instrumentation. If a research instrument—questionnaire, survey, checklist—is used, the report needs to discuss conceptual and operational definitions of variables, a copy of the instrument used or questions asked, and the reliability and validity of measures.

■ Discussion
The "meat" of research reports discusses findings and recommendations. The analysis contains a discussion of the patterns derived from the data gathered and presents tables and other graphic information. Then the researcher draws conclusions from the facts gathered and makes recommendations based on his or her findings.

References & Resources

Articles

Breisch, Roger E. "Are You Listening?" *Quality Progress,* January 1996, pp. 59-62.

Chaudron, David. "The Right Approach to Employee Surveys." *HRFocus,* March 1997, pp. 9-10.

Devlin, T., et al. "Selecting a Scale for Measuring Quality." *Marketing Research,* Summer 1993, pp. 12-17.

Hamermesh, Daniel S. "A Data User's Look Back from 2015." *Monthly Labor Review,* April 1990, pp. 9-12.

Hastings, Thomas E. Jr. "Fast-tracking the Survey Process." *HRMagazine,* December 1995, pp. 71-73.

Kearsley, Greg. "Analyzing the Costs and Benefits of Training: Part 4—Data Collection." *Performance and Instruction Journal,* June/July 1986, pp. 8-10.

Nowack, Kenneth M. "Getting Them Out and Getting Them Back." *Training & Development Journal,* April 1990, pp. 82-85.

Paul, Karen B., and David W. Bracken. "Everything You Always Wanted to Know About Employee Surveys." *Training & Development,* January 1995, pp. 45-49.

Sahl, Robert J. "Company-Specific Attitude Surveys." *Personnel Journal,* May 1990, pp. 46-51.

Saltzman, A. "Improving Response Rates in Disk-by-Mail Surveys." *Marketing Research,* Summer 1993, pp. 32-39.

Starner, Tom. "Electronic Surveyors." *Human Resource Executive,* March 1998, pp. 55-57.

Thach, Liz. "Using Electronic Mail to Conduct Survey Research." *Educational Technology,* March/April 1995, pp. 27-31.

Yaney, Joseph P. "Questionnaires Help in Problem Analysis." *Performance Improvement,* September 1997, pp. 28-33.

Books

Alreck, Pamela L., and Robert B. Settle. *The Survey Research Handbook.* (2nd edition). Chicago: Irwin, 1994.

Berdie, Douglas R., et al. *Questionnaires: Design and Use.* (2nd edition). Metuchen, New Jersey: Scarecrow Press, 1986.

Clardy, Alan. *Studying Your Workforce: Applied Research Methods and Tools for the Training and Development Practitioner.* Thousand Oaks, California: Sage Publications, 1997.

Fink, Arlene, and Jacqueline Kosecoff. *How to Conduct Surveys: A Step-by-Step Guide.* (2nd edition). Thousand Oaks, California: Sage Publications, 1998.

Head, Glenn E. *Training Cost Analysis.* (rev. edition). Alexandria, Virginia: ASTD, 1993.

Keeves, John P. (ed.). *Educational Research, Methodology, and Measurement: An International Handbook.* (2nd edition). New York: Pergamon Press, 1997.

Kirkpatrick, Donald L. (comp.). *More Evaluating Training Programs.* Alexandria, Virginia: ASTD, 1988.

Miller, David W., and Samuel T. Barnett (eds.). *How-to Handbook on Doing Research in Human Resource Development.* Alexandria, Virginia: ASTD, 1986.

Rossi, Peter H., et al. (eds.). *Handbook of Survey Research.* New York: Academic Press, 1985.

Siegal, Sidney, and N. John Castellan Jr. *Nonparametric Statistics for the Behavioral Sciences.* New York: McGraw-Hill, 1988.

Sudman, Seymour, and Norman M. Bradburn. *Asking Questions.* San Francisco: Jossey-Bass, 1982.

Sudman, Seymour, et al. *Thinking About Answers.* San Francisco: Jossey Bass, 1996.

Swanson, Richard A. (ed.). *Human Resource Development Research Handbook.* San Francisco: Berrett-Koehler, 1997.

Tracey, William R. *Human Resources Management & Development Handbook.* (2nd edition). New York: AMACOM, 1994.

Weisbert, Herbert F., et al. *An Introduction to Survey Research, Polling, and Data Analysis.* (3rd edition). Thousand Oaks, California: Sage Publications, 1996.

Zemke, Ron, and Thomas Kramlinger. *Figuring Things Out: A Trainer's Guide to Needs and Task Analysis.* Reading, Massachusetts: Addison-Wesley, 1982.

Zikmund, William G. *Business Research Methods.* (4th edition). Chicago: Dryden Press, 1994.

How to Evaluate a Research Study

The following checklist is a handy tool for ensuring the validity of a study, whether it is conducted through questionnaire, interview, or observation.

Does the Study Have Implications for Practice?

☐ Yes ☐ No

1. Who cares about the study?

_____

_____

_____

_____

2. Does it

- add new concepts? ☐ Yes ☐ No
- identify new skills? ☐ Yes ☐ No
- test new theories? ☐ Yes ☐ No
- suggest new policies? ☐ Yes ☐ No
- organize a fragmented area? ☐ Yes ☐ No
- refute conventional wisdom or practice? ☐ Yes ☐ No
- answer a critical question? ☐ Yes ☐ No

3. Does it inform practice—directly or indirectly?

☐ Yes ☐ No

Does the Study Break Any Critical Technical Rules?

☐ Yes ☐ No

1. Is it designed to get an answer rather than prove a point?

☐ Yes ☐ No

2. Does the study provide a mechanism to check frequency of responses as well as percentages?

☐ Yes ☐ No

3. Has it been tested for sampling bias?

☐ Yes ☐ No

4. Are the variables controlled?

☐ Yes ☐ No

5. Are measurement techniques adequate?

☐ Yes ☐ No

6. Are answers of "no difference" provided for?

☐ Yes ☐ No

Does the Study Speak Directly to Its Audience?

☐ Yes ☐ No

1. Is the study clearly written?

☐ Yes ☐ No

2. Does it contain little or no jargon?

☐ Yes ☐ No

3. Does it have practical relevance?

☐ Yes ☐ No

4. Does it speak to its audience?

☐ Yes ☐ No

Testing for Learning Outcomes

Issue 8907

Testing for Learning Outcomes

AUTHOR:

Deborah Grafinger Hacker
PowerVision Corporation
Senior Instructional Designer
8945 Guilford Road
Columbia, MD 21046-2620
Tel. 410.312.7243
Fax 410.312.9970
E-mail
dhacker@powervision.com

Deborah Hacker has her master's degree in ISD and bilingual education from the University of Maryland. She has been in instructional design for 14 years —designing, writing, and teaching principals of design, and working in distance education and industry. She is currently at PowerVision Corporation, a company that concentrates on IT and training development.

Revised 1998

Editor
Cat Sharpe

Designer
Steven M. Blackwood

Contributing Editor
Ann Bruen

Testing for Learning Outcomes

Test!
Quiz!
Exam!
Performance Appraisal!
Evaluation!

Do these words make your palms sweat? Increase your heart rate? Keep you awake at night? If so, don't feel alone. Dread of being evaluated is a feeling shared by grade school students and company executives alike. Of course, the company line is that it is for your own good, which is true—provided the evaluation is done right and results are used constructively.

Unfortunately, most of us have had a bad experience somewhere along the way that has made us nervous about tests. Here are just a few typical testing and evaluation nightmares that are responsible for our test phobias.

- After listening to their instructor for an entire course, learners still don't have the slightest idea of what they will be tested on.

- Learners work hard to master complex skills and ideas covered in a particular course, but the evaluation consists of multiple-choice and true-false questions that test their memories for minor details.

- Test questions are written so badly that learners cannot figure out what is being asked.

- The instructor, annoyed with restless learners, punishes the class by giving a surprise pop quiz.

- Learners find trick questions designed so that no one gets a perfect score. (Too many "A" grades make the course seem too easy.)

- An employee evaluation is based on an unrealistic job description; the employee is evaluated on irrelevant job skills, while critical skills are ignored.

If you haven't experienced any of these situations, you are a lucky person and probably have no trouble sleeping the night before you are evaluated. Before you get complacent, however, consider that while *you* may have no problem, you may inadvertently be the cause of someone else's nightmares. If you've ever written a test, chances are you've written a bad test question. The best

way to eradicate test phobia is for evaluators themselves to try to understand and adopt good evaluation practices.

Let's look at some of the main testing methods. You've probably experienced most of these methods, but one or two are a bit exotic, not often seen outside special training situations. Written test items can be divided into two major groups: objective items and subjective items.

Objective Tests

Objective test items are those that have only one correct answer. They include the following:

- multiple-choice

- matching columns

- true-false

- fill-in or completion items (when the correct answer is only a word—or its synonym—or phrase)

They are called *objective* items because they can be objectively graded. Anyone with an answer key can grade them with identical results, and the grader doesn't need to make any decisions. Objective questions are used in computerized testing because the correct answers can be easily programmed. See pages 4 and 5 for tips on writing objective test items.

Objective tests have the following advantages and disadvantages:

■ *Time and Effort*
Good objective test items are difficult to write and take a lot of thought. But once they are developed, they can be administered by one person, and are easy to correct. They can even be corrected by a machine or by an assistant unfamiliar with the subject matter.

■ *Cost*
The main expense of using objective tests is in the initial development. But once developed, the test items can be reused with minimal cost.

■ *Relevance*

Objective test items are not appropriate for every learning objective. They are generally suitable when the objective calls for selecting or identifying correct information.

■ *Computer-Based or Online Testing*

Objective test items lend themselves to computer-graded testing. Just make sure that your learning objectives can be properly tested with multiple-choice, matching columns, true-false, or short-answer questions.

While objective tests are economical (after they have been developed), they are sometimes misused because they aren't always the appropriate means for testing learning objectives.

Subjective Tests

An instructor or subject matter expert (SME) must grade each item and decide whether or not it meets the criteria of acceptability. See the sidebar on page 207 for hints on writing good subjective test items.

Subjective test items have many possible answers. Examples of subjective items include the following:

- essay questions (usually several paragraphs or pages)

- short-answer items (requiring a short explanation of a few sentences)

Subjective tests have the following advantages and disadvantages:

■ *Time and Effort*

Subjective test items are easier to write than objective items, but the developer should take care that the questions are clearly written and well organized. The decision-making process of grading is time consuming, as is writing a detailed answer key to ensure that tests are graded using the same criteria.

■ *Cost*

Cost of development is generally low, but grading costs are higher since only instructors or subject matter experts can grade them.

■ *Relevance*

Subjective test items are appropriate when learners are expected to produce the correct information themselves. Subjective questions are suitable for testing a broad range of learning tasks from low-level objectives (for example, reproduction of a memorized definition) to objectives using multiple, high-level skills (such as analyzing a problem, applying complex concepts to find a solution, and organizing an explanation and defense of that solution).

■ *Computer-Based or Online Testing*

While a subjective test item can be administered online it must be graded by humans with adequate expertise in the field to correct the answer. Nevertheless, it may be advantageous to administer online subjective tests to students being tested at a distance.

Oral Tests

Oral test items are usually subjective. Types of oral testing in training include the following:

- panels of subject matter experts who gauge the depths of the learner's knowledge

- walk-throughs, in which the learner walks through a task and explains a procedure or points out locations of components in a plant or on equipment

- talk-throughs, in which the learner explains, step by step, how a particular task is carried out

The use of oral tests has the following advantages and disadvantages:

■ *Time and Effort*

Since the tests usually are administered with one or more instructors (or subject matter experts) and one learner, oral tests are time consuming.

■ *Cost*

The cost factor of the instructor's time makes oral testing expensive.

■ *Relevance*

Oral testing is appropriate whenever a more accurate evaluation of the learner's knowledge can be gained through conversation than from a written test. This includes situations such as the following:

● Learners have problems answering in writing.

● The examiner wants to question learners in depth on their responses.

● The examiner wants to clarify questions or add details at the learner's request.

■ *Computer-based or Online Testing*

While this seems unlikely, Internet software that allows for synchronous video and sound between an instructor and learner would make it possible for oral testing to be administered online at a distance.

Certain advantages exist for the learner in an oral testing situation that do not exist in a written testing environment. For example, if the learner does not understand a question, the instructor can reword it. The instructor may also prompt the learner to give more information by asking further questions. Oral testing is a good way to explore the depths of a learner's knowledge because there is always an opportunity to ask more questions.

Psychomotor Tests

Psychomotor skills are tested through the actual performance of a physical task using real equipment or a simulator. These tests allow the instructor to see if the learner has the physical and intellectual skills to perform given tasks. Any time an objective asks the learner to perform a physical skill, such as measuring, adjusting, operating, or repairing, it should be tested by actual physical performance of that task.

Physical skills should be tested in the same or a similar environment and under conditions similar to those on the job. If a mechanic is being tested on car repairs, he or she should be tested in a garage that has the same equipment used on the job. Sometimes it isn't possible to test in the actual environment because of costs or dangers involved in on-the-job testing. Examples include nuclear plant operations or fire control training. In those cases, tasks may be tested in a shop, laboratory, or simulator.

An instructor or supervisor monitors and rates the learner's performance. In order to ensure that each performer is rated by the same standards, he or she uses checklists that define the standards of acceptable performance. See the sidebar "Steps for Psychomotor Testing" for hints on developing psychomotor checklists.

The use of psychomotor tests has the following advantages and disadvantages:

■ *Time and Effort*

Psychomotor tests are time consuming because the learner and instructor are usually in a one-to-one testing environment.

■ *Cost*

In addition to the cost of the instructor's time, psychomotor tests can be expensive because they usually involve the use of costly equipment or simulators.

■ *Relevance*

Despite the cost, a physical demonstration is the only valid way to test psychomotor skill. For example, some electrical utilities use simulators to train the personnel who buy and sell electricity on the national grid. These people must make quick decisions that will affect the cost of electricity to the consumer.

■ *Computer-Based or Online Testing*

While this seems unlikely, Internet software that allows for synchronous video and sound between an instructor and learner would make it possible for oral testing to be administered online at a distance.

Writing Objective Test Items

There are four types of objective test items: true-false, multiple-choice, matching column, and fill-in or completion.

True-False Test Items

True-false test items often are used because they are:

- easy to write
- easy to correct
- don't take up much class time

True-false testing should be used cautiously. True-false questions should be used only to test knowledge objectives. They are valid only for objectives that ask learners to recognize or identify correct information rather than to state or recall it. The method can be invalid and unreliable because questions are easy to guess (there is a 50 percent chance of being correct), and knowledgeable learners tend to be tricked by them because they are aware of exceptions.

Guidelines for True-False Items

1. Test only one idea at a time. Learners may know the answer to one part of the question, but not the other. Then it is impossible to know what they know and what they do not know. More than one statement in a question also may be confusing.

   Example: *Thomas Edison invented the light bulb and Henry Ford invented the automobile.* This is a weak true-false item because it asks about unrelated events.

2. Avoid ambiguous questions. Words like "seldom," "often," and "possible" tend to confuse.

   Example: *It seldom rains in Greece during the summer.* How often is seldom—once a week? Once a month? Where in Greece? In the mountains? On the islands? In the north?

3. Avoid using "always," "never," and "none." Many learners realize that such definite statements usually are false, so they will guess without really reading the question. Or they may get the question right for the wrong reason.

   Example: *Pure water always boils at 212° C.* The learner may get this item right for the wrong reason. He or she may answer "false" because of the word "always," rather than because water boils at 212° F.

Multiple-Choice Items

Multiple-choice items are most appropriate for knowledge-based objectives in which the learner needs to choose correct information, or simple problem-solving skills where it is appropriate to select a certain solution. Multiple-choice questions are difficult to write. They are commonly used because they are easy to grade and do not use a lot of class time to administer. The problem is that often they are misused and poorly written.

Guidelines for Multiple-Choice Items

1. Put any blanks toward the end of the main part of the question (the stem). This makes it easier for learners to read and understand what is being asked.

2. The stem is usually followed by four or five possible responses. There should be only one correct response; the rest should be distracters—words or phrases meant to distract the learner's attention away from the correct response.

3. Writing good distracters is the most difficult part of constructing good multiple-choice items. All distracters should be believable. One or more obviously wrong distracters makes the correct answer easier to guess.

   Example: *The capital of Maryland is (a) Baltimore (b) Aberdeen (c) Columbia (d) Annapolis.*

   or:

   The capital of Maryland is (a) Miami (b) New York City (c) Kansas City (d) Annapolis.

The first of these items has more plausible distracters. The second item has such poor distracters that the correct answer is obvious to most people. Distracters should agree grammatically with the stem so they don't provide clues to the learner. Distracters should be about the same length as the correct response. A response that is substantially longer than the rest often is the correct one.

The correct responses should be placed in random positions. Test-wise learners know that (c) and (b) are favorite spots for correct responses. It is important not to develop a pattern of correct responses across the test.

Using Multiple-Choice for Math Problems

Multiple-choice items should be used to test calculation objectives only with extreme caution. Test-wise learners often can pass multiple-choice math tests with minimum knowledge because of implausible distracters.

Multiple-choice items should be used to test math problems only if the distracters are very good. One way to construct good distracters is to go through the problems, making different common mistakes for each distracter. Warning: Changing the decimal point is not a difficult-enough distracter to fool all learners (unless it is a common mistake for that particular problem).

Matching Column Items

Matching column items are a lot like multiple-choice items, so many rules of construction are the same. The matching items have directions, the problems, and the distracters.

Example: *Directions: Match the part of a gas combustion engine to the function it performs. Only use answers once.*

Part (problems)	Function (distracters)
____ 1. Alternator	a. Cools the engine
____ 2. Carburetor	b. Ignites fuel
____ 3. Spark plug	c. Keeps track of mileage
____ 4. Radiator	d. Mixes oil with gas
	e. Mixes gas and air
	f. Recharges the battery

Guidelines for Matching Column Items

1. All the problems should be related so the distracters sound reasonable.

2. Distracters should agree grammatically.

3. There should be more responses than problems so the last problem won't automatically match the last response.

4. Responses should be in a logical order, such as alphabetical order, or, if numbers are used, in numerical order.

5. Every item should have directions. If responses can be used more than once, the directions should so indicate.

Fill-In or Completion Items

Fill-in items are generally easy to construct. They cannot be used for information recall, or for short responses to mathematical problems.

Examples: *A univalve is a mollusk with one*

_____.

or:

The area of a square with three-inch sides is_____ square inches.

Guidelines for Fill-In Items

1. The context of the question must be included; the learner should not have to guess what the question is asking.

   Examples: *An alligator is a(n)*

   _____.

   Better: *An alligator is in the phylum*

   _____.

In the first example, the learner can't tell how to answer the question. The instructor would be forced to accept any correct response, such as animal, lizard, reptile, and so forth.

2. The blank should come toward the end of the statement to lessen confusion.

   Examples: *A(n) _____ is a hybrid from a donkey and a horse.*

   Better: *The hybrid offspring of a donkey and a horse is a(n)*
   _____.

3. No grammatical clues should be given. Using "a/ an, a(n), he or she, him or her" will prevent the learner from eliminating items through grammatical clues.

If you use fill-in items in a computer-graded test, you must determine all synonyms and spellings (correct and incorrect if spelling is not an issue) and program your software to accept them. Otherwise you may mark acceptable answers as wrong.

Using Objectives

One of the most important things to remember when developing a test item is that it must match an objective, that is, the statement that defines the following:

- what the learner should know how to do by the end of the course

- conditions under which the task is to be performed

- criteria by which acceptable task performance will be determined (how performance will be evaluated)

It is difficult—if not impossible—to determine what should be tested and how it should be done without linking testing with objectives. Objectives are the heart of education and training. They tell learners the skills and knowledge they will be expected to acquire, and how they will be tested.

Some of the problems learners face when being evaluated are directly related to the absence of objectives. Objectives help course designers and instructors make decisions about evaluating. Proper use of objectives helps to ensure that:

- important skills and information are covered in class

- support materials match the class work and test items

- important skills and knowledge are evaluated

- appropriate types of test items are used

In a systematic approach to course or program development, the objectives and test items are developed together—before the course is even written. This is a good time to develop test items because, in the design and development stage, the course designer can make sure the written objectives are testable before writing the materials to support them.

Selecting Testing Methods

Every objective should be tested, when possible, by performance of the objective. Depending upon whether you are testing for knowledge, skills, or attitude, here are some guidelines to follow.

Knowledge should be tested as the specific objective indicates. If the objective says, for example, to *list* or *state,* then the objective should require that the learner recall and reproduce the information. If the objective says to *identify*, then the learner is only required to select the appropriate answer (as with multiple-choice or completion items).

Intellectual skills such as calculating, analyzing, or using knowledge can be evaluated in a written test (though an oral test might also be appropriate). The test item should require the learner to *perform* the skill, not *describe* how it is done.

A **psychomotor** or physical skill such as calibrating, repairing, or parking can be tested *only* by performance of the skill. The testing situation should be under the same conditions (noise, distractions, equipment used, and so forth) as those encountered on the job. If the objective is to park a fully loaded truck at a loading dock, the dock should meet typical conditions. The truck should be filled with a load of similar weight and volume carried so the truck handling properties will be the same.

Although many training professionals test for **attitude,** it is very difficult to do since any attitude evaluation will be, by definition, subjective. Training and testing for attitude change should be undertaken with care, because any evidence of coercion or use of peer pressure could have serious legal and moral implications touching on the rights of the individual and free will. When appropriate, attitude can best be evaluated through questionnaires or surveys (see the sidebar on surveying attitudes).

Writing Subjective Items

A subjective test should not test the learner's ability to understand complex questions and organize essays *unless* that is clearly a requirement for the course. In order to avoid testing essay *writing* as a hidden skill, write essay questions so they require only a few paragraphs each. It should be made clear—both orally and in writing—that brief answers are expected.

Questions should be short and concise. If one question covers a lot of information, break it up into sections. This helps the learner to understand the question, and the instructor to organize the answer. Look at the following examples of subjective questions for customer sales representatives at a bank. Which one is easier to understand?

Describe the procedure for selling and opening a money market account: how to determine who's a prospective customer, advantages of a money market account over other investments, and rates of interest and paperwork to be completed.

or:

Write short descriptions of the steps for selling a money market account. Include in your answer:

● *determining the customer's needs*

● *introducing the idea of a money market account*

● *describing the advantages of a money market account over other investments*

● *explaining interest rates and how interest accrues*

● *completing the paperwork for the customer*

The second item organizes the learner's response and lets the learner know exactly what the instructor wants.

Follow these steps when writing subjective questions and grading keys:

1. Write a question. Check it for clarity. Compare it with the objective to ensure a match.

2. Write the expected answer.

3. Ask a colleague to read the question, checking it for clarity and writing an answer.

4. Revise the question (if needed), based on the answers written by the instructor (if you are not the instructor) and your colleague.

5. Construct a grading key. The key should include all components of a correct answer, and the point value for each piece of the answer. Make sure that point values assigned to different parts of the answer are weighted according to their importance.

6. The first time you administer the test, ask another instructor to grade copies of some of the questions using the answer key. Compare your results. Ask the other instructor about problems he or she had using the key. If the other instructor's results differ greatly from yours, discuss the differences and determine how the key can be improved.

Evaluating Tests

The two key goals of creating an evaluation instrument are that it must be valid and reliable. Validity is the measure of whether a question tests the intended skills and knowledge. Reliability measures whether an item differentiates between individuals who know the information and those who do not.

Measuring the validity and reliability of test items requires collecting and analyzing test score data. While we are not going to get into determining validity and reliability at this time, we can help you assess whether a test item is likely to be valid and reliable by examining certain characteristics.

Validity

A valid test is one that tests what it is meant to test. In other words, it tests the specific skills and knowledge defined in the objectives. To assess the potential validity of a test item, we need to ask the following questions:

- Does the question test the intended objective, matching the performance described in the verb as well as any predefined conditions and standards?

- Is the material in the question important information or incidental detail?

- Was the material in the test item covered in the training?

If an objective states that the learner must install an Omega model 105 dishwasher, then the only valid test of that skill is for the learner to install that specific brand and model of appliance. It is not a valid test for the learner to install another brand or model of dishwasher. The differences in design between the two models may require other skills and knowledge. It is also not a valid test for the learner to *describe* installation of the dishwasher. That would only test the learner's *knowledge* of how to perform the task, and not the actual *skills* needed for performance.

Sometimes the difference between the objective and the test item can be seen clearly. For example, an objective may state that the learner is to install a dishwasher, while the test item asks the learner to describe how the installation is done. It is easy to see in this case that the objective and test item do not match. Sometimes the difference between

the objective and the test item is so subtle that it is difficult to recognize that an item is invalid. For example, look at the following objective:

List the steps for starting up the engine room boiler, in procedural order.

Now look at this test item:

Number the following steps in procedural order for starting up the engine room boiler.

_____ *Open the choke.*

_____ *Light the burner.*

_____ *Open the fuel line.*

_____ *Check the air intake valve.*

_____ *Check the fuel level.*

The second test item does not really test the knowledge required by the objective. The learner does not need to know the steps for boiler start-up to answer the question correctly. The test item only requires the learner to put the steps in order. It does not tell us if the learner can remember all of the steps without prompting. This may seem like a small difference, but if one of the safety steps is missed, it could cause an accident. In order to ensure that test items are valid, it is a good idea to get a second opinion from a colleague on whether or not test items truly match objectives.

Reliability

A reliable test item is one that consistently measures the learner's ability to perform the objective. A test item that consistently differentiates learners who can do a task from learners who cannot is a reliable item.

To assess the potential reliability of a test item we need to ask the following questions:

- Is the answer to the question common sense?

- Does the question's wording make it easy to guess the correct answer?

- Does the item contain tricks that might fool learners into picking the wrong answer?

Steps for Psychomotor Testing

Here is one possible sequence for developing psychomotor checklists:

1. Analyze an expert performing the task. Determine the critical steps and key decisions that must be made by the learner in order to perform the task correctly. Have a colleague check your results.

2. Set the guidelines for checklist construction. They will be dependent on the types of skills or procedures you are testing and your grading criteria. Checklists can be organized in a number of ways, including:

   Product measure. Arrange the checklist according to the products that are created throughout the test. This measure is most appropriate where product quality is more important than process.

   Performance criteria. These checklists specify a task or procedure at the top and list the areas of applicable criteria below. The examiner has a copy of the procedure and related standards to check against. This type of checklist would be appropriate for procedures that have several applicable criteria (for example, speed, safety, product, technique, and accuracy).

   Sequential order. Set up the checklist of tasks in their sequential order. This type of checklist lends itself to testing procedures or tasks that must be done in sequence.

3. Determine the rating scales to be used. Will there be:

   - a two-point scale (such as yes/no or pass/fail)?

   - a numerical scale grading performance from 1 to 10?

   - a graphic rating scale? (See the example below.)

4. Spell out guidelines for rating learner performance. Remember, there is a certain amount of subjectivity to rating the performance of physical tasks. In order to ensure that all raters will grade by the same criteria, it is necessary to write a set of guidelines and discuss them with raters before the test is administered.

Graphic Rating Scale

Engine starts immediately.   Engine hesitates.   Engine doesn't start.
                                      There are knocks and pings.

Pass   Fail

- Are negatives or absolutes used within the question that might lead to misinterpretation?

We know that a test item is *unreliable* if it falls into the following categories:

- It is easy to guess because it fails to separate skilled, knowledgeable learners from those who cannot perform the task.

- It is difficult to understand because some learners who can perform the task will not understand what they are being asked to do.

- It is evaluated differently for different learners, such as in an essay test.

To ensure the reliability of essay tests, it is important to define an acceptable answer before the test is given; and to determine whether or not partial credit will be given and, if so, how many points each part of the answer is worth. Reliability can be affected by the conditions under which a test is given. Learners who are tested in an uncomfortable, noisy room are not likely to perform as well as those tested in a comfortable, quiet environment.

Learners should be given the same amount of time to take the same test with the same tools, materials, and resources. If one learner is allowed to take an open-book test, and another takes the test with no resources, the results will not be consistent because one of the learners had advantages the other did not.

Look at the following objective:

Replace the spark plugs, wires, and distributor cap on a Ford Escort at recommended manufacturer's internals, within 30 minutes, given the necessary tools and manuals.

If some learners are asked to perform this task without the required manuals, it would be an unreliable test. Without the manual to look up the specifications, learners would not have the opportunity to demonstrate their ability to perform the task correctly. Having learners perform this task without a time limit also invalidates the test. It would not show which learners could perform the task in the allotted time and which could not.

Here are some additional steps you can take to help ensure reliability.

- Ask colleagues to review test items. They should be clearly written and easily understood, but not easy to guess.

- Define acceptable answers for essay items before the test is given. Determine how they will be marked. If more than one person will grade the tests, make sure all graders apply the standards in the same way.

- Choose a comfortable, quiet environment for testing learners unless a different setting more closely approximates the actual job conditions.

- Make sure that all learners are taking the test under the same conditions (with the same tools, materials, resources, and time limitations).

Playing Fair

Every time instructors or course designers construct a test item, they should make sure that it is as fair as possible, while giving learners who know the material a chance to prove what they know. *The main point of evaluation is to determine what skills and knowledge a learner possesses.*

■ *Keeping Learners Informed*
Objectives serve the purpose of informing learners what is expected of them. Each session should begin with an introduction addressing objectives to be covered during that session. This way, learners constantly know where they are in the course and what is to be accomplished.

Objectives should also be used for review before testing. Learners should be told which objectives are being covered by the test and how they will be tested. Informed learners are motivated and in control of their learning process. They are more likely to succeed than those who do not know what is expected of them.

■ *Writing Clear, Concise Test Items*
It is difficult to write good test items that are easily understood. One way to ensure good test construction is to have someone else review the test to make sure it is written clearly. The instructor can also ask the reviewer to answer the questions to see if the test yields the expected answers.

Surveying Attitudes

Writing a good attitude survey is as difficult as writing a good test. Here are some steps for developing a good questionnaire adapted from *Handbook of Training Evaluation and Measurement Methods* by Jack Phillips.

1. Determine the information needed. List subjects, skills, or abilities covered. An outline form is helpful for grouping related questions.

2. Select the type of questions. Keep in mind the kind of information to be gathered and how it will be used.

3. Develop the questions. Base them on the type of questions planned and the information needed, keeping them simple and concise.

4. Test the questions. If possible, test the questions on a group of participants in a pilot program. Or test them on a group of employees with skills that approximate those of potential participants. Revise questions as needed. Testing a control group (people not involved in the training program) allows for comparison of responses with those of participants.

5. Develop the complete questionnaire and prepare a data summary. Integrate questions and write clear instructions. Develop a summary sheet for quick tabulation and interpretation.

Types of Questions on Attitude Surveys

Several types of questions can be used in a survey:

Short-answer questions, in which learners explain their thoughts.

Selection or multiple-choice questions, in which learners check off items on a list or pick an answer that best expresses their opinions.

Yes-no questions, in which a learner agrees or disagrees with a statement.

Ranking scales, in which a learner ranks the importance of different ideas or determines their degree of agreement or disagreement with given statements.

Here are some typical examples of these question types.

Short-answer Question
What can you do to transform the workplace into a safer environment?

_____

_____

_____

Selection Questions
What do you think are the three most important qualities of a customer service representative? (May be in multiple-choice format.)

☐ Administration skills
☐ Communications skills
☐ Good rapport with customers
☐ Good rapport with service technicians
☐ Knowledge of company policy
☐ Product knowledge
☐ Telephone skills
☐ Troubleshooting

Yes-no Questions
Do you think that present company policies on handling toxic materials are sufficient for protecting employees?

☐ Yes   ☐ No

Ranking Scales
The plant technicians are given sufficient opportunities to express their ideas on company policy.

☐ Strongly agree
☐ Agree
☐ Neutral
☐ Disagree
☐ Strongly disagree

■ *Giving Away the Answers*

Objective test items are notoriously easy to guess by test-wise learners. The following are some of the common clues found in test items:

● grammatical hints—disagreement among the number and tenses in distracters, or use of "a" and "an" instead of "a/an" in the question

● poor distracters—wrong selections in multiple-choice or in matching columns—sensible enough to provide the learner possible choices or to make guessing easy

● word cues—using a key word in a question that is also in the distracter or in the answer, such as asking what piece of equipment transforms current into voltage and writing "transformer" as the answer

■ *Hidden Skills*

Test items should test only the skills and knowledge they were meant to test. But sometimes items test hidden skills. That means that a learner is required to do or know something outside the prerequisites and requirements of the course. For example, asking a bank teller trainee for a well-organized essay on customer service would call for written communications skills unnecessary for the training program and the job.

■ *Good Grading Practices*

Subjective tests should be graded using the same criteria—a difficult challenge. Here are some problems and possible solutions.

There are grading differences among instructors. If a test is standard and given by more than one instructor, or more than one person is grading, learners may be rated differently. A key should be used, detailing the grading criteria. All raters should meet and discuss how these criteria will be applied. Decisions to give partial credit must be uniform. Ensure continuity by having each instructor grade selected questions across the entire test and one person look over all tests at the end of the grading process to standardize marks.

The order in which tests are graded is also an issue. It is difficult to rate performance by consistent criteria. If the initial performances are very good, the grader tends to judge the following ones harder. If initial performances are poor, succeeding ones tend to be judged more leniently. Reviewing all papers a second time helps to ensure equal application of criteria. It is also helpful to grade one question across all learners before moving on to the next. You can shuffle the papers between questions to make sure you grade each test item in a different sequence.

Prejudice based on past performance can also influence an instructor during grading. When a grader rates a learner he or she knows, it is difficult to separate current performance from past performance. Good past performance tends to work favorably for the learner, while poor past performance may unfavorably color the rater's evaluation of current performance. On written tests, names should be covered or numbers assigned.

■ *Trick Questions*

Some instructors try to fool learners by asking them trick questions. Unless an item tests for recognition of a specific tricky situation that is part of the necessary training, trick questions are simply not a fair test of a learner's skills and knowledge. Sometimes an instructor will inadvertently write a trick question. He or she must be open to removing or changing an unfair question when it is pointed out.

Evaluating Test Results

There are two methods of evaluation that you should be familiar with:

1. Norm-referencing—a traditional and familiar means of evaluating learner performance. It is how we frequently were graded in school, but it is not always the best way to evaluate performance.

2. Criterion-referencing—another perspective on evaluation. It compares performance with objective standards.

Norm-Referenced Evaluation

Do you remember back in school when the class did badly on a test but the teacher assured us that it would be "graded on the curve"? Do you remember the importance of class rank for students who wanted to get into certain colleges? Class ranking and grading on the curve are artifacts of norm-referenced evaluation.

Norm-referenced evaluation compares an individual's performance with that of all the others taking a particular test or in the same class. The worse the rest of the population performs, the higher the scores of those in the top 50 percent of the class.

When a large number of people take a standardized test, their marks usually fall within a normal range. This range, when plotted, forms a bell-shaped curve like the one shown here. It shows the performance of most people falling in the middle, with a few doing very well and a few doing very poorly. When scores are marked on a curve, marks are adjusted so that they still form a bell curve, but instead of an "A" starting at 100 percent, it may begin at 75 percent or 80 percent.

This seems like a strange way to evaluate whether or not a learner can perform a task or demonstrate knowledge. If the best mark is an 80 percent, does that mean that none of the learners was able to perform the task completely?

The truth of the matter is that norm-referencing evaluation should not be used to determine who can and who can't perform a task. The purpose of norm-referencing is to identify the best and worst performances by comparing each individual to the rest of the group. It may be used in cases like the following:

- There is room in a training program for five learners. The company wants to give the spots to the best five applicants.

- A scholarship will be given to the top quarter of the class. They need to be identified.

- An organization is offering remedial math and reading courses. Employees who need them most will be admitted into the courses first.

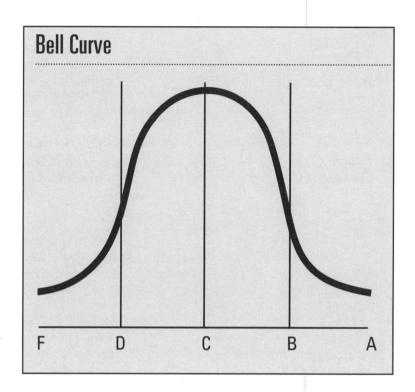

Bell Curve

F   D   C   B   A

Criterion-Referenced Evaluation

Criterion-referencing means that an individual's performance is measured against the standards of the objectives being tested. This type of evaluation should be used in any program in which learners must master particular skills or knowledge before continuing. Criterion-referenced evaluation enables learners to compete against their own performance rather than that of others. In order to reach their goals, they must meet the necessary objectives. Most organizations are interested in whether or not an individual has the skills to perform a particular job. They aren't interested in the individual's ranking among 20 other trainees who may or may not have the necessary skills.

Still, instructors tend to compare learners' performances without knowing whether or not any of them have the skills and knowledge it takes to continue. This is a mistake made in both educational and training environments. Criterion-referenced evaluation is based on meeting the objectives. The most appropriate way of grading a course that uses criterion-referenced evaluation is pass-fail. When learners pass, it means they have mastered all the skills and knowledge needed to perform specific tasks.

References & Resources

Articles

Anonymous. "Testing Buyers' Guide." *Human Resource Executive,* November 1994, pp. 62-66.

Blair, David, and Steve Giles. "Evaluating Test Questions: More Than Meets the Eye." *Technical & Skills Training,* May/June 1996, pp. 23-24.

Jones, Paul E. "Three Levels of Certification Testing." *Performance & Instruction,* October 1994, pp. 22-28.

Lapp, H.J. "Rate Your Testing Program." *Performance & Instruction,* September 1995, pp. 36-38.

Lee, William W., and Robert A. Mamone. "Design Criteria That Make Tests Objective." *Journal of Instruction Delivery Systems,* Summer 1995, pp. 13-17.

Marrelli, Anne F. "Writing Multiple-choice Test Items." *Performance & Instruction,* September 1995, pp. 24-29.

Parshall, Cynthia G. "Practical Issues in Computer-Based Testing." *Journal of Instruction Delivery Systems,* Summer 1995, pp. 13-17.

Reynolds, Angus. "The Basics: Evaluation." *Technical & Skills Training,* August/September 1994, pp. 5-6.

Schriver, Rob. "Testing Employee Performance: A Review of Key Milestones." *Technical & Skills Training,* April 1997, pp. 27-29.

Shrock, Sharon A. "Testing Triage: Maximizing Effectiveness in Assessment With Minimal Investment." *Performance Improvement,* March 1997, pp. 46-50.

Sidick, John T., et al. "Three-Alternative Multiple-choice Tests: An Attractive Option." *Personnel Psychology,* Winter 1994, pp. 829-835.

Stape, Christopher J. "Techniques for Developing Higher-Level Objective Test Questions." *Performance & Instruction,* March 1995, pp. 31-34.

Weekley, Jeff A., and Casey Jones. "Video-Based Situational Testing." *Personnel Psychology,* Spring 1997, pp. 25-49.

Books

Berk, R.A. (ed.). *Criterion-Referenced Measurement: The State of the Art.* Baltimore, Maryland: Johns Hopkins University Press, 1980.

Birnbrauer, Herman (ed.). *The ASTD Handbook for Technical and Skills Training.* Vol. 2. Alexandria, Virginia: American Society for Training & Development, 1986.

Briggs, Leslie J. *Instructional Design: Principles and Application.* Englewood Cliffs, New Jersey: Educational Technology, 1981.

Craig, Robert L. (ed.). *Training and Development Handbook.* New York: McGraw Hill, 1987.

Deming, Basil S. *Evaluating Job-Related Training.* Alexandria, Virginia: American Society for Training & Development, 1982.

Fitch, Brian. *Testing in Employment and Training Programs.* Columbus, Ohio: National Center for Research in Vocational Education, 1983.

Finch, Curtis R., and Robert McGough. *Administering and Supervising Occupational Education.* Englewood Cliffs, New Jersey: Prentice-Hall, 1982.

References & Resources

Books

Gagne, Robert J., and Leslie J. Briggs. *Principles of Instructional Design.* 4th ed. New York: Holt, Rinehart & Winston, 1986.

Heinich, Robert, et al. *Instructional Development and the New Technologies of Instruction.* New York: John Wiley & Sons, 1982.

Kirkpatrick, Donald L. (ed.). *More Evaluating Training Programs.* Alexandria, Virginia: American Society for Training & Development, 1987.

Lutterodt, Sarah A., and Deborah J. Grafinger. *Measurement and Evaluation: Basic Concepts.* Columbia, Maryland: GP Courseware, 1985.

————. *Measurement and Objective Test Items I.* Columbia, Maryland: GP Courseware, 1985.

Mager, Robert F. *Measuring Instructional Results or Got a Match?* Atlanta, Georgia: Center for Effective Performance, 1997.

Morris, Lynn Lyons, et al. *How to Measure Performance and Use Tests.* Newbury Park, California: Sage Publications, 1987.

Tenopyr, Mary L., and Robert L. Craig (eds.). *The ASTD Training and Development Handbook: A Guide to Human Resource Development.* New York: McGraw-Hill, 1996.

Wentling, Tim L. *Evaluating Occupational Education and Training Programs.* 2nd ed. Boston, Massachusetts: Allyn and Bacon, 1980.

Info-lines

Long, Lori. "Surveys From Start to Finish." No. 8612.

Martelli, Joseph T., and Dennis Mather. "Statistics for HRD Practice." No. 9101.

O'Neill, Mary. "How to Focus an Evaluation." No. 9605.

Robinson, Dana Gaines. "Tracking Operational Results." No. 9112.

Waagen, Alice K. "Essentials for Evaluation." No. 9705.

Internet Sites

American Society for Training & Development
http://www.astd.org

http://www.assess.com/b-advanc.html

http://www.nprdc.navy.mil/wworks/read2.5.htm

http://www.thebok.com/nwba/professional.html

http://www.press.uchicago.edu/cgi_bin/hfs.cgi/99/johns-hopkins/84047955.ct1

http://www.nprdc.navy.mil/wworks/find3.8.htm

http://www.nis.za/crcn/page2.htm

Job Aid: How to Test a Learning Outcome

Use the following worksheet to make decisions regarding *how* to test and to help in the actual *writing* of the test.

Determine the type of test item to be used:

1. Look at the objective. What type of objective is it (knowledge, skills, or attitude)?

   _____

2. What are the best ways of testing this type of objective?

   _____

   _____

   _____

   _____

   _____

3. List any constraints on testing. (Is there a time limit? Are there enough instructors to administer or grade the test? Is the equipment available?)

   _____

   _____

   _____

   _____

   _____

4. How will any of the constraints affect your choice of test item types?

   _____

5. What type of testing will you use?

   _____

Surveys from Start to Finish

Issue 8612

Surveys from Start to Finish

A U T H O R :

Lori Long

Editorial staff for 8612

Editor
Gerry Spruell

ASTD Internal Consultant
Eileen West

Revised 1998

Editor
Cat Sharpe

Contributing Editor
Ann Bruen

ASTD Internal Consultant
Michael Czarnowsky

Surveys from Start to Finish

How comfortable is your corporate climate? How effective is your technical training? What kind of courses, if any, do supervisors need to advance your company's customer service aims?

When you want the inside story from employees on a particular corporate question, a survey may be the answer. It brings out opinions, insights, and facts about a current situation by questioning the people involved. Whether conducted in person, sent through the mail, or conducted over the phone, a survey can provide valuable information about training and performance needs and results. But a survey can provide accurate data only if it is conducted correctly.

Once you thoroughly understand the information needs of your client, you must determine on a case-by-case basis whether a survey will efficiently meet those needs. Perhaps information already available would suffice. When you feel confident that a survey is suitable, you must then determine the type of survey to conduct, the size and nature of the group of people to survey, the type of questions to ask, and the appropriate means for tabulating and analyzing the answers. And in doing all of this, you must follow proper survey ethics. These include some of the following:

- You may not betray confidences.

- You may not twist the truth.

- You may not play with numbers or statements to make survey analyses easier on the brain or the ear.

Following proper survey ethics is easier said than done, as are all of the other tasks of surveying.

This issue of *Info-line* will help you determine when to conduct a survey, what type of survey to use, whom to survey, what to ask, and how to get the information you need. For background and additional information, see the following *Info-line*s: No. 8502, "Be a Better Needs Analyst"; No. 9808, "Task Analysis"; No. 8907, "Testing for Learning Outcomes"; No. 9008, "How to Collect Data"; and No. 9101, "Statistics for HRD Practice."

Types of Surveys

Surveys vary greatly in amount of time and money required and in complexity. Choose the type of survey that will best provide the data you need—not necessarily the one that is fastest, cheapest, and easiest to do. Another factor to consider is that you may need to use more than one type of survey to obtain different kinds of data about the same topic.

Some of the considerations for determining what survey type(s) to use are as follows:

- What kind of issue do you need to resolve?

- How many people must you survey?

- What is the sensitivity of the questions you must ask?

- How much time and money are available to collect and analyze data?

- What amount of time will respondents be willing to invest in supplying the data?

- How easily can you access the prospective respondents?

Three popular types of surveys are the face-to-face interview, the telephone interview, and the written questionnaire. Electronic surveys are a fourth option for gathering information—a modern delivery mechanism for written questionnaires. Guidelines for when to use each of these survey types, plus their advantages and disadvantages, are discussed on the following pages.

Pre-Survey Checklist

Before you mail a list of questions, dial a number, or knock on a door, you must be sure of one thing: Should you be doing a survey in the first place? The following questions will help you determine whether, with the task at hand, a survey is necessary, appropriate, affordable, and feasible.

What data are needed?
Are these data available elsewhere? Did you check with colleagues, various company departments, libraries, and other sources to ensure that the data you need have not already been collected?

How strong is the need for data?
Is the need strong enough and is the information topic important enough to justify the time and effort involved in a survey?

Who will sponsor the survey?
Will respondents willingly answer a request from this sponsor? Will respondents be intimidated and answer untruthfully?

How will the data be used?
Is your client's goal in collecting information to gain insights? Get ideas? Support decisions? Are information needs too varied for one survey? Are there methods more effective than surveying, considering the intended use of the collected data?

Who will respond?
Does the respondent group you plan to use have the knowledge to answer accurately? Are these respondents a reliable source of information? Are they willing to invest the time and effort required by a survey?

When are the data needed?
Did you ask several potential respondents the best time to be surveyed (season, month, day), based on their work load? Does this time coincide with your deadline?

How will the data be analyzed?
Do you have the means necessary for appropriate analysis? For example, if statistical analysis is required, do you have access to a computer and the proper software, or do you have the time necessary to tabulate results manually? If you wish to ask respondents to brainstorm ideas, can you take the great amount of time necessary to summarize the results?

Is enough money available to perform a survey?
What are the estimated time and dollar costs for each phase of the survey (researching, preparing, pretesting, conducting, tabulating, analyzing)? If you cannot meet these costs, can you narrow the scope of your proposed survey or take shortcuts without sacrificing quality of data? Or would you wind up with a "quick and dirty" survey yielding dubious results?

Face-to-Face Interviews

Use this type of survey to explore complex questions that require explanatory answers. Following are some examples of when to use face-to-face interviews:

- when part of a needs analysis—surveying managers about whether training is needed, and if so, why, what kind, and for whom

- when asking highly sensitive questions

- when all possible responses to an issue cannot be anticipated

- when respondents are experts in the field or are in upper management

- when survey time and dollars are plentiful (but only if exploratory or sensitive questions are necessary)

If survey time and dollars are tight, consider combining two survey types: Conduct face-to-face interviews, asking open-ended questions of a small portion of the survey sample; also use telephone interviews or written questionnaires with forced-choice questions for the entire survey sample.

Following are the advantages and disadvantages of face-to-face interviews:

Advantages

- Interviewers can clarify questions respondents do not understand.

- Interviewers can ask spontaneous questions based on new thought paths respondents pursue.

- Interviewers can gain insights and get ideas from respondents.

- Interviewers can pick up nonverbal cues. A respondent's body language is a strong indicator of personal comfort or uneasiness with a question, affecting the accuracy of the response.

- Interviewers can change the tone and style of the questions to match individual conversation styles of respondents.

Disadvantages

- Respondents may get distracted as the interviewer takes notes.

- Respondents may doubt that their answers will remain confidential and, therefore, not answer truthfully.

- Interviewer training may be necessary.

- Face-to-face interviews are the most expensive type of survey, and they are extremely time consuming because they survey many people.

Tips for Face-to-Face Interviews

Before the face-to-face interview, call or write the respondent to request an interview appointment. During the call, introduce yourself—include your job title and a little bit about what you do. Explain the reason for the interview request. Name the sponsor of the survey and explain the purpose and the scope of the survey. Describe the nature and size of the sample. Tell the person how much time you expect the interview to take. Make the appointment for a time and place convenient to the respondent. Ask to be alone with the respondent; interruptions and the presence of others can influence responses.

Preparation

Make up a detailed outline of interview questions, using the following guidelines:

1. Write one or two simple and interesting *yes/no* questions for the start of the interview in order to put the respondent as ease and gain interest; make the rest of the questions open ended. (Remember, you should not be doing a face-to-face survey if your purpose is to get brief answers to structured questions.)

2. Write a few different versions of key questions so you can ask them more than once (without irritating the respondent); this will ensure that you get full answers. Space out different versions of the same question.

3. Cluster questions on like topics together.

4. Sequence questions from general to specific.

5. Alternate tough and easy questions to give respondents necessary breaks from thinking so hard.

6. Do not put sensitive questions at the beginning of the interview. They are better asked after the respondent answers other questions and feels comfortable with you.

7. Do not put important questions at the end of the interview. The respondent may become tired and may answer inaccurately; or the respondent may terminate the interview due to lack of time before you ask an important question.

8. Put demographics questions at the end. They are easy to answer, and they flag the interview's finish.

Face-to-Face Interview Outline

The following survey questions might be asked of sales managers as part of a needs analysis designed to find out why sales are dropping.

1. Do you have more than five salespeople on staff?

2. Are most of them experienced or fairly new to sales?

3. How experienced is your top performer?

4. Do you think the company offers enough formal training to supplement the coaching you give your staff?

5. What skills could your salespeople strengthen?

6. What knowledge areas could they strengthen?

7. Would your salespeople benefit more from attending training programs or from being coached by you after you have attended programs? Why?

8. What more can the company do about training?

9. Do you think you could use more management training? Why or why not?

10. How long have you been in sales?

11. Do you have other ideas on training or further comments?

Practice asking the questions. Make sure you are pronouncing words correctly and enunciating clearly. Explain each question to respondents who do not understand the question the first time they are asked. Learn everything you can about the respondent. This knowledge will help you answer any questions the respondent has and will help you gain respondent cooperation and confidence. Try to find out information such as age, job, number of years with company, number of years in professional field, and the jargon of the respondent's professional field (in case the respondent uses it; you, however, should avoid all jargon).

When leaving for the interview, take along any sources of information, such as reports or published data, that pertain to your questions. The respondent may not have the materials on hand or may have never seen them. Get to the interview a little early.

Beginning the Interview

Put the respondent at ease by initiating everyday conversation. Try to pick up signals from the respondent as to how much small talk is appropriate. This can create a smooth transition to the questions. After the small talk, state your job title and what you do; the sponsor of the survey; the purpose of the survey; and the size and nature of the sample.

Before questioning begins, determine how you will record the answers. If you want to tape answers, ask the respondent for permission. Even if permission is granted, do not use a tape recorder if the respondent seems uncomfortable; his or her uneasiness will affect the responses. If you take notes, do so accurately and immediately after each response, even if you must periodically ask the respondent for a few moments to write or type notes on particularly important and lengthy answers.

During the Interview

Use the same friendly, conversational tone of voice with every respondent and avoid implying the answer you expect; you must sound neutral, as though all answers are equal. Here are some guidelines to use when conducting the interview:

- Make sure your body language communicates self-confidence and interest in the respondent's thoughts.

- Observe the respondent's body language. Blushing, hesitation, quizzical expressions, and nervous mannerisms can mean you should change the way you are conducting the survey.

- Keep your line of questioning flexible. Spontaneously follow the respondent's line of thinking if it digresses from your interview outline, so long as you think the new thought path can provide meaningful data. Then get the interview back on track; interject a smooth transition to your next question.

- Keep your comments to a minimum; telling the respondent your opinion could color subsequent responses.

- Listen with a questioning mind to responses. Jot down additional questions as you think of them.

- If you do not understand an answer, ask the respondent to clarify. If your mind happens to wander, ask the respondent to repeat what was said.

- Tactfully ask the respondents to qualify answers that sound like exaggerations or sweeping generalizations.

Remember that the respondents are the subject matter experts (SMEs). Do not make them feel as though you are testing them, and do not argue with them about answers. Admit any errors you make. If you find the interview lasting longer than you said it would, ask the respondent if he or she would mind answering a few more questions. If the respondent is agreeable, ask *only* a few more. If necessary, request an additional interview and set a date.

Closing the Interview

Ease the interview to a conclusion. Once you finish asking questions, invite the respondent to make comments or ask questions. Thank the respondent for his or her time and thoughts. After the interview, review any notes you took and fill in impressions you did not have time to write down during the interview.

Telephone Interviews

Use this type of survey to gather nonsensitive *yes/no* or range of *like/dislike* answers to specific, tightly focused questions. Following are some examples of when to use a telephone interview:

- when part of a training evaluation—surveying people who have completed a program as to how transferable the training was to their job

- when gathering strictly numerical data (usually requires two calls, one to state the need and another to get the numbers)

- when most or all possible responses to an issue can be anticipated

- when time available for the survey is tight and exploratory or sensitive questions are not essential

If exploratory or sensitive questions are essential, consider combining two survey types: Phone the survey sample and ask forced-choice questions; also conduct face-to-face interviews, asking open-ended questions of a small portion of the sample.

Following are the advantages and disadvantages of telephone interviews:

Advantages

- Interviewers can clarify questions respondents do not understand.

- Respondents generally are more relaxed when speaking with a stranger by telephone than when speaking face to face. And the more relaxed respondents are, the more truthful their answers tend to be.

- Interviewers can read questions from a script and take notes without concern about distracting respondents.

- Respondents cannot read the interviewer's body language. The interviewer need only concentrate on his or her voice, without concern for nervous mannerisms.

- Telephone interviews are the fastest way to collect information and the least expensive type of survey.

Disadvantages

- Respondents often feel that a telephone survey is an invasion of their professional or personal life.

- Interviewers have little opportunity to "loosen up" the respondent; small talk does not work well by telephone.

- Interviewers cannot read respondents' body language to determine if they are anxious about answering any questions.

- The scope of the survey is limited because respondents tire quickly during telephone interviews, and the interviewer does not have the opportunity to draw out thoughtful, insightful responses.

- Interviewer training may be necessary.

Tips for Telephone Interviews

Before the telephone interview, plan and practice your questions, create a checklist for recording data, and devise a means for tracking respondents.

Preparation

Make up a list of simple, straightforward, forced-choice questions—true/false, yes/no, multiple choice—or direct questions that can be answered with one or two words. Use the following guidelines:

1. Exclude sensitive questions or ones that require explanatory answers. (If you need that kind of information, you should be using face-to-face interviews.)

2. Order the questions logically, one leading smoothly to the next.

3. Put the easiest-to-answer, qualifying questions first. Qualifiers confirm that the respondent fits your needs; the simplicity of these questions puts the respondent at ease.

4. Put a particularly interesting, though simple, question at the beginning to gain the respondent's interest.

5. Do not save important questions for the end of the interview. The respondent may become tired and may answer inaccurately, or terminate the interview early due to lack of time.

Practice asking the questions. Make sure you are pronouncing words correctly and enunciating clearly. Make up a simple checklist answer form to complete as you ask the questions. Prepare this even if you would rather tape-record responses, because to do so you need the respondent's permission and you may not get it. (Remember that if you tape-record, you must replay the tape and go through the whole interview again to tabulate the data.) Create a log for numbers called, respondents reached, busy signals received, and messages taken so you have a record of whom you contacted and whom you need to try again.

Beginning the Interview

When the respondent answers the phone, state your name and give a short introduction of the sponsor, purpose, and scope of the survey. Ask if the respondent has time to answer a few questions. Mention how much time you expect the survey to take (set your maximum time at 10 minutes).

Speak clearly, but mention all the above elements without a silence long enough for the respondent to break in. If the respondent is busy, set a time to call back. If you would like to tape-record the interview, ask the respondent for permission; it is illegal to tape a phone conversation without informing the respondent.

Telephone Interview Questions

The following questions might be asked of post-program participants as part of a training evaluation.

1. Are you still doing secretarial work, as you were during the word processor training you participated in last month? (Yes/no) If "no," terminate the interview; if "yes," continue.

2. How often do you use your word processor: every day, a few days a week, or less than once a week?

3. How would you rate your word processor training: very helpful, adequate, or not helpful?

4. How would you rate the job aids you took back to work: very helpful, adequate, or not helpful?

5. How often do you use the job aids: every day, a few days a week, or less than once a week?

6. Do you think you could have learned just as much about your word processor from reading a manual? (Yes/no)

7. Those are all the questions I have. Do you have any questions or comments?

During the Interview

Use the same upbeat, friendly, conversational tone of voice with every respondent. Avoid implying the answer you expect; you must sound neutral, as though all answers are equal. Following are some guidelines to use when conducting the interview:

- Do not talk too fast. Pronounce words correctly and enunciate clearly.

- Listen for commotion on the respondent's end of the line; if you hear distractions, set up an appointment to call back.

- Stick to the prepared questions. Do not let respondents ramble; get the interview back on track by tactfully interjecting your next question.

- If you find the interview lasting longer than you said it would, ask the respondent if he or she would mind answering a few more questions. If the respondent is agreeable, ask *only* a few more.

Closing the Interview

Once you finish asking questions, invite the respondent to make comments or ask questions. Thank the respondent for his or her time and information. Enter the call on your log.

Written Questionnaires

Use this type of survey to gather broad, quantifiable nonsensitive data. Some examples of when to use a written questionnaire are as follows:

- when part of an organizational assessment—determining employee opinions about professional development opportunities (keeping respondents anonymous if some of the data is sensitive)

- when surveying a large or geographically dispersed population

- when all possible responses to an issue can be anticipated

- when dollars available for the survey are tight, and exploratory or sensitive questions are not essential

If exploratory or sensitive questions are essential, consider combining two survey types: Send written questionnaires with forced-choice questions to the survey sample; also conduct face-to-face interviews, asking open-ended questions of a small portion of the sample.

Following are the advantages and disadvantages of written questionnaires:

Advantages

- Respondents may answer quite accurately due to the tension-free nature of questionnaires sent through the mail. Questions can be answered at the respondents' convenience and personal pace, without probing by an interviewer.

- Since all respondents receive the exact same questions in printed form, answers are not susceptible to the biases that can slip into personal interviews—for instance, when questions are posed with different wordings to different respondents.

- Filling out questionnaires is simple, which advances the response rate and the number of accurate responses.

- Written questionnaires are usually the least expensive type of survey as well as the easiest to administer; tabulating and analyzing results also are easy.

- More people can be reached with written questionnaires than with any other type of survey.

Disadvantages

- Respondents may not understand or may misinterpret questionnaire instructions or the questions themselves. If the questionnaire comes through the mail, there is no facilitator to clarify questions. As a result, respondents may answer some questions inaccurately, or they may not answer them at all.

- Respondents often are irritated by "another dumb survey," so response rate or accuracy may be poor.

- Some respondents may not feel comfortable with the impersonal nature of the questionnaire; they may deem the survey sponsor "cold" and may not respond, or respond untruthfully.

- Results may be misleading, because only those respondents particularly interested in the topic or outcome may respond.

- Results also may be misleading because people not in the target sampling may respond. They may complete questionnaires mailed to people no longer employed at the firm or to residential occupants who have moved. Even when a questionnaire reaches the right person, that person may ask someone else, perhaps a subordinate, to fill it out.

- The scope of the survey is limited. Respondents can offer no insights by answering the structured questions of the written questionnaire, and respondents can offer no explanations with questions they feel forced to answer only somewhat accurately.

Tips for Written Questionnaires

When preparing a questionnaire to mail, choose an appropriate format; decide question topic groups and question structures. (Stay flexible; revise the format as needed once you begin writing questions.)

Preparation

Develop short, straightforward questions with various forced-choice structures—true/false, yes/no, multiple choice, ranking. Follow these guidelines when making up questions:

1. Vary question structure to promote accuracy of responses; respondents will read more carefully.

2. Write as few questions as possible to gather the data you need; this will encourage respondents to finish. But do write some extremely easy questions to scatter throughout the questionnaire; these will give respondents necessary breaks from hard thinking.

3. Order the questions within a topic group logically, one leading smoothly to the next. (Do not forget to alternate tough and easy questions.) Order the topic groups logically.

4. Put a few extremely easy and particularly interesting questions at the beginning to gain respondent interest.

5. Do not save the most important questions for the end of the survey; respondents may quit answering before they get to the last questions.

6. Put demographics questions at the end.

7. As the final question, ask for comments. Leave an appropriate amount of space for these comments or you will irritate respondents.

After developing questions, conclude your preparation steps by doing the following:

- Write clear and simple instructions for completing and returning the questionnaire; put instructions at the top of the questionnaire.

- Write a cover letter to introduce yourself—include your job title and a little bit about what you do. Explain the reason for the survey, identifying the sponsor of the survey, the purpose and scope of the survey, and the size and nature of the sample.

- Specify the date by which you would like the completed questionnaire returned; also state the return address and mention an enclosed postage-paid envelope.

- Encourage the respondent to return the completed questionnaire soon. Mention the importance of the survey information, and thank the respondent for contributing to the survey.

- Have the questionnaire and cover letter produced with the most sophisticated methods you can afford, either typed and copied or typeset and printed. Use high-quality paper.

- Have two types of envelopes printed: (1) *response envelopes*—self-addressed envelopes with postage-paid indicia for return of questionnaires (this boosts the response rate); and (2) *package envelopes*—envelopes with your company's return address and indicia for mailing the questionnaire, cover letter, and response envelope.

- Order respondent address labels, and arrange for questionnaire package labeling, stuffing, and mailing.

Follow-up

Unless respondents are to remain anonymous, keep track of whom you send questionnaires to and who responds. Send follow-up letters to remind and encourage people who did not respond to do so. Include another questionnaire and another response envelope.

On-site Completion

When preparing a questionnaire to hand out to a group for completion on the spot, follow all the tips for preparing a questionnaire to mail, with a few changes. Turn the cover letter into a memo requesting attendance at a particular site and on a particular day to complete the questionnaire, and mention how much time the survey will take. Mail only the memo. For continuity, prepare a short introduction from the information on the memo to present before the respondent group begins the survey. There is no need in this case for response envelopes; respondents can simply drop completed questionnaires in a box at the door as they leave the room.

Written Questionnaire Questions

The following questions might be the start of a written questionnaire used in an organizational assessment.

1. How interested are you in advancing at this company?

☐ very interested

☐ somewhat interested

☐ not at all interested

2. How far would you like to advance?

☐ chief executive officer

☐ upper management

☐ middle management

☐ happy where I am

3. How would you describe the professional development opportunities at this company?

☐ nonexistent

☐ scarce

☐ numerous

☐ abundant

4. I have taken advantage of professional development opportunities offered.

☐ true ☐ false

Electronic Surveys

The increase in the use of e-mail and the Internet/intranets has opened new options for gathering information with written questionnaires. Software is currently available to post surveys on your World Wide Web page or on your corporate intranet for respondents to complete. The survey can be completed online and often submitted directly to a database, thereby significantly reducing or even eliminating data entry. The results of the survey can be updated automatically after respondents complete the questionnaire, providing them with immediate feedback on how their responses compare with those of others who have completed the questionnaire. Software is also available to distribute questionnaires via e-mail. Respondents can then return their responses via e-mail either to a data entry person or directly to a database.

Advantages of Electronic Surveys

The most notable advantage of electronic surveys over mailing or faxing questionnaires is a very quick turnaround of responses. You often can get responses in a few hours. Also, after the initial investment of dollars to purchase the software and training time to learn the software, the cost of distribution and analysis of the survey is minimal. There is no postage and in many cases few if any data entry requirements, since the software often captures the responses for you. Many software packages also provide rudimentary data analysis components giving you virtually instant tabulations and graphs of your data.

Disadvantages of Electronic Surveys

There are, however, some serious disadvantages to using such software. First and foremost, many of the people in your target population may not have access to computers, e-mail, or the Web. Or, you may not have e-mail addresses for all members of the population. If you decide to include in your sample only those people who have access and for whom you have an e-mail address, you will likely get a rather biased sample. Second, there may be a significant investment of time and money necessary to procure the appropriate software and learn how to use it. If you do not have adequate start-up funds or have little time to launch the survey, the electronic version may not be the best choice.

Questions to Consider

When contemplating using e-mail or the Internet/intranet to distribute a questionnaire, ask the following questions:

- Is the population computer literate enough to complete the questionnaire?

- Which sections of the population will you be missing if you use this method? (Who does not have access to computers or the Web?)

- Will this method of surveying intimidate or scare some people away?

- Will this method of surveying bias any of the responses?

- How much money can you invest in software? (Software can run from less than $100 to several thousand dollars, depending upon your needs and specifications.)

- Do you have the time and interest necessary to learn a new piece of software? Does your organization already have the expertise to help you?

- If sending by e-mail, do you have e-mail addresses for the sample?

- If sending by e-mail, are the respondents' e-mail servers able to handle the format for the software you have selected? (This is expected to become less of a problem as time goes on.)

- If posting the questionnaire on the Internet or a corporate intranet, how will you get people to come to the page to complete the survey?

- How will you track to ensure that each person is responding only one time?

- How will you ensure that only the people you want included in your sample respond to the survey?

- How will you screen out responses from people who just happened to find your page?

Software Considerations

Software is available from a wide variety of companies, too varied and too frequently changing to list here. Search the Web for the most currently available software. Most established vendors will have a Web site and often will have a demo version or trial version that you can download directly from their site. Determine which software is compatible with the computer system you have available. Many currently available software products include a library of questions to help you design your questionnaires, but some may not be able to handle certain types of questions, such as ranking or open-ended questions. Consider how you plan to analyze the data collected. If the software does not include a data analysis component, check to see if it saves the data in a format that you can import into the software you plan to use for analysis. Check out a few different software products to determine which is right for you, and check whether the company offers a money-back guarantee if the software does not meet your needs.

Administering Surveys

A number of areas of concern are associated with the administration of surveys. They include sampling techniques, the types of questions to ask, pretesting, tabulating and analyzing results, and ethical behavior.

Sampling

Should you survey every employee about the corporate culture, or just a few people at each level? Should you request feedback on recent automation training just from learners or from their supervisors, too? It would be nice if you could always survey everybody who could provide information on your topic—the whole survey *population*. Population size and survey deadlines and dollars often make that ideal impossible, however. Many times you can survey only some of the potential respondents—a *sample*.

■ Criteria for Sample
First, the sample must be a *cross section* of the population, with all the characteristics of the population represented. For instance, with a corporate culture survey, every employee of the company is a member of the survey population; but if your company is large, you may be able to survey only a sample. To ensure that all characteristics of the population are represented in your sample, include some employees at every level. In a training evaluation survey, the population generally consists of the learners and the people directly affected by the learners' work—supervisors and subordinates. Representatives of all these groups must be included in your sample. Remember, in order to survey a cross section of the population, you may have to use different versions or different types of surveys with different groups of people in the sample. For example, the survey you devise to question support personnel about corporate culture may not be appropriate for managers. Second, the sample must be large enough to be *reliable*—that is, the odds of having a question answered a certain way are statistically equal.

To ensure that your sample meets these criteria, investigate the population to determine how large it is and the *primary* and *secondary* traits of its members. A primary trait is one the whole population has in common. The secondary trait is one that some, but not all, members of the population have in common. For example, when studying opinions about whether automation training was transferable to the job, your population consists of the employees trained and their supervisors. The primary trait of the population members is that their work is affected by the automation (and, therefore, by the training). Two secondary traits of the population are that some people use the new automated methods for work and others do not, but these others depend on the work produced with the automated methods.

■ *Methods of Sampling*

Choose a sampling method that allows for any primary and secondary traits the population displays. Following are the two most common sampling methods:

1. **Random sampling.** Every individual in the population has an equal chance of being chosen for the sample. Choosing every 10th person from an alphabetical list of names, for example, provides a random sample.

2. **Stratified random sampling.** The population is divided into constituent parts; then sample members are chosen randomly from the constituent parts. This is done to provide a more representative sample than the random sample. For example, dividing the population into age groups (10-20, 21-30, 31-40, and so forth), then randomly choosing people from each age group, provides a stratified random sample.

■ *Size of Sample*

The size of the sample needed for your survey depends on the following factors: the size of the population; how accurate you want the results to be (that is, how much error is acceptable); and how confident you want to be that the results were not caused by chance.

Findings from samples are actually estimates for the overall population, and therefore have some degree of inaccuracy or error. Think about all the various political and news polls you see on television and in the newspaper. These polls typically give an error rate, such as ± 3.5 percent, to indicate how accurate the figures are relative to the overall population. This indicates that the actual figure for the overall population is within ± 3.5 percent of the estimate given. In general, the larger the sample size relative to the size of the population, the more accurate the estimate.

When using a sample, there is also a possibility that the findings you get are caused merely by the random sample you selected, rather than a true reflection of the population. You will need to decide how "confident" you want to be that the findings you get are real and not caused by chance. It is typically acceptable to have one time in 20 that the findings were caused by chance. This is called a 95 percent confidence interval, meaning that 19 times out of 20, or 95 percent of the time, you are confident that the findings are real. In some cases you may decide that it is acceptable to have one time in 10 that the findings were caused by chance (90 percent confidence interval).

If you know how large your population is and can decide in advance what you find to be an acceptable error rate and how confident you want to be with your results, you can determine how large a sample you need to target to meet those criteria.

The graph on page 13 shows the sample size needed (in terms of percent of population) to have an error rate of ± 3.5 percent with both a 95 percent interval confidence and a 90 percent confidence interval. Use this tool to help determine how large a sample you need to have respond to your survey. For example, if your population size is 200 and you want to be 95 percent confident of your results, you should target to get 80 percent of your population, or 160 people, to complete your survey. If your population size is 1500, you will need to target only 34 percent of your total population.

Questions

Using questions correctly is the key to achieving successful survey results. The following list of guidelines for questions will help you get accurate answers.

■ Structure

Questions have two basic structures: open ended and forced choice. Open-ended questions are those that respondents answer in their own words. Information obtained from these questions is insightful and often most accurate, but quantifying and analyzing the responses are difficult. Consider using these questions with a subsample instead of the whole sample.

Forced-choice questions are those in which respondents choose from the answers listed. Quantifying and analyzing responses to these questions are easy, but the information obtained may include inaccuracies. It may not represent exactly what respondents would say if allowed to choose their own words. When using these questions, make sure you offer all possible answers, including "don't know" or "indifferent," and make answers mutually exclusive.

■ Specific Purpose

Each question should have one of the following specific purposes: to provide background information and help you describe and theorize about your sample; or to provide the specific data you are trying to obtain in the survey. Asking for information that is simply nice to know makes respondents doubt your credibility.

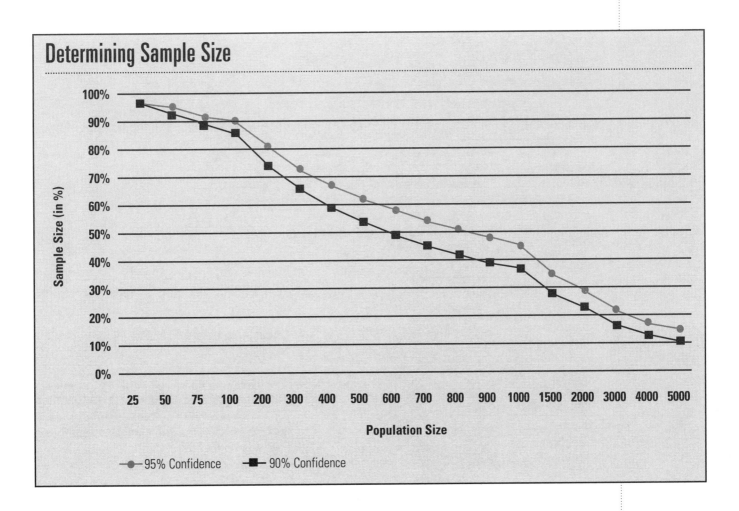

Determining Sample Size

Sample Size (in %) vs. Population Size

Legend: ● 95% Confidence   ■ 90% Confidence

■ **Bias**

Questions must not give the respondent any clue to the response you expect. For example, the question "Don't you feel that it is really unfair to expect everybody to get to work on time every day?" will usually provoke a "yes" answer.

■ **Negativity**

Negative questions are often hard to understand. Reword them. For example, "Shouldn't the government deny foreign access to military information?" can be reworded as "Should the government allow foreign access to military information?"

■ **Repetition**

With written questionnaires, if you wish to repeat a question to test how carefully respondents considered the survey items, remember that respondents may become irritated, even if you reword the repeat questions.

■ **Sensitivity**

Questions about personal or moral issues can elicit emotional responses. Be cautious when asking sensitive questions so you do not lose respondent cooperation. When you ask sensitive questions, word them tactfully and do not use them as the first or last questions of the survey. Remember, sensitive questions generally are reserved for face-to-face interviews.

■ **Clarity**

Questions must be understood and interpreted correctly to be answered accurately. To ensure clarity, follow these guidelines when writing questions:

- Use fewer that 20 words per question.

- Exclude unnecessary words. In the question "Are you currently in the process of automating your work methods?" the words *in the process of* are unnecessary.

- Make sure questions are grammatically correct.

- Make sure wording is exact. For example, if you want to know how many people use audiovisual equipment—perhaps not as expertly as possible—for presentations, do not ask, "Do you ever show slides in client meetings?" Respondents who have used only overhead projectors may reply, "No."

- With written questions, underline or italicize where necessary to highlight important words or to show respondents where the emphasis in the question belongs. For example, true or false: "I know how to operate an *advanced* widget."

- Ask for only one piece of information per question. Two-part questions can confuse respondents and provide you with data you did not mean to ask for or cannot use.

- Do not include jargon, technical words, or pretentious language even if you think respondents should understand. What if they do not? Either they will get frustrated and stop cooperating, or they will guess and answer inaccurately.

Pretesting

You left a vital question out of your interviews. Questions and instructions that seemed perfectly clear to you were misinterpreted by your questionnaire respondents. Spelling mistakes and solid answer boxes you missed caught some of your respondents' eyes, destroying the professional appearance of your questionnaire. To help avoid problems like these, pretest your survey before administering it. The more ways you pretest, the safer you are in assuming the accuracy of results. There are a number of ways to pretest your survey:

- Send drafts of questions to the client for review, checking that you have asked for all the data needed.

- Circulate drafts of questions to colleagues for comments.

- Test the survey on a small sample population to make certain that instructions and questions are clear and answerable, have all appropriate options listed, and can be completed in a reasonable length of time.

- Ask the data analysts to perform a trial-run analysis with the responses from the trial survey. If you are using a computer for analysis, ask the data entry operator to make some trial entries. You may find that data supplied as you requested are difficult to analyze and that survey structure and format need to be revised.

- Have two people besides yourself proofread final questionnaires before you copy them or have them printed.

Tabulating and Analyzing Results

After you collect the responses, you will need to tabulate and analyze them. Several books provide detailed instructions for these tasks. Primarily, you will want to use good judgment when analyzing survey results; question the results that do not "feel" right. There are some general tips for completing this final step in the survey process.

With telephone surveys and written questionnaires, be prepared for incomplete surveys and incomplete responses. Decide whether you are going to disregard all of a respondent's answers if he or she did not complete the survey.

If you are using a computer to tabulate results, check for data entry errors, especially when the operator is entering the first responses. This will prevent the recurring errors created when the operator misunderstands a task. If a staff is manually tabulating results, make sure everybody is using the same tabulating system. Be sure that anyone tabulating results understands the criteria for making decisions on questionable responses. Paraphrase carefully; do not change the meaning of a response.

Use charts and graphs to make the result of each question evident at a glance. Use a cross-tab table for a pictorial comparison of results of two or more questions. (Computers are very useful for doing this.) Cross-tab tables can help you analyze cause-and-effect and complementary relationships. For example, the cross-tab between a question about age and a question about professional development might lead you to report that 20 percent of the employees over age 50 want professional development opportunities.

Ethics

A lot of people hate surveys. Why? Because too many times when these people were told that the information they supplied would be used for one purpose, they later discovered that it was used for another. Because when they were told that their responses would remain confidential, they were betrayed. Because results were manipulated. You must conduct your survey ethically if you want valid results. Respondents who feel they cannot trust you will not answer questions accurately.

There are a number of rules to follow in order to ensure that you are behaving ethically toward respondents. Never mislead respondents about why the survey is being done. Explain who is being surveyed and what will be done with the data obtained. Do not use the data for any other purpose. If you assure respondents that individual answers will remain confidential, keep that confidentiality. That means confidentiality from the public, such as not publishing a person's response in a newsletter. It also means more personal confidentiality, such as refraining from telling a colleague "this funny anecdote." Destroy surveys and list of respondents after results have been tabulated. If you tell respondents they will receive a copy of the survey results, send it.

To ensure that you are behaving ethically toward your client, always approach the survey with an open mind. If you are trying to prove or disprove a personal theory, your desires will bias your questions. You also should approach the survey results with an open mind. If results are not what you expected and you are not convinced they are accurate, research to find out why. Do not throw out responses that contradict the expected outcome. Report the results honestly and directly to the client. Do not withhold information. Do not qualify or downplay results.

Surveys can provide valuable information. Choosing the appropriate type of survey instrument and observing the guidelines covered in this issue of *Info-line* can ensure success in this important method of information gathering and analysis.

References & Resources

Articles

Chaudron, David. "The Right Approach to Employee Surveys." *HRFocus,* March 1997, pp. 9-10.

———. "Survey Methods Questioned." *Human Resources Professional,* Summer 1993, pp. 30-32.

Fink, Arlene. "Short List, Long-term Memory, and Vice-versa." *American Demographics,* February 1996, p. 8.

Frazier, Shirley. "Seeking Solutions Through Surveys." *Incentive,* April 1997, pp. 61-62.

Futrell, David. "Ten Reasons Why Surveys Fail." *Quality Progress,* April 1994, pp. 65-69.

Garee, Michael L., and Thomas R. Schori. "Focus Groups Illuminate Quantitative Research." *Marketing News,* June 9, 1997, p. H25.

Greilsamer, Marc. "Post-survey Blues." *Across the Board,* March 1995, pp. 62-63.

Hodges, Kris. "Ask a Silly Question…" *American Demographics,* May 1997, pp. 20-25.

Long, Steven A. "Pretesting Question-naires Minimizes Measurement Error." *Marketing News,* May 27, 1991, p. 12.

Mehta, Raj, and Eugene Sivadas. "Comparing Response Rates and Response Content in Mail Versus Electronic Mail Surveys." *Journal of the Market Research Society,* October 1995, pp. 429-439.

Nogami, Glenda Y. "Eight Points for More Useful Surveys." *Quality Progress,* October 1996, pp. 93-96.

Nowack, Kenneth M. "A True Training Needs Analysis." *Training & Develop-ment Journal,* April 1991, pp. 69-73.

Rollins, Thomas. "Performance Surveys: Quality Tools Emerging for the 1990s." *Employment Relations Today,* Summer 1992, pp. 119-125.

Seymour, Harry. "Conducting and Using Customer Surveys." *Marketing News,* June 9, 1997, pp. H24, H39.

Zinober, Joan Wagner. "Do's and Don'ts of Client Satisfaction Surveys." *Law Practice Management,* May/June 1996, pp. 38-40.

Books

Babbie, E.R. *Survey Research Methods.* (2d edition). Belmont, California: Wadsworth, 1990.

Bateson, J. *Data Construction in Social Surveys.* London: Allen and Unwin, 1984.

Berdie, D.R., et al. *Questionnaires: Design and Use.* (2d edition). Metuchen, New Jersey: Scarecrow Press, 1986.

Bulmer, M. (ed.). *Censuses, Surveys and Privacy.* New York: Holmes and Meier, 1980.

Dunham, R.B., and F.J. Smith. *Organiza-tional Surveys: An Internal Assessment of Organizational Health.* Glenview, Illinois: Scott, Foresman, 1979.

Gallup, G. *The Sophisticated Poll Watcher's Guide.* Princeton, New Jer-sey: Princeton Opinion Press, 1972.

Kesselman-Turkel, J., and F. Peterson. *Research Shortcuts.* Chicago: Contem-porary Books, 1982.

Laird, D. *Approaches to Training and Development.* (2d edition). Reading, Massachusetts: Addison-Wesley, 1985.

Patton, M.Q. *Qualitative Evaluation and Research Methods.* (2d edition). Thou-sand Oaks, California: SagePublica-tions, 1990.

Reynolds, P.D. *Ethics and Social Science Research.* Englewood Cliffs, New Jersey: Prentice-Hall, 1982.

Schuman, H., and S. Presser. *Questions and Answers in Attitude Surveys.* (reprint). Thousand Oaks, California: Sage Publications, 1996.

Singer, P. *Practical Ethics.* (2d edition). Cambridge: Cambridge University Press, 1993.

Stewart, C.J., and W.B. Cash Jr. *Interview-ing Principles and Practices.* (7th edi-tion). Dubuque, Iowa: Brown and Benchmark, 1993.

Sudman, S., and N.M. Bradburn. *Asking Questions: A Practical Guide to Questionnaire Design.* San Francisco: Jossey-Bass, 1982.

Zemke, R., and T. Kramlinger. *Figuring Things Out: A Trainer's Guide to Needs and Task Analysis.* Reading, Massachu-setts: Addison-Wesley, 1982.

Info-lines

Callahan, Madelyn (ed.). "Be a Better Needs Analyst." No. 8502.

———. "Be a Better Task Analyst." No. 8503 (out of print).

Gilley, Jerry W. "How to Collect Data." No. 9008 (revised 1998).

Hacker, D.G. "Testing for Learning Out-comes." No. 8907 (revised 1998).

Martelli, J. T., and D. Mather. "Statistics for HRD Practice." No. 9101.

Survey Plan

1. State the purpose of the survey (25 words or less). Include the name of the survey sponsor.

    _____

    _____

    _____

    _____

    _____

    _____

    _____

2. List the data needed.

    _____

    _____

    _____

    _____

    _____

    _____

    _____

3. List the ways in which your client will use the data obtained.

    _____

    _____

    _____

    _____

    _____

    _____

    _____

4. Describe the survey respondents.

    Size of population: _____

    Primary traits of population: _____

    Secondary traits of population: _____

    Size of sample: _____

    ☐   Sample is a cross section of the population.

    ☐   Sample is large enough to be reliable.

Job Aid

5. Check the type(s) of survey you will conduct.

- ☐ Face-to-face interview
- ☐ Telephone interview
- ☐ Written questionnaire
- ☐ Electronic questionnaire

6. Timetable for each type of survey you will conduct:

	Research	Prepare	Pretest	Conduct	Analyze
● Face-to-face interview					
● Telephone interview					
● Written questionnaire					
● Electronic questionnaire					

7. Estimate the cost of each type of survey you will conduct.

   - Face-to-face interview

   Wages + Interview training + Data tabulation/analysis costs + Other =   Total _____

   - Telephone interview

   Wages + Interview training + Telephone charges + Data tabulation/analysis costs + Other =   Total _____

   - Written questionnaire

   Wages + Paper/printing + Postage + Data tabulation/analysis costs + Other =   Total _____

   - Electronic questionnaire

   Wages + Software/design costs + Online charges + Data tabulation/analysis costs + Other =   Total _____

8. Question checklist (complete for each question):

   ☐ has specific purpose
   ☐ is unbiased
   ☐ is positive, not negative
   ☐ if open ended, is not vague
   ☐ if forced choice, offers all possible choices
   ☐ if sensitive, is tactful
   ☐ if a repeat, is reworded
   ☐ is clear and concise

Job Aid

9. Rough drafts of questions should be circulated for survey pretest to:

Client(s): _____

_____

Colleagues:_____

_____

Small sample population: _____

_____

Data analysts: _____

_____

Data entry operators: _____

_____

10. State your plan for keeping track of which respondents have/have not been contacted.

_____

_____

_____

_____

_____

_____

_____

_____

11. What steps will be taken with results of incomplete surveys/questions?

_____

_____

_____

_____

_____

_____

_____

_____

12. Can you guarantee confidentiality?............................ ☐ yes   ☐ no

13. Can you approach the survey and its results with an open mind?...... ☐ yes   ☐ no

14. Can you report the results honestly? .... ☐ yes   ☐ no

Author Biographies

Jack Phillips

Jack Phillips, Ph.D. has more than 27 years professional experience in HRD and management, and has served as training and development manager at two Fortune 500 firms, senior HR executive at two firms, president of a regional bank, and management professor at a major state university. He is the founder of Performance Resources Organization (PRO), an international consulting firm specializing in accountability issues including ROI. PRO's clients are located throughout North America, Europe, Asia, Africa, and the South Pacific. A regular presenter at numerous conferences, he is also the author of several books and articles on training evaluation and also acts as series editor for the award winning and best selling *In Action* series published by ASTD.

Wendy L. Combs

Wendy L. Combs, Ph.D., is a Process Improvement Manager for the Wireless Networks of Nortel. In this capacity she is actively involved in a large-scale change initiative focused on preparing the business for process and software application changes associated with an integrated supply chain and millennium compliance by the year 2000. Wendy has consulted in public schools, local and state government, higher education, and corporate settings. She has also presented at professional conferences and is a co-author of a book on training evaluation that will be published in late 1999.

Malcolm J. Conway is currently a Performance Consultant in IBM Global Services' Performance and Competency Management Consulting practice. He has previously held positions as principal and founder of his own consulting firm, as Director of Continuing Education Services for Educational Testing Service, and in various research management positions for the New Jersey and New York State Education Departments. Among his consulting clients was a major telecommunications company for whom he developed and taught courses on various group process topics, trained facilitators, and facilitated a variety of strategic and tactical meetings. He has extensive experience designing and facilitating computer and non-computer assisted group meetings. Malcolm has also been an Adjunct Professor at George Washington University and Monmouth University where he taught courses on various measurement and quantitative topics.

Salvatore V. Falletta, Ed.D., is the Southeast Regional Manager for Training and Development at 360 Communications. Prior to joining 360 Communications, Sal was a Senior Evaluation Specialist for the Nortel Technical Education Centers in the United States and Canada. At Nortel, he led a comprehensive evaluation initiative that served over 25,000 students annually across a training portfolio of 200 courses. Sal has a doctoral degree in Training and Development and is co-author of a book on training evaluation that will be published in late 1999.

Salvatore V. Falletta

H. Steve Giles is a Senior Consultant with Tenera Energy's Technology Enhanced Training Division in San Francisco, California. He has over 15 years experience managing training functions and has served as the training manager for the Oak Ridge National Lab and Performance Technology Services within Lockheed Martin Energy Systems responsible for designing and developing computer and Web-based tests and other aspects of performance technology. He has a Masters degree in Human Resource Development, has authored articles in *Technical Training* magazine and the *Journal of Southeastern Association of Educational Opportunity Program Personnel*. He has also been a presenter at numerous professional conferences.

H. Steve Giles

Deborah Grafinger Hacker is a Senior Instructional Designer with PowerVision Corporation in Columbia, Maryland where she develops on-line testing and training, systems training and user documentation for proprietary systems for Motorola, Armstrong World Industries and other clients. She has a Master's Degree in Instructional Systems Design and Bilingual Education from University of Maryland Baltimore County (UMBC). She formerly worked for General Physics Corporation, concentrating in developing classroom and self-paced training for the nuclear industry and other utility clients; as a project manager for the Competencies and Standards study for HRD conducted by ASTD; for the University of Maryland University College supervising the development of Nuclear Science and Engineering Distance Education Program; and as an adjunct faculty member teaching both undergraduate and graduate level courses on ISD.

Deborah Grafinger Hacker

Daniel J. McLinden, Ed.D has 15 years experience in consulting, with an emphasis in evaluation and performance measurement. He is currently affiliated with the Metrus Group and Monar Consulting, firms specializing in strategic measurement and performance improvement. Previously, Dan directed Evaluation & Performance Measurement for Andersen Consulting's Center for Professional Education. His client experience has included program evaluation, strategy implementation, needs assessment, testing, and organizational assessment with a wide variety of organizations in both the United States and Europe. He regularly presents at conferences and has authored and co-authored a number of articles and books including *Return-on-Investment* Volume 1, published by ASTD.

Daniel J. McLinden

Sandra I. Pettit-Sleet

Sandra I. Pettit-Sleet is an Assistant Vice President and Team Leader at First Union National Bank in Charlotte, North Carolina. She has a background in public and private accounting and taught accounting for six years at a business college. In 1995 Sandra took over the Level 1 Evaluation process at First Union National Bank and was challenged to create a smooth-flowing, efficiently-run operation that services 6 internal areas, more than 400 courses, and approximately 70,000 employees. She has an MBA, specializes in the financial and marketing arenas of business, and has 13 years professional experience in four diverse areas—evaluation of training, education, public and private accounting, and business consulting.

Patricia Pulliam is Vice President, Business Development of Performance Resources Organization (PRO), responsible for cultivating international and domestic alliances, client relations, and the development of the ROI Resource Center™, a Web-based evaluation tool and case study library. She has more than 13 years experience in marketing, planning, evaluation, and customer and employee satisfaction, including work for major utility and service industries. She provides consulting support in measurement and evaluation and serves as Executive Director of the ROI Network™. She is contributing author to several publications including *Evaluating Training Programs* 2nd Edition, by Donald Kirkpatrick, (1998), and *HRD Trends Worldwide* by Jack Phillips (1999).

Connie Schmidt is an Assessment Evaluation Specialist with Illinova University. She has over 20 years of corporate experience in the fossil and nuclear side of the utility industry, finance and accounting, human resources division, and training areas of Illinova/Illinois Power Corporation. Her career accomplishments include pioneering a peer group program to increase staff knowledge of the company, leading the development of computerized programming for succession planning for the executive branch, and the design and implementation of a results-based approach to evaluation at Illinova University. She is a member of the ROI Network™, an elite organization of evaluation research practitioners.

Robert Schriver

Robert Schriver, Ph.D., has 13 years experience as an instructional designer and training project leader with two Fortune 100 companies. Currently, he is the program leader for training evaluation in the Center for Continuing Education at Lockheed Martin Energy Systems (LMES). He is a certified instructor in Mager's Criterion-Referenced Instruction, Harless' Job Aids Workshop, and Phillips' Measuring Return-on-Investment in Training. He has published nine articles in ASTD's *Technical Training* magazine and has been an adjunct faculty member at the University of Tennessee and on the advisory board at Pellissippi State Community College.

Ronnie Drew Stone is the Vice President and Chief Consulting Officer of Performance Resources Organization (PRO). In this capacity he consults on numerous evaluation projects with a broad range of international clients. Ron has more than 30 years experience in the HRD field, including extensive work in the aerospace and electric utility industries. He provides consulting and services in measurement and evaluation, training design, budgeting, and strategic planning, as well as workshops on ROI. He is a frequent presenter at HRD conferences and a contributing author to ASTD's *In Action* series.

Alice Waagen Ph.D. has focused her career on applying the principles of education and learning to meet business goals. She heads up Workforce Learning, a management consulting firm specializing in designing learning programs that support business strategies. Alice has a varied background in learning applications, from experience in elementary, secondary and higher education to heading up training units in major Fortune 500 companies. Her corporate expertise encompasses industries like computer software, finance, transportation, and utilities. Under her leadership, these organizations have developed full systems for learning measurement and evaluation of issues such as cost of training, volume and activity, customer satisfaction and training ROI. She also has a background in systems analysis and workforce training automation, and has assisted numerous clients in the design of fully automated systems to manage learning activity and results.

Joan O. Wright is the Vice President and Director of Learning Services for First Union National Bank's First University in Charlotte, North Carolina. Joan manages a unit with the primary responsibilities of providing performance consulting and training needs assessment, design, delivery, and measurement to six internal areas and approximately 70,000 employees. She has 16 years professional and managerial experience in human resources with Citicorp, General Electric, and First Union National Bank.

Joan O. Wright